Lecture Notes in Computer Science   7423

Commenced Publication in 1973
Founding and Former Series Editors:
Gerhard Goos, Juris Hartmanis, and Jan van Leeuwen

Young-Bin Kwon   Jean-Marc Ogier (Eds.)

Graphics Recognition

New Trends and Challenges

9th International Workshop, GREC 2011
Seoul, Korea, September 15-16, 2011
Revised Selected Papers

 Springer

Volume Editors

Young-Bin Kwon
Chung-Ang University
Department of Computer Science and Engineering
221 Heuksukdong, Dongjakku
156-756 Seoul, South Korea
E-mail: ybkwon@cau.ac.kr

Jean-Marc Ogier
Université de La Rochelle
Laboratoire L3i, Avenue Michel Crépeau
17042 La Rochelle Cedex 1, France
E-mail: jean-marc.ogier@univ-lr.fr

ISSN 0302-9743   e-ISSN 1611-3349
ISBN 978-3-642-36823-3   e-ISBN 978-3-642-36824-0
DOI 10.1007/978-3-642-36824-0
Springer Heidelberg Dordrecht London New York

Library of Congress Control Number: 2013932192

CR Subject Classification (1998): I.7.5, I.4.1, I.4.5-7, I.4.9-10

LNCS Sublibrary: SL 6 – Image Processing, Computer Vision, Pattern Recognition,
and Graphics

Typesetting: Camera-ready by author, data conversion by Scientific Publishing Services, Chennai, India

Printed on acid-free paper

Springer is part of Springer Science+Business Media (www.springer.com)

Preface

This book contains refereed and improved papers presented at the 9th IAPR Workshop on Graphics Recognition (GREC 2011), held in Seoul, Korea, during September 15–16, 2011. The GREC workshops provide an excellent opportunity for researchers and practitioners at all levels of experience to meet colleagues and to share new ideas and knowledge about graphics recognition methods. Graphics recognition is a subfield of document image analysis that deals with graphical entities in engineering drawings, sketches, maps, architectural plans, musical scores, mathematical notation, tables, diagrams, etc. GREC 2009 continued the tradition of past workshops held at Penn State University, USA (GREC 1995, LNCS Volume 1072, Springer Verlag, 1996); Nancy, France (GREC 1997, LNCS Volume 1389, Springer Verlag, 1998); Jaipur, India (GREC 1999, LNCS Volume 1941, Springer Verlag, 2000); Kingston, Canada (GREC 2001, LNCS Volume 2390, Springer Verlag, 2002); Barcelona, Spain (GREC 2003, LNCS Volume 3088, Springer Verlag, 2004); Hong Kong, China (GREC 2005, LNCS Volume 3926, Springer Verlag, 2006); Curitiba, Brazil (GREC 2007, LNCS Volume 5046, Springer Verlag, 2008); and La Rochelle, France (GREC 2009, LNCS Volume 6020, Springer Verlag, 2010).

The program of GREC 2011 was organized in a single-track two-day workshop. It comprised several sessions dedicated to specific topics. For each session, there was an invited presentation describing the state of the art and stating the open questions for the session's topic, followed by a number of short presentations that continued by proposing solutions to some of the questions or by presenting results of the speaker's work. Each session was then concluded by a panel discussion. Session topics included structural approaches for recognition and indexing, techniques toward vectorization, sketching interfaces, on-line processing, symbol and shape segmentation, description and recognition, historical document analysis, indexing, spotting, and performance evaluation and ground truthing. In addition, a panel discussion on the state of the art and new challenges was organized as the concluding session of GREC 2011.

Continuing with the tradition of past GREC workshops, the program of GREC 2011 included graphics recognition contests. In particular, three contests were held: an arc segmentation contest, organized by Hasan S.M. Al-Khaffaf, Abdullah Zawawi Talib, and Mohd Azam Osman; a symbol recognition contest, organized by Ernest Valveny, Mathieu Delalandre, Bart Lamiroy, and Romain Raveaux; and a music scores: writer identification and staff removal, organized by Alicia Fornés, Anjan Dutta, Albert Gordo, and Josep Lladós. In these contests, for each contestant, test images, and ground truths were prepared in order to have objective performance evaluation conclusions on their methods.

After the workshop, all the authors were invited to submit enhanced versions of their papers for this edited volume. The authors were encouraged to include the ideas and suggestions of two or three reviewers. At least one reviewer was assigned from the workshop attendees. Papers appearing in this volume were selected, and most of them were thoroughly revised and improved, based on the reviewers' comments. The structure of this volume is organized in seven sections, reflecting the workshop session topics.

We want to thank all paper authors and reviewers, contest organizers and participants, and workshop attendees for their contributions to the workshop and this volume. In particular, we gratefully acknowledge the group of organizers of the Chung-Ang University for their great help in the local arrangements of the workshop.

The 10th IAPR Workshop on Graphics Recognition (GREC 2013) is planned to be held in the USA.

November 2011   Young-Bin Kwon
                                                       Jean-Marc Ogier

Organization

General Chair

Young-Bin Kwon

Program Chair

Jean-Marc Ogier

Local Arrangements Chair

Jaehwa Park

Program Committee

Sébastien Adam, France
Karell Bertet, France
Dorothea Blotein, Canada
Jean-Christophe Burie, France
Bertrand Coüasnon, France
Mathieu Delalandre, France
David Doermann, USA
Philippe Dosch, France
Alicia Fornés, Spain
Alexander Gribov, USA
Pierre Héroux, France
Xiaoyi Jiang, Germany
Young-Bin Kwon, Korea
Bart Lamiroy, France
Rafael Lins, Brazil
Marcus Liwicki, Germany
Josep Lladós, Spain

Tong Lu, China
Simone Marinai, Italy
Jean-Marc Ogier, France
Umapada Pal, India
Jaehwa Park, Korea
Sitaram Ramachandrula, India
Jean-Yves Ramel, France
Romain Raveaux, France
Marçal Rusiñol, Spain
Salvatore-Antoine Tabbone, France
Karl Tombre, France
Ernest Valveny, Spain
Nicole Vincent, France
Muriel Visani, France
Toyohide Watanabe, Japan
Su Yang, China

Additional Referees

Yao-Yi Chiang, USA
Gunter Drevin, South Africa
Akio Fujiyoshi, Japan
Aurélie Lemaitre, France
Long-long Ma, China

Koji Nakagawa, Japan
Nibal Nayef, Germany
Feng Su, China
Zhengxing Sun, China
Abdullah Zawawi Talib, Malaysia

Sponsoring Institutions

Chung-Ang University
The Korean Institute of Information Scientists and Engineers (KIISE)
Suprema Inc.
Triple Aims

Table of Contents

Session 4: Performance Evaluation

Session 5: Challenge Processing

A Region-Based Method for Sketch Map Segmentation

Klaus Broelemann and Xiaoyi Jiang

Department of Mathematics and Computer Science, University of Münster,
Einsteinstr. 62, D-48149 Münster, Germany
{broele,xjiang}@uni-muenster.de

Abstract. Sketch maps are an intuitive way to display and communi-
cate geographic data and an automatic processing is of great benefit for
human-computer interaction. This paper presents a method for segmentation of sketch map objects as part of the sketch map understanding
process. We use region-based segmentation that is robust to gaps in
the drawing and can even handle open-ended streets. To evaluate this
approach, we manually generated a ground truth for 20 maps and conducted a preliminary quantitative performance study.

Keywords: sketch segmentation, sketch classification, sketch maps.

1 Introduction

During the last years, applications using Geographic Information(GI) contributed
by the public became widely used in people's daily life, e.g. Google Map, Flicker,
Wikimapia and OpenStreetMap. Such user-generated content of Geographic Information is so-called Volunteered Geographic Information (VGI) which allows
the general public to contribute Geographic Information via an open framework
on the web (see Goodchild [5]). While the abilities and complexity of existing
VGI systems are continuously increasing, there is still an absence of easy-to-use
interaction methods. Compared with WIMP (window, icon, menu and point-
ing device) interfaces that current VGI systems use, people are more familiar
with other human-human communication approaches in everyday life such as
freehand sketch maps. According to Schlaisich and Egenhofer [15] hand-drawn
sketch maps are an intuitive way to interact with a VGI system.

There are two aspects that characterize hand-drawn sketch maps. One is the
fact that they are drawn on a paper, a whiteboard or a tablet PC by hand
and, thus, show a lack of accurately. The other aspect is the difference between
metric maps and sketch maps. Metric maps display a region accurately based
on a mathematical projection. In contrast to metric maps, sketch maps are not
drawn accurate. They show conceptual image of a region that has distorted
metric information like lenghts, angles, and scales, but can be drawn by everyone.
While the second aspect leads to challenges for sketch map matching, e.g. against
a geographic database, the inaccuracies in drawing are challenges for previous
processing steps like the segmentation.

Y.-B. Kwon and J.-M. Ogier (Eds.): GREC, LNCS 7423, pp. 1–14, 2013.

One application for sketch maps are volunteer geographic information systems, which allow users to annotate, add and modify content of maps. Using sketch maps as input would enable users to provide automatic systems with their knowledge in a natural way and also to share it with other users.

There are two ways to process sketch maps in an automatic way: on-line with pen-based input devices and off-line using images of sketch maps. While most sketch processing systems use pen-based input devices, we deal with photos of sketch maps. Thus, our approach does not rely on special input devices, but can also deal with photos or scans of a sketch map drawn on a paper.

One essential part of automatic understanding of sketch maps for VGI is the localization and recognition of objects, since the VGI operations are based on this information: Adding, changing or removing objects means to know the objects location and meaning.

In this paper, we present an algorithm for such an automatic localization of objects by using a region-based segmentation. The algorithm has to deal with inaccuracies of hand-drawn sketches, as discussed later.

We structure this paper as follows: First, we will give a brief description of related work. Section 2 is used to describe our segmentation method. A preliminary evaluation of our algorithm is presented in Section 3. Finally, in Section 4 we will give a conclusion and an outlook on future work.

1.1   Related Work

Sketch recognition has been subject of research for several years. Most of the previous work concentrates on pen-based sketch recognition. The first task in sketch recognition is to recognize geometric primitives such as rectangles or circles. Low-level recognizers have been proposed to recognize such primitives [14]. Based on such methods, sketch recognition has been used for different applications including UML diagrams [7], presentation slides [11], and electric circuit diagrams [4]. To cover different applications, Hammond and Davis presented the language LADDAR [6] that allows the user to define complex elements based on geometric primitives and to recognize these elements based on low-level recognizers. Still, all these works process the sketches on-line and, thereby, use a segmentation into single strokes and the drawing order of these strokes. For our off-line approach, this information is not available. Thus, different methods have to be applied to recognize elements of the sketch.

Beside the on-line approaches, there is also work addressing the problem of finding and recognizing elements of documents using off-line methods. One group of such elements are symbols. Symbol spotting methods address the localization and recognition of symbols in documents. Recent methods can even deal with hand-drawn symbols. Bhuvanagiri et al. [1] presented a method for hand-drawn symbol spotting based on a sub-graph matching. Dutta et al. [3] presented another method based on graph paths and applied this method also to hand-drawn symbols. Though symbol spotting can be useful for sketch map understanding, these methods do not solve the problem of finding region-based objects like streets that are represented by their border lines. Since these bordered objects

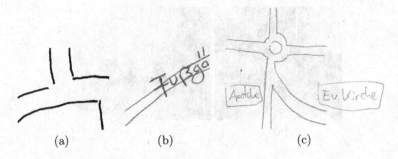

Fig. 1. Challenges for sketch map segmentation: (a) Gaps between lines, (b) intersection of text and graphics, and (c) open-ended streets

can have a very broad range of possible appearances, symbol spotting methods fail to recognize them.

Szwoch [16] presented a method that deals with bordered objects in flow chart drawings by finding loops in the drawn lines. This work does not deal with problems like gaps between border lines or intersection with text elements. Thus, this method is not applicable for typical sketch maps.

Map segmentation and classification has been object of research for several years, including raster maps [8], topographic maps [10] and satellite images [20]. Since the input format for these methods differs from binary line drawings, they are not very helpful for sketch map segmentation. One class of algorithms for image segmentation are watershed [2] and flooding algorithms [13]. These algorithms segment the image by iteratively growing regions. To our knowledge region based methods have not been applied to sketch maps yet.

2   Sketch Map Segmentation

Sketch maps contain several different elements. These can be symbols, bordered objects and also text. The aim of our segmentation method is to find bordered objects, like buildings, streets or parks.

As sketch maps are drawn by hand, the segmentation has to deal with typical inaccuracies of hand-drawn images: lines that should be connected have gaps in between, objects can overlap each other due to drawing order of streets, connected streets can be separated by street border lines and text might be drawn inside the objects. Another issue for the segmentation of sketch maps are streets that are not drawn completely and have an open end. Figure 1 shows examples for these challenges.

Our segmentation method is based on a flooding method that stops at gaps and open street endings. This leads to a strong oversegmentation, which is subsequently reduced by merging segments.

In this section we will initially give a brief description of the sketch map preprocessing. In a second part, the flooding algorithm that is used to create an

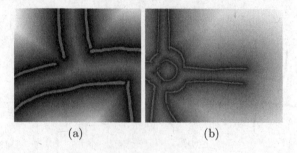

(a)   (b)

Fig. 2. Examples of distances to drawn pixels. (a) It can be seen, that at gaps between lines the distances are lower than in the connected areas. (b) Surrounding areas have much higher distances than the streets.

oversegmentation of the map will be presented. At the end of this section, we will describe the merging algorithm.

2.1 Preprocessing

Prior to the segmentation, we perform some preprocessing operations to prepare the image, reduce artefacts and improve the segmentation results. Since sketch maps are drawn in black and white as binary images, our first step is a binarization of the image. To be able to deal with both scanned images and photos we use an adaptive binarization that compares each pixel with the average value of a local surrounding. By doing so, the algorithm can work on inhomogeneously illuminated photos.

Though text is an important element of sketch maps, it is often written inside of objects and, thereby, disturbs the segmentation method. To reduce the impact of text on the segmentation, we perform a text separation method that was proposed by Tombre *et al.* [18].

A subsequent closing operation followed by the removal of small connected components reduces possible artefacts due to binarization and text separation.

2.2 Flooding

We start the sketch map segmentation with a flood-filling algorithm. The goal is to stop the flooding at gaps between lines and at open endings of streets. Gaps are small holes between broader regions. Open street endings connect a slim street with a broad region.

Starting with a seeding point, the algorithm finds a segment by flooding to all connected pixels that fulfill certain constraints. This is repeated with new seeding points until the whole image is segmented, having one segment for each seeding point. Again, the function of our constraints is to ensure that the flooding stops at gaps and open street ends.

Gaps between lines can be characterized as parts with small distances to drawn pixels that connect areas of high or medium distances. Similar to this,

- $segmentID = 1$
- while unlabeled pixel exists
  1. Find seeding point (x_s, y_s) with maximal $D_s = D(x_s, y_s)$ and label it with $segmentID$
  2. While segment has unvisited neighbor (x, y)
     (a) if $D(x, y) \geq D_s - T$ then label (x, y) with $segmentID$
     (b) if (x, y) has a labeled neighbor (x_n, y_n) with $D(x_n, y_n) > D(x, y)$ then label (x, y) with $segmentID$
  3. $segmentID = segmentID + 1$

Fig. 3. Flooding Algorithm

open street ends are parts where an area with medium distances to drawn pixels is connected to an area of high distances. Figure 2 shows this characterization schematically. In order to make use of this, we perform an Euclidean distance transform (see Maurer *et al.* [12] for more details). This gives us the distance $D(x, y)$ of each pixel (x, y) to its nearest drawn pixel.

Based on these characteristics, we start at high-distance points flood to points with lower distance. Thus, we select always the unsegmented point with the highest distance as seeding point. By doing so, the flooding will start in surrounding areas of open street ends. Due to the flooding to pixels with lower distance, the flooding will stop at gaps as well as open street ends.

By strictly flooding to pixels with lower distances to drawn pixels, the size of a segment is directly limited by its highest distance pixel. This would lead to a high oversegmentation, especially for long, slim elements like streets. To avoid this oversegmentation, we introduce a tolerance parameter T and allow the flooding to pixel if distance $D(x, y) \geq D_s - T$ where D_s is the distance value of the seeding point. A higher tolerance T leads to larger segments but increases also the risk that open street ends and gaps will not stop the flooding.

Our flooding algorithm is displayed in in Fig. 3 and an example showing the flooding directions is shown in Fig. 4. By allowing flooding to both pixels of width $\geq D_s - T$ and pixels nearer to drawn lines, the created segments will be of homogeneous width and connected to the drawn lines. The disadvantage of this algorithm is an oversegmentation, especially for small T. To overcome this oversegmentation, a subsequent merging of segments is performed.

2.3   Segment Merging

The aim of the segment merging is to reduce the number of segments without creating an undersegmentation. Thus, we use a conservative strategy. The merging is divided into three steps that correspond to three criteria for merging. We show examples for all three steps in Fig. 5.

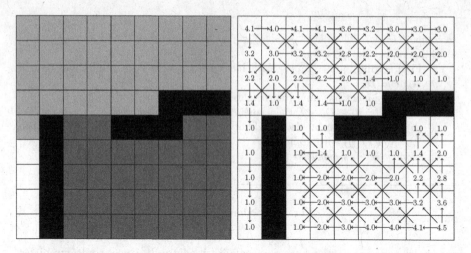

Fig. 4. Example for the flooding algorithm with $T = 3$. (a) The resulting segmentation. (b) The computed distance values and the flooding directions.

The flooding algorithm needs a small tolerance value T to stop at gaps and open street ends. This leads to oversegmented regions. In order to merge segments that belong to the same sketch object we loosen in a first step the constraint of homogeneous distances. We define the width of a segment as the maximal distance value of its pixels and allow the merging of segments with higher width differences than the tolerance value T for the flooding. We introduce another constraint to prevent merging at gaps and open street ends. This constraint is based on inner lines: inner lines are drawn lines that are on both sides connected to the same segment. After removing text, most of the drawn lines are border lines between regions instead of lying inside a region. Thus, we allow the merging of two segments only, if the amount of inner lines of the resulting segment lies below a given threshold.

For our experiments we used the following parameters. Two adjacent segments can only be merged if their width differs by less than 10 pixels and the amount of inner lines of the resulting segment is less than 10 percent of the total border. See Fig. 5 (c) for an example of this merging step.

One result of the oversegmentation are some small segments. These artefacts occur near drawn lines and have, due to their small size, a small width. Some of these segments remain after the first merging step. To overcome these artefacts, we perform a subsequent merging step for small segments. We merge the small segments with the neighbor segment with which they share the longest not drawn border. Our experiments have shown a size of $S \leq 200$ pixels as limit for small segments to be a good value. An example that shows the necessity of this step can be seen in Fig. 5 (d).

In a third merging step, we deal with fragmented objects. In some cases, the text separation does not remove all text pixels from the graphics. This leaves some objects fragmented into multiple segments. Since drawn objects often have a compact shape, we merge segments that result in a segment with higher

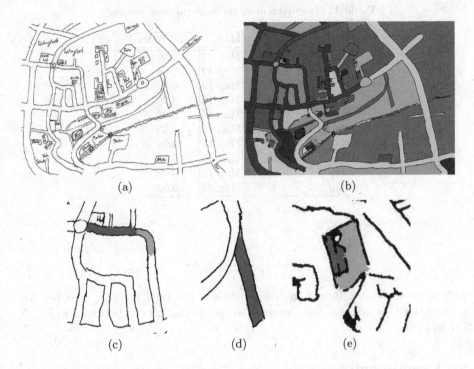

Fig. 5. Examples for the segmentation with intermediate merging steps: (a) The original sketch map. (b) The resulting segmentation. (c) Inaccurate drawing leads to different street widths and thus to oversegmented streets. The shown merging will continue with other parts and create one segment for the street. (d) The flooding leads to a small artefact at the top corner of the shown street. The size threshold merges both segments. (e) Leftovers from text separation cause an oversegmentated rectangle. The merging leads to a compacter segment.

compactness than the weighted geometric average of both parts. We compute the compactness C_s of a segment s using the maximal width W_s and its size S_s:

$$C_s = \frac{\sqrt{S_s}}{W_s} \tag{1}$$

The term for the weighted average is:

$$\bar{C}_{s,t} = C_s^{\frac{S_s}{S_s+S_t}} \cdot C_t^{\frac{S_t}{S_s+S_t}} \tag{2}$$

Using the unmodified compactness as criterion can lead to the merging of segments that are separated by a drawn line and have only a small connection. To avoid these wrongly merged segments, we use the fraction $F_{s,t}$ of the border between two segments that is drawn in the sketch map. The modified condition is:

Table 1. Measurement of the segmentation results

Map	Rand Index	Map	Rand Index
Map 1	0.96	Map 11	0.80
Map 2	0.96	Map 12	0.99
Map 3	0.65	Map 13	0.90
Map 4	0.97	Map 14	0.96
Map 5	0.92	Map 15	0.96
Map 6	0.96	Map 16	0.95
Map 7	0.85	Map 17	0.96
Map 8	0.88	Map 18	0.97
Map 9	0.94	Map 19	0.92
Map 10	0.96	Map 20	0.99

$$\frac{\bar{C}_{s \cap t}}{\bar{C}_{s,t} \cdot (1 + F_{s,t})} \geq t_C \tag{3}$$

with a threshold t_C. Based on this condition, the final merging is done. An example for this merging and the resulting segmentation can be found in Fig. 5 (b) and (e).

3 Experiments

In this section, the results of our algorithm will be presented. At first, we describe our evaluation method and present our results. In a second part, we show the robustness of our algorithm against parameter alterations. At the end of this section, we give a brief discussion of the quality of our ground truth.

3.1 Evaluation and Results

To evaluate our segmentation method, we used 20 different sketch maps that are displayed in appendix A. These sketch maps were taken from four different datasets to ensure a broad range of drawing task and drawing habits. For these maps we manually created a ground truth segmentation. These ground truth segmentations were compared to the result of our algorithm using the Rand index.

The Rand index for image segmentations compares two segmentations by counting the pairs of pixels that find agreement of both segmentations. Given an image $\mathcal{I}$ and two segmentations

$$S_1, S_2 : \mathcal{I} \to \mathbb{N}$$

there are four possibilities for a pair of pixels $p, q \in \mathcal{I}, p \neq q$:

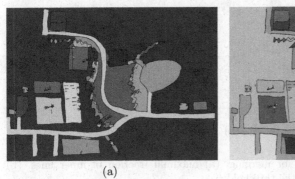 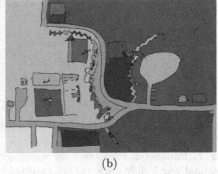

(a)   (b)

Fig. 6. Segmentation of Map 3: (a) Ground truth and (b) Results of the algorithm

1. $S_1(p) \neq S_1(q)$ and $S_2(p) \neq S_2(q)$. The number of such pairs is N_{00}.
2. $S_1(p) \neq S_1(q)$ and $S_2(p) = S_2(q)$. The number of such pairs is N_{01}.
3. $S_1(p) = S_1(q)$ and $S_2(p) \neq S_2(q)$. The number of such pairs is N_{10}.
4. $S_1(p) = S_1(q)$ and $S_2(p) = S_2(q)$. The number of such pairs is N_{11}.

$S1$ and $S2$ agree upon a pair of pixels, if both consider the pixels of pair belonging to the same segment or both consider the pixels belonging to different segments. Thus, the number of pairs upon which $S1$ and $S2$ agree is $N_{11} + N_{00}$. With the number of pixels N, then the Rand index is defined by

$$\mathcal{R}(S_1, S_2) = \frac{N_{11} + N_{00}}{N(N-1)/2} \tag{4}$$

Since $N(N-1)/2$ is the total number of pairs and $N_{11} + N_{00}$ is the number of a subset of pairs, it is necessarily

$$0 \leq N_{11} + N_{00} \leq N(N-1)/2 \iff \mathcal{R}(S_1, S_2) \in [0, 1]$$

with higher similarities leading to higher values. For a further description of the Rand index see Jiang *et al.* [9]. An overview of the Rand index of our results can be seen in Table 1.

The mean Rand index for our experiment is 0.92. Besides the good values of most maps, there are some maps that get only medium values. These values are the result of an oversegmentation of the sketch map. There are different reasons for the oversegmentation: One reason are text and symbols that interfere with other elements and can not completely be removed by the text separation technique that we use. The remaining text and symbols are considered as drawn borders and prevent a merging of segments that are divided by these elements. This leads to several small segments. Another reason for oversegmentation is a narrow drawing style. The effects of a narrow drawing style are similar to the previously mentioned effects of text and symbols.

Beside these minor effects, an oversegmentation of the background leads to low Rand index. This can especially be seen at Map 3. The background that

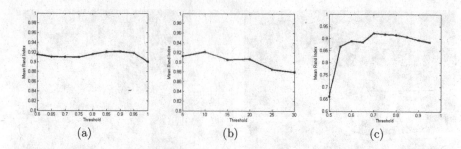

(a)   (b)   (c)

Fig. 7. Parameter robustness for merging: (a) maximal fraction of inner lines, (b) maximal width difference, (c) the threshold t_C

is represented by one segment in the ground truth is divided into four parts in the result of the algorithm (as can be seen in Fig. 6). In this sketch map, the connections between the background parts are small and slightly longer streets or a cropped image would lead to four background parts in the ground truth. Due to this fact, the oversegmentation does not have big effects on further processing of the sketch map.

3.2 Parameters

The algorithm is based on some parameters. To assure the robustness against parameter variations and determine the best values, we searched the parameter space and measured the results by the mean Rand index over all 20 sketch maps. The examined parameters are three thresholds for the merging steps: For the first merging step the maximal amount of inner lines and the maximal difference between the width of both segments. For the final merging step we examined the threshold t_C.

Our experiments showed best results for a maximum of 10% of inner lines, a maximal difference of 10 pixel and $t_C = 0.7$. The results are stable due to changes of these parameters though the values can not be chosen arbitrarily. Figure 7 shows the average Rand index for altered parameter values. For these diagrams, we fixed two parameters to the best values and altered the third one.

3.3 Effects of Ground Truth Inaccuracies

Creating the ground truth manually is a process that leads to some inaccuracy on pixel level. To increase the quality of the ground truth, we applied an automatic postprocessing method to label pixels correctly near drawn borders. Yet, there can remain wrongly labeled pixels in the ground truth. This can lead to slight errors in the resulting Rand index. In the following we will estimate this error and show that the inaccuracies in the ground truth labeling have little effect on the Rand index.

Given an image $\mathcal{I}$ and three segmentations

$$S, GT, GT^* : \mathcal{I} \mapsto \mathbb{N}$$

with the resulting segmentation S of our algorithm, the manually created ground truth GT and the perfect ground truth GT^*. Let M be the number of pixels in which GT and GT^* differ. Then the maximal error between the Rand index based on GT and the one based on GT^* can be estimated by:

$$E = |\mathcal{R}(S, GT) - \mathcal{R}(S, GT^*)| \leq \frac{M(N-1)}{N(N-1)/2} = 2\frac{M}{N} \qquad (5)$$

The inequation is valid because the computation of $\mathcal{R}(S, GT)$ and $\mathcal{R}(S, GT^*)$ can only differ in pairs that are different in GT and GT^*. An upper bound for such pairs is $M \cdot (N - 1)$. In fact for this bound the $M(M - 1)/2$ pairs with two pixels in which GT and GT^* differ are counted twice, but for our rough estimation this is good enough.

Thus, the worst-case error can be calculated based on the number of mislabeled pixels. Assuming a high rate of 1% of mislabeled pixels, the Rand index will not differ by more 0.02. Due to our postprocessing of the ground truth, the rate of mislabeled pixels will be lower than 1%.

3.4 Processing Times

We used a MATLAB implementation for our experiments. Only the flooding algorithm was written in C. The experiments were conducted on a computer with a 2.8 Ghz dual core CPU. For scanned images with 1654×2340 pixels, the flooding needs in average 3 seconds. The subsequent merging needs between 10 and 30 seconds, depending on the number of resulting segments. We expect that this time can strongly be reduced by using a more performant C implementation.

4   Conclusion and Future Work

In this paper we have presented a region based segmentation algorithm that is able to deal with inaccuracies of sketch maps like missing connections between lines and open ended streets. This algorithm produces good results. Furthermore, it could be shown that the algorithm is robust to the choice of parameter values. Only in one case the algorithm results in a medium oversegmentation. Since some oversegmentation can not be avoided, we plan to deal with the oversegmentation during a subsequent classification, using a hierarchical approach similar to an approach of Todorovic and Ahuja [17].

Beside the optimization of sketch map segmentation, a further step towards sketch understanding and processing is the classification of segments. This will enable automatic systems to understand what is drawn in the sketch map. Another step is the alignment of sketch maps that can be used to integrate the information of sketch maps into other maps. Some basic research on sketch maps that can be used to develop such a matching method has previously been done [19].

Acknowledgment. K. Broelemann is supported by the International Research Training Group 1498 "Semantic Integration of Geospatial Information" funded by DFG (German Research Foundation).

References

1. Bhuvanagiri, K., Daga, A.V., Ramachandrula, S., Kompalli, S.: Hand-drawn symbol spotting using semi-definite programming based sub-graph matching. In: Proceedings of the 12th International Conference on Frontiers in Handwriting Recognition, pp. 283–288 (2010)
2. Cousty, J., Bertrand, G., Najman, L., Couprie, M.: Watershed cuts: Minimum spanning forests and the drop of water principle. IEEE Transactions on Pattern Analysis and Machine Intelligence 31, 1362–1374 (2009)
3. Dutta, A., Llados, J., Pal, U.: Symbol spotting in line drawings through graph paths hashing. In: Proceedings of the 11th International Conference on Document Analysis and Recognition, pp. 982–986 (2011)
4. Feng, G., Viard-Gaudin, C., Sun, Z.: On-line hand-drawn electric circuit diagram recognition using 2D dynamic programming. Pattern Recognition 42(12), 3215–3223 (2009)
5. Goodchild, M.: Citizens as sensors: the world of volunteered geography. Geo Journal 69, 211–221 (2007)
6. Hammond, T., Davis, R.: LADDER, a sketching language for user interface developers. Computers & Graphics 29(4), 518–532 (2005)
7. Hammond, T., Davis, R.: Tahuti: a geometrical sketch recognition system for UML class diagrams. In: ACM SIGGRAPH 2006 Courses, SIGGRAPH 2006. ACM, New York (2006)
8. Henderson, T.C., Linton, T., Potupchik, S., Ostanin, A.: Automatic segmentation of semantic classes in raster map images. In: Proceedings of the 8th International Workshop on Graphics Recognition (2009)
9. Jiang, X., Marti, C., Irniger, C., Bunke, H.: Distance measures for image segmentation evaluation. EURASIP Journal on Applied Signal Processing, 209 (2006)
10. Leyk, S., Boesch, R., Weibel, R.: Saliency and semantic processing: Extracting forest cover from historical topographic maps. Pattern Recognition 39(5), 953–968 (2006)
11. Mas, J., Sanchez, G., Lladós, J.: SSP: Sketching Slide Presentations, a Syntactic Approach. In: Ogier, J.-M., Liu, W., Lladós, J. (eds.) GREC 2009. LNCS, vol. 6020, pp. 118–129. Springer, Heidelberg (2010)
12. Maurer, C., Qi, R., Raghavan, V.: A linear time algorithm for computing exact euclidean distance transforms of binary images in arbitrary dimensions. IEEE Transactions on Pattern Analysis and Machine Intelligence 25, 265–270 (2003)
13. Meyer, F., Lerallut, R.: Morphological Operators for Flooding, Leveling and Filtering Images Using Graphs. In: Escolano, F., Vento, M. (eds.) GbRPR. LNCS, vol. 4538, pp. 158–167. Springer, Heidelberg (2007)
14. Paulson, B., Hammond, T.: PaleoSketch: Accurate primitive sketch recognition and beautification. In: Proceedings of the 13th International Conference on Intelligent User Interfaces, pp. 1–10 (2008)
15. Schlaisich, I., Egenhofer, M.: Multimodal spatial querying: What people sketch and talk about. In: Proceedings of the 1st International Conference on Universal Access in Human-Computer Interaction, pp. 732–736 (2001)
16. Szwoch, W.: Recognition, understanding and aestheticization of freehand drawing flowcharts. In: Proceedings of the 9th International Conference on Document Analysis and Recognition, pp. 1138–1142 (2007)
17. Todorovic, S., Ahuja, N.: Region-based hierarchical image matching. International Journal of Computer Vision 78, 47–66 (2008)

18. Tombre, K., Tabbone, S., Pélissier, L., Dosch, P.: Text/Graphics Separation Revisited. In: Lopresti, D.P., Hu, J., Kashi, R.S. (eds.) DAS 2002. LNCS, vol. 2423, pp. 200–211. Springer, Heidelberg (2002)
19. Wang, J., Mülligann, C., Schwering, A.: An empirical study on relevant aspects for sketch map alignment. In: Proceedings of the 14th AGILE International Conference on Geographic Information Science (2011)
20. El Zaart, A., Ziou, D., Wang, S., Jiang, Q.: Segmentation of sar images. Pattern Recognition 35(3), 713–724 (2002)

A Sketch Map Dataset

The sketch maps that we used for our experiments are shown below to give an expression of the performed task.

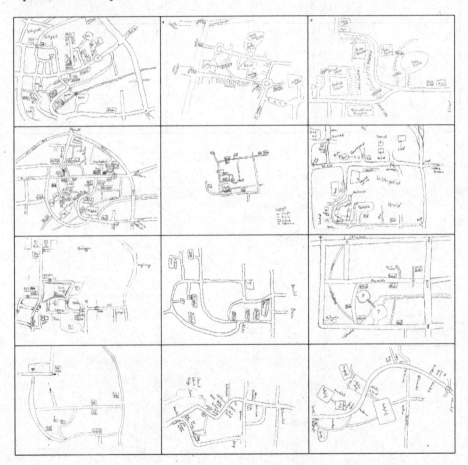

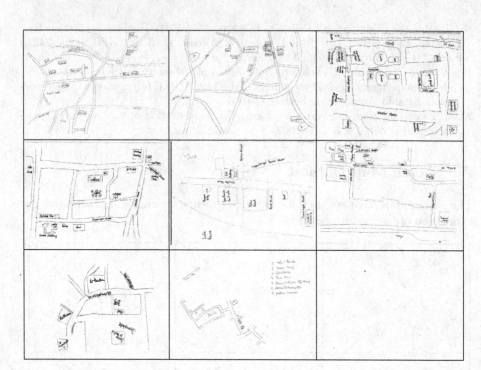

Ancient Documents Denoising and Decomposition Using Aujol and Chambolle Algorithm

Mickael Coustaty[1], Sloven Dubois[2], Michel Menard[1], and Jean-Marc Ogier[1]

[1] Laboratoire d'Informatique, Image et Interactions
Université de La Rochelle, Avenue Michel Crepeau
17042 La Rochelle, France
{mcoustat,mmenard,jmogier}@univ-lr.fr
[2] Université de Lyon, F-42023, Saint-Étienne, France
CNRS, UMR5516, Laboratoire Hubert Curien, F-42000, Saint-Étienne, France
Université de Saint-Étienne, Jean Monnet, F-42000, Saint-Étienne, France
Bâtiment F 18 Rue du Professeur Benoît Lauras, 42000 Saint-Étienne
sloven.dubois@univ-st-etienne.fr

Abstract. With the improvement of printing technology since the 15th century, there is a huge amount of printed documents published and distributed. These documents are degraded by the time and require to be preprocessed before being submitted to image indexing strategy, in order to enhance the quality of images. This paper proposes a new pre-processing that permits to denoise these documents, by using a Aujol and Chambolle algorithm. Aujol and Chambolle algorithm allows to extract meaningful components from image. In this case, we can extract shapes, textures and noise. Some examples of specific processings applied on each layer are illustrated in this paper.

Keywords: Historical documents, decomposition, denoising, Aujol and Chambolle.

1 Introduction

With the improvement of printing technology since the 15th century, there is a huge amount of printed documents published and distributed. At this period, the printed book quickly becomes a regular object in the world. By 1501, there were 1000 printings shops in Europe, which were at the basis of the production of 35,000 titles and 20 million copies. Since that time, most of these books have been falling into decay and degrading. With the disappearing of these books, the knowledge of our ancestors is also vanishing. Therefore, there are a lot of attempts to keep, organize and restore ancient printed documents. With the better digital technology, one of the preservation methods of these old documents is digitizing. This explains the large number of digitizing campaigns that one can find all over the world. However, digitizing documents is not beneficial without the ability to retrieve and extract the information from them which could be done by using techniques of document analysis and recognition. The extraction of this kind of information requires the use of high level features extraction techniques,

Y.-B. Kwon and J.-M. Ogier (Eds.): GREC, LNCS 7423, pp. 15–24, 2013.

which can be trongly altered if images are degraded. This paper proposes a set of contributions related to the use of Aujol and Chambolle algorithm for the enhancement of the quality of images.

2 NaviDoMass and Historical Document Challenges

2.1 NaviDoMass

NAVIDOMASS (Navigation into Documents Masses) is a french collaborative project. With the collaboration of seven laboratories in France, the global objective of this project is to build a framework to derive benefit from historical documents. It aims at preserving and providing public accessibility to this national heritage. NAVIDOMASS was a three-year project completed in 2010. It was established on four principles: anywhere (global access), anyone (public and multilingual), anytime and any media (accessible through various channels such as world wide web, smartphone, etc.). The focus of NAVIDOMASS was on five studies: (1) user requirement, participative design and ground truthing, (2) document layout analysis and structure based indexing, (3) information spotting, (4) structuring the feature space [8,9] and (5) interactive extraction and relevance feedback.

As a part of NAVIDOMASS project, this paper focuses on the preprocessing part, or enhancing the graphical part of the document in order to use it in indexing. However, the main interest of this study is based on specific graphics called drop caps and is inspired by [14] and [16]. Even if the use case of this paper is reduced to drop caps analysis (also called dropcaps or ornemental letters), the aim of this study is to develop complex graphic pre-processing techniques. By complex graphic, we mean here any graphic document which does not respect a rigourous structure, as one can find in the domain of symbol recognition for instance.

2.2 Historical Documents Specificities

Historical documents are specific in many different points. The first difference between historical and actual documents relies on the structure and the variation of structure of these documents. Actually, when you buy a newspaper, you can usually find texts, graphics and images. All these elements, and their spatial organization, compose the structure of the document. In contemporary documents, this structure is generally well-defined, can be clearly identified, and is the same for a category of document (all books have a title, a subtitle, ...). In the case of heritage documents, the structure was specific to each document and to each printer. An example of this heterogeneity can be observed in Figure 1, where documents from different libraries are presented.

The second difference relies on the method used to print these documents. At the beginning of the print technology, a machine applied a wood stamp on paper to deposit ink. These stamps degrades themselves with time and the number of impressions. The usury of stamps deteriorate the quality of books, texts and illustrations which create a big quantity of variations for a same model. For example, one can see in Figure 1 that the same image differs in different books.

Fig. 1. Different types of documents and variations of an image

From these two problems, we can see that historical documents are hard to segment and to retrieve in database. The variations of structure prevent to create a unique treatment to compare documents and their contents. Moreover, these documents are rich in term of information and complexity and identifying an element only by a global description of the document is impossible.

Finally, heritage documents are subjected to the ageing, and all the marks of time (mildew, thining of paper, ...). All these problems create a non uniform background in which we can find the text of the back page, variation of gray-levels and differents elements which make though the extraction and the segmentation of content of documents. In this next of this paper, we propose a new method, based on the use of the Aujol and Chambolle algorithm, to denoise images of documents and to simplify them by decomposing each image in different layers of information. We first work on a treatment adapted to image containing principally text and in a second time images of drop caps.

3   Grayscale Decomposition Model of J-F Aujol and A. Chambolle

Decomposing an image into meaningful components appears as one of major aims in recent development in image processing. This kind of model comes from well known ill-posed problem in image processing, the aim of which is to recover an ideal image u, from a degraded observation f as follow: $f = Au + v$ (with A a linear operator representing blur and v the noise, often additive). Retrieving the original image can then be seen as a deconvolution which is an ill-posed problem: operator A is not boundedly invertible in $H = L^2(a, b)$ (A is compact in H).

The first goal was image restoration and denoising, but following the ideas of Yves Meyer [11], in total variation minimization framework of L. Rudin, S. Osher and E. Fatemi [10], image decomposition into geometrical and oscillatory (i.e texture) component appears as useful and very interesting way for our image analysis case. Indeed, we want to obtain the main structure of images in order to properly segment drop caps, independently of textured parts and avoid aquisition problems like noise.

Our aim is to catch the pure geometrical component in an image independently of texture and noise. For this, in [2], J-F. Aujol and A. Chambolle propose a decomposition model which splits a grayscale image into three components: the first one, $u \in BV$ [1], containing the structure of the image, a second one, $v \in G$ [2], the texture, and the third one, $w \in E$ [3], the noise. For better comprehension of differents spaces, see [1,2,3,7]. One of the main advantage of this decomposition is its reversibility, as when an image has been decomposed, we are able to reconstruct it, with a precision related to the rounding errors.

This decomposition model is based on a minimization of this discretized functional F:

$$\inf_{(u,v,w)\in X^3} F(u,v,w) = J(u) + J^*\left(\frac{v}{\mu}\right) + B^*\left(\frac{w}{\lambda}\right) + \frac{1}{2\alpha}\|f - u - v - w\|_{L^2}$$

where $J(u)$ is the total variation related to the extraction of the geometrical component, $J^*\left(\frac{v}{\mu}\right)$, $B^*\left(\frac{w}{\lambda}\right)$ are the Legendre-Fenchel transforms[4] of respectively J and B [3] for the extraction of texture and noise components, parameter α controls the $L^2 - norm$ of the residual $f - u - v - w$ and X is the discrete euclidean space $\mathbb{R}^{N \times N}$ for images of size $N \times N$.

For minimizing this functionnal, Chambolle's projection algorithm is used [2]. The Chambolle's projection P on space λB_G [5] of f is denoted $P_{\lambda B_G}(f)$ and is solved by an iterative algorithm. This algorithm starts with $P^0 = 0$ and for each pixel (i,j) and at each step $n+1$ we have:

$$P_{i,j}^{n+1} = \frac{P_{i,j}^n + \tau \left(\triangle div\left(P^n\right) - \frac{f}{\lambda}\right)_{i,j}}{1 + \tau \left|\triangle div\left(P^n\right) - \frac{f}{\lambda}\right|_{i,j}} \tag{1}$$

---

[1] $BV(\Omega)$ is the subspace of functions $u \in L^1(\Omega)$ such that the following quantity, called the total variation of u, is finite:

$$J(u) = sup\left\{\int_\Omega u(x)div(\xi(x))dx\right\}$$

such that $\xi \in C_c^1(\Omega, \mathbb{R}^2), \|\xi\|_{L^\infty(\Omega)} \leq 1$.

[2] G is the subspace introduced by Meyer for oscillating patterns. G denotes the Banach space composed of the distributions f which can be written $f = \partial_1 g_1 + \partial_2 g_2 = div(g)$ with g_1 and g_2 in $L^\infty(\Omega)$. On G, the following norm is associated:

$$\|v\|_G = inf\{\|g\|_{L^\infty(\Omega, R^2)}/v = div(g),$$
$$g = (g_1, g_2), |g(x)| = \sqrt{(|g_1|^2 + |g_2|^2)(x)}\}$$

[3] E is another dual space to model oscillating patterns. $\dot{B}_{1,1}^1$ is the usual homogeneous Besov space and the dual space of $\dot{B}_{1,1}^1$ is the Banach space $E = \dot{B}_{-1,\infty}^\infty$.

[4] The Legendre-Fenchel transform of F is given by $F^*(v) = sup_u(\langle u, v\rangle_{L^2} - F(u))$, where $\langle .,.\rangle_{L^2}$ stands for the L^2 inner product [15].

[5] $\lambda B_G = \{f \in G/\|f\|_G \leq \lambda\}$.

In [4] a sufficient condition ensuring the convergence of this algorithm is given: $\tau \leqslant \frac{1}{8}$. To solve (3), the authors propose the algorithm of figure 2.

Algorithm :
Initialization: $u = v = 0$

1. u and v have been previously computed, we estimate: $\tilde{w} = P_{\delta B_E} \left(f - u - v \right)$
2. then we compute: $\tilde{v} = P_{\mu B_G} \left(f - u - \tilde{w} \right)$
3. and we finally obtain: $\tilde{u} = f - u - \tilde{v} - \tilde{w} - P_{\lambda B_G} \left(f - \tilde{v} - \tilde{w} \right)$

This operation is repeated until :

$$max(|\tilde{u} - u|, |\tilde{v} - v|, |\tilde{w} - w|) \leqslant \varepsilon$$

Fig. 2. Grayscale image decomposition algorithm

In [2], the authors replace $P_{\delta B_E}(f - u - v)$ by $f - u - v - W_{ST}(f - u - v, \delta)$ where $W_{ST}(f - u - v, \delta)$ stands for the wavelet soft-thresholding of $f - u - v$ with threshold δ defined by :

$$S_\delta \left(d_i^j \right) = \left\{ \begin{array}{cc} d_i^j - \delta sign \left(d_i^j \right) & if \quad |d_i^j| > \delta \\ 0 & if \quad |d_i^j| \leqslant \delta \end{array} \right. \tag{2}$$

where d_i^j is the wavelet coefficient, j the resolution and $i \in \{x, y, xy\}$. The figure 3 shows the application of grayscale decomposition model of J-F Aujol and A. Chambolle into an image.

In the next section, the benefits of this algorithm on historical documents are presented.

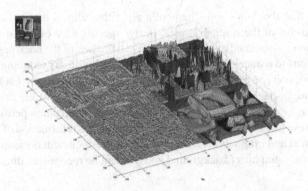

Fig. 3. Image decomposition. From top to bottom and left to right: Texture component (v), original noisy image (f), noise component (w) and regular or geometrical part (u).

4   Pre-processing for Historical Documents Based on the Aujol and Chambolle Algorithm

In all this section , we will call "shape layer" the image associated to the regular and geometrical part, and "texture layer" the texture component, obtained by the Aujol and Chambolle algorithm.

4.1   Denoising Text

We can see in the Figure 4(a) that images of old documents are degraded and some see through text of the back page appear. The Aujol and Chambolle algorithm is used on old documents images to separate informations in three layers. The two first layers (shapes and texture layers) are exposed in Figure 4(b) and in Figure 4(c).

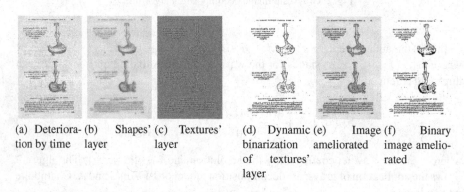

(a) Deteriora- (b)   Shapes' (c) Textures'   (d) Dynamic (e)   Image (f)   Binary
tion by time   layer   layer   binarization ameliorated image amelio-
                                                  of   textures'   rated
                                                  layer

Fig. 4. A page degraded by time. The three layers extract with the Aujol and Chambolle algorithm (a, b, c) and image ameliorated for segmentation (d, e, f)

One can see that the Aujol and Chambolle algorithm allows to distinctly separate shapes from textures of the original image. In our specific case of literal and graphic document, the layer associated to texture contains all the text of the back page while the shape layer permits to reduce effect of time on the background. By reducing the number of colours to two, one can easily isolates textures of the front from the back one. Once we get the texture of the front page, we add it to the shape layer of the original image to obtain the image in Figure 4(e). And finally, a classical binarization permits to obtain the document presented in Figure 4(f) which contains all the information of the original document with text and graphics. The new version of the document is easier to segment in three parts : text / graphics / background and text can be recognized directly.

4.2   Simplifying Drop Caps

Images composed only of graphics, like drop caps, are very rich in information. One can see in Figure 5 that Aujol and Chambolle algorithm simplifies the image and permits to obtain three layers of information on which we can apply specific preprocessings. For example, shapes' layer permits a better and easier shapes' extraction for recognition. In addition, shapes obtained are cleaned, allowing us to abstain from the noise, what offers greater robustness for segmentation and description.

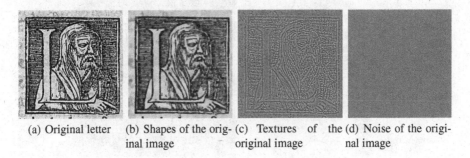

(a) Original letter   (b) Shapes of the orig- (c) Textures   of   the (d) Noise of the origi-
                         inal image   original image   nal image

Fig. 5. An example of drop cap using Aujol and Chambolle algorithm

This decomposition gives us simplified images and particularly we have worked on shapes' layer to extract most significant shapes like the letter or faces [6], arms, legs [5], etc. All these elements are useful for historians to retrieve similar images by content. Another application we have developed consisted in applying a segmentation process on textures to extract relevant ones which correspond to important elements, like in [12].

Furthermore, we can see that fundamental elements of drop caps are composed of one or many shapes, mixed with one or many textured regions. A global approach, the aim of which is to describe an image without dissociating these two kind of information, can't precisely describe this kind of elements and these images (main features are dedicated to one kind of information). It becomes then necessary to separate shapes from textures, by simplifying the image.

One solution, to simplify images, consists in using a decomposition that allows separating different kind of elements in the image in different layers. Each layer is then composed of elements with the same properties (only textured regions, only shapes, ...). It is then possible to apply classical features computation adapted to the content of the layer to get a specific description of the layer content. Finally, the global description of the image relies on the combination of all these descriptions.

4.3 Evaluation

The evaluation of such a system is a fundamental point because it guarantees its possible usability by the users, and because it permits to have an objective regard on the system. In the context of such a project, the implementation of an objective evaluation device is quite difficult, because of the variability of the user requirements on the one hand (historians researchers, netsurfers, are likely to retrieve many different information which can be very different the one from the others), and because this filtering stage in a preliminary process in the global indexing system. However it appears to be important

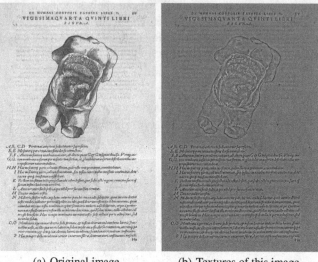

(a) Original image   (b) Textures of this image

Fig. 6. An example of surimpressing

to evaluate it. In the context of NAVIDOMASS project, considering the fundamental aspect of this filtering stage, we propose to use signal processing evaluation criteria: the Signal Noise Ratio (SNR). In the context of such images databases, the main difficulty is to implement a groundtruth for the evaluation of a processing. Considering this difficulty, we decided to use a synthetic noise generator applied on a set of cleaned images, and to evaluate the capacity of our system to remove this noise.

The protocol that we have implemented is the following one:

1. We considered a significant set of images of newspaper documents (see Figure 7). We chose images of newspaper because they have an homogenous background, a good contrast between text and background and no initial noise
2. We generated some additive synthetic noise on these images by using different parameters for this additive noise
3. On each of these images, we applied Aujol and Chambolle algorithm, in order to separate the different layers: shape, texture and noise
4. A binarization stage is applied on the texture layer in order to separate the texture corresponding to the text layer, and the texture coming from issuing from surimpressing. As one can see on Figure 6, thanks to this dynamic binarization stage ([13]), all the layer issuing from the background character layer is removed
5. A combination XOR of the texture layer remaining at the issue of the stage 4, and the shape layer is operated in order to build the filtered image
6. At the issue of this stage 5, the resulting image is the filtered image. A computation of its SNR is operated and compared to the original image one

As one can see, this protocol has been applied on a set of document images, on which we have applied different additive synthetic noises, with different statistics. With this

(a) Original image   (b) Noised image

Fig. 7. An example of newspaper

protocol, more than 86% of the 29 images of newpapers which have been tested gave a better SNR. The results are very satisfying, since, the removal of the noise is very efficient (evaluation based on the SNR). These excellent results are validated and confirmed by our historian experts, in terms of pre-processing for further indexing operations.

5   Conclusion and Perspectives

This paper present a new method to simplify and denoise old documents images in order to index them. This process relies on a Aujol and Chambolle algorithm which allow to obtain three layers of information: 1) regularized one which contain shapes, 2) textures one which contain all the oscillating elements and 3) noise one which correspond to the original image less the two first layers. From this decomposition, one can apply specific treatments on one or many layers. In our case, we used shapes' and textures' layers in two example: first one to pick out text of back page and a second one to extract region of interest. Experimentations are promising and we will ameliorate these results in future works. One interesting perspective that we plan to study consists in conjointly analysing the spatial organisation of the shapes regions against the textures ones. This analysis will permit to take into account the semantic of these complex images.

References

1. Aujol, J.F., Aubert, G., Feraud, L.B., Chambolle, A.: Image decomposition into a bounded variation component and an oscillating component. Journal of Mathematical Imaging and Vision 22(1), 71–88 (2005), http://dx.doi.org/10.1007/s10851-005-4783-8
2. Aujol, J.-F., Chambolle, A.: Dual norms and image decomposition models. International Journal of Computer Vision 63(1), 85–104 (2005), http://dx.doi.org/10.1007/s11263-005-4948-3

3. Aujol, J.-F., Gilboa, G., Chan, T., Osher, S.: Structure-texture image decomposition - modeling, algorithms, and parameter selection. International Journal of Computer Vision 67(1), 111–136 (2006), http://dx.doi.org/10.1007/s11263-006-4331-z

4. Chambolle, A.: Total Variation Minimization and a Class of Binary MRF Models. In: Rangarajan, A., Vemuri, B.C., Yuille, A.L. (eds.) EMMCVPR 2005. LNCS, vol. 3757, pp. 136–152. Springer, Heidelberg (2005)

5. Coustaty, M., Bouju, A., Bertet, K., Louis, G.: Using ontologies to reduce the semantic gap between historians and image processing algorithms. In: IEEE International Conference on Document Analysis and Recognition, Beijing, China, pp. 156–160 (2011)

6. Coustaty, M., Pareti, R., Vincent, N., Ogier, J.-M.: Towards historical document indexing: extraction of drop cap letters. IJDAR 14(3), 243–254 (2011)

7. Elhamidi, A., Menard, M., Lugiez, M., Ghannam, C.: Weighted and extended total variation for image restoration and decomposition. Pattern Recognition 43(4), 1564–1576 (2010)

8. Chouaib, H., Tabbone, S., Ramos, O.: Feature selection combining genetic algorithm and adaboost classifiers. In: ICPR 2008, Florida (2008)

9. Jouili, S., Tabbone, S.: Applications des graphes en traitement d'images. In: ROGICS 2008, pp. 434–442. University of Ottawa, University of Sfax, Canada, Tunisia (2008)

10. Rudin, L., Osher, S., Fatemi, E.: Nonlinear total variation based noise removal. Physica D 60, 259–269 (1992)

11. Meyer, Y.: Oscillating patterns in image processing and nonlinear evolution equations. In: The Fifteenth Dean Jacqueline B. Lewis Memorial Lectures (2001)

12. Nguyen, T.T.H., Coustaty, M., Ogier, J.M.: Bags of strokes based approach for classification and indexing of drop caps. In: IEEE International Conference on Document Analysis and Recognition, Beijing, China, pp. 349–353 (2011)

13. Otsu, N.: A threshold selection method from grey scale histogram. IEEE Trans. on Syst. Man and Cyber (1979)

14. Pareti, R., Vincent, N.: Ancient initial letters indexing. In: ICPR 2006: Proceedings of the 18th International Conference on Pattern Recognition, pp. 756–759. IEEE Computer Society, Washington, DC (2006)

15. Starck, J.L., ELad, M., Donoho, D.: Image decomposition via the combination of sparse representation and variationnal approach. IEEE Trans. Image Process (2005)

16. Uttama, S., Loonis, P., Delalandre, M., Ogier, J.-M.: Segmentation and Retrieval of Ancient Graphic Documents. In: Liu, W., Lladós, J. (eds.) GREC 2005. LNCS, vol. 3926, pp. 88–98. Springer, Heidelberg (2006)

Efficient and Robust Graphics Recognition from Historical Maps

Yao-Yi Chiang[1], Stefan Leyk[2], and Craig A. Knoblock[3]

[1] Information Sciences Institute and Spatial Sciences Institute,
University of Southern California, 4676 Admiralty Way, Marina del Rey, CA 90292, USA
yaoyichi@isi.edu
[2] Department of Geography, University of Colorado, UCB260, Boulder, CO 80309, USA
stefan.leyk@colorado.edu
[3] Department of Computer Science and Information Sciences Institute,
University of Southern California, 4676 Admiralty Way, Marina del Rey, CA 90292, USA
knoblock@isi.edu

Abstract. Historical maps contain rich cartographic information, such as road networks, but this information is "locked" in images and inaccessible to a geographic information system (GIS). Manual map digitization requires intensive user effort and cannot handle a large number of maps. Previous approaches for automatic map processing generally require expert knowledge in order to fine-tune parameters of the applied graphics recognition techniques and thus are not readily usable for non-expert users. This paper presents an efficient and effective graphics recognition technique that employs interactive user intervention procedures for processing historical raster maps with limited graphical quality. The interactive procedures are performed on color-segmented preprocessing results and are based on straightforward user training processes, which minimize the required user effort for map digitization. This graphics recognition technique eliminates the need for expert users in digitizing map images and provides opportunities to derive unique data for spatiotemporal research by facilitating time-consuming map digitization efforts. The described technique generated accurate road vector data from a historical map image and reduced the time for manual map digitization by 38%.

Keywords: Color image segmentation, road vectorization, historical raster maps, image cleaning.

1 Introduction

Maps contain valuable cartographic information, such as locations of historical places, contour lines, building footprints, and hydrography. Extracting such cartographic information from maps (i.e., creating spatial layers that can be processed in a GIS) would support multiple applications and research fields. For example, there are numerous cases in which historical maps have been used to carry out research in land-cover change and biogeography [Kozak et al., 2007; Petit and Lambin, 2002], and urban-area development [Dietzel et al., 2005].

Y.-B. Kwon and J.-M. Ogier (Eds.): GREC, LNCS 7423, pp. 25–35, 2013.

Today, thousands of such maps and map series are available in scanned raster format (i.e., digital map images) in a variety of digital archives. Previous work on extracting cartographic information from raster maps typically requires intensive user intervention for training and parameter tuning, in particular, when processing historical maps of poor graphical quality [Gamba and Mecocci, 1999; Leyk and Boesch, 2010]. Consequently, most studies that utilize cartographic information from historical maps for their analysis are based on time-consuming manual map digitization, which introduces subjectivity because of the missing reproducibility and the limited number of maps that can be digitized. More advanced semi- or fully- automated procedures for cartographic information extraction from historical maps would allow the advancement of such studies by including historical spatial data that are derived from a variety of maps, underlie repeatable procedures with reproducible results, and cover large areas.

In this paper, we present an interactive graphics recognition technique based on straightforward user training processes to minimize the required user effort for processing raster maps, especially for the raster maps that have limited graphical quality. We demonstrate this approach using a historical U.S. Geological Survey (USGS) topographic map in a road vectorization example, which builds on our previous work on color image segmentation (CIS) [Leyk, 2010] and road vectorization [Chiang et al., 2008; Chiang and Knoblock, 2011]. The USGS topographic map suffers from poor graphical quality and thus represents a particularly challenging research object.

The remainder of this paper is organized as follows. Section 2 discusses related work. Section 3 presents our graphics recognition technique using an example of road vectorization from a historical USGS topographic map. Section 4 reports on our experimental results. Section 5 presents the conclusions and future work.

2   Recent Work

Here we provide a brief review of recent map processing research; a more detailed review can be found in [Chiang, 2010; Chiang and Knoblock, 2011]. Extracting cartographic information from raster maps is challenging due to poor image quality caused by scanning or image compression processes, as well as the aging of the archived paper material, which often causes effects of false coloring, blurring or bleaching [Chen et al., 2006; Dhar and Chanda, 2006; Gamba and Mecocci, 1999]. The complexity of raster map contents increases if there are overlapping map layers of geographic features, such as roads, contour lines, and labels in different or similar colors. Color image segmentation has been investigated as a preprocessing step to separate individual map color layers [Chen et al., 2006; Chiang, 2010; Leyk, 2010; Leyk and Boesch, 2010]. However, there are still limitations when processing poor quality images of historical maps [Leyk, 2010].

Much research has been devoted to extracting geographic features from particular map series. For example, Itonaga et al. [2003] describe a road-line vectorization approach from computer-generated maps that cannot be applied to scanned maps. Dhar and Chanda [2006] extract geographic features from Indian survey maps based on user-specified image processing filters that exploit the geometric properties of these features. Another exemplary approach that is highly customized to a specific map series is the work by Raveaux et al. [2008] on extracting quartiers from historical French cadastral maps. As with many other recent approaches, the described extraction procedures from Itonaga et al. [2003], Chanda [2006], and Raveaux et al. [2008] have limited applicability to other map series or types and require expert knowledge for parameter tuning.

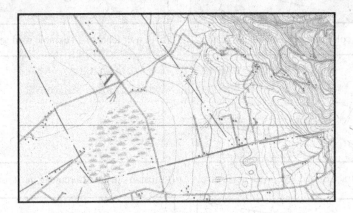

Fig. 1. A sample USGS historical topographic map

3 Methods: Road Vectorization from a Historical USGS Topographic Map

We demonstrate our approach using a road vectorization example. Figures 1 shows a sample USGS historical topographic map. Typical problems existed in old maps (and can be seen here too) that limit the graphical image quality are bleaching and blurring effects as well as mixed or false coloring as consequences of archiving paper material and scanning procedures. Figure 2 illustrates the different steps and the user interface of the described technique. Our graphic recognition approach consists of three major steps: (i) separation of homogeneous thematic map layers using color image segmentation (CIS) [Leyk, 2010], (ii) interactive extraction and cleaning of these separated map layers, and (iii) subsequent raster-to-vector conversion of the cleaned map layers [Chiang et al., 2008; Chiang and Knoblock, 2011].

3.1 Color Image Segmentation

As an important preprocessing step, color image segmentation (CIS) separates thematic homogeneous colored map layers. CIS is of critical importance since the outcome directly determines the image processing methods to be applied in all subsequent stages of data extraction. In our previous work, a hierarchical CIS approach based on homogeneity computation, color space clustering, and iterative global/local color prototype matching has been implemented and tested on historical USGS topographic maps (Figures 1 shows a sample map) [Leyk, 2010]. The only input parameters for this

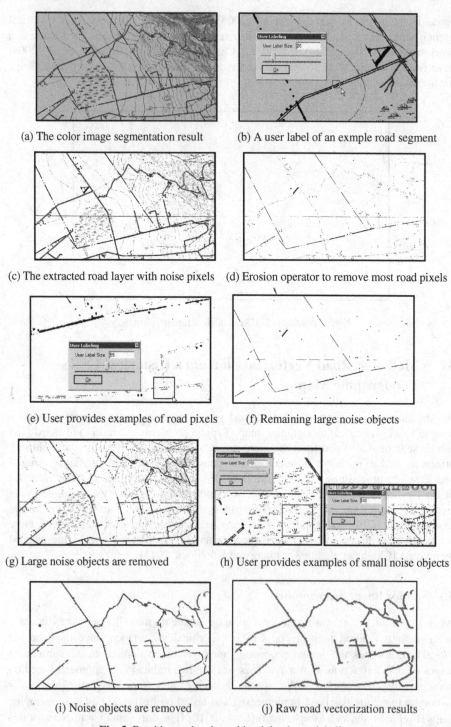

(a) The color image segmentation result   (b) A user label of an exmple road segment

(c) The extracted road layer with noise pixels   (d) Erosion operator to remove most road pixels

(e) User provides examples of road pixels   (f) Remaining large noise objects

(g) Large noise objects are removed   (h) User provides examples of small noise objects

(i) Noise objects are removed   (j) Raw road vectorization results

Fig. 2. Road layer cleaning with minimal user labeling

CIS approach are the number and types of color layers. The approach has been improved for this paper to overcome some reported limitations in the final region-growing step, such as merging of nearby elevation or road line features. Constraining the final segments to maximum widths and enforcing connectivity between homogeneous portions was incorporated in order to avoid such merging effects and thus improve the final CIS output.

Figure 2(a) shows the result of CIS of the original USGS topographic map portion (Figure 1). While the performance of the segmentation is visually satisfying (i.e., individual map layers are shown in unique colors), there are some remaining merging and mixing effects at places with dense elevation contours and road lines as well as gaps in road lines where they intersect with elevation contours; these problems are caused by issues of graphical quality as described earlier. Although this CIS procedure could be further tuned to provide better results, the raw and unrepaired segmentation outcome is used to test the robustness of the subsequent cleaning and road vectorization steps when using a general non-post-processed (and thus sub-optimal) CIS outcome.

3.2 Road Layer Extraction and Cleaning by Example

Road Layer Extraction by Example. To extract the road layer (the black layer in the CIS result) from the segmented map, first one sample area (approximately) centered on a road line has to be identified by a user. Figure 2(b) shows the user interface for the road-vectorization approach. Using this interface a user labels a rectangular area of 20-by-20 pixels to provide a "road sample." The thematic map layer that has the same color as the identified road lines (i.e., the road-like features) are automatically identified in the entire map image and the road type (e.g., parallel lines or single lines) and road width are determined [Chiang and Knoblock, 2011]. This step is carried out in a rotation-invariant way. Figure 2(c) shows the identified road layer. In this example, the majority of the detected linear features have a width of one pixel.

Road Layer Cleaning by Example. The identified road layer might contain non-road pixels depending on the quality of the input maps and the CIS result. Therefore, prior to generating the road vector data, the road layer has to be cleaned. Commercial products for raster-to-vector conversion, such as R2V[1] and Vextractor,[2] generally include image-processing tools, such as morphological or structural operators that can be selected and adjusted by the user to manually clean the raster image. However, this manual process requires expert knowledge and is very time consuming. In order to overcome such limitations, in this paper, we present an interactive technique, which incorporates simple user training processes for removing the undesired (non-road) pixels. This technique exploits user provided "noise samples" in order to identify appropriate image-processing filters and to generate parameter sets. These parameterized image-processing filters are then applied to efficiently clean the map image and remove existing noise.

---

[1] http://www.ablesw.com/r2v/
[2] http://www.vextrasoft.com/vextractor.htm

In this road vectorization example, the first step of our cleaning process removes large non-road objects (noise objects that are thicker than road lines); the second step removes small non-road objects. To identify large non-road objects in the road-layer-extraction result (Figure 2(c)), first, an image (Figure 2(d)) is created in which the majority of road lines are eliminated by applying the erosion operator and thus non-road objects remained. The number of iterations for erosion is determined by the detected road width (one pixel according to the one collected sample) [Chiang and Knoblock, 2011].

The identified large noise objects (Figure 2(d)) contain some road pixels that are not eliminated by the erosion operator. This is because some of the road lines are thicker than the identified road width. To remove these road pixels from the identified large noise objects, the user provides an example containing road pixels that are not removed by the erosion operator (Figure 2(e)). The connected components in Figure 2(d) that have a similar length, width, and number of pixels as the ones in the new user label (Figure 2(e)) are removed automatically; they represent parts of road features and will be preserved. Figure 2(f) shows the remaining large noise objects that exceed the detected (sampled) typical road width. Removing the objects in Figure 2(f) from Figure 2(c) results in the image shown in Figure 2(g) which contains road pixels and small noise objects.

To remove the remaining small noise objects in Figure 2(g), the user again provides local areas containing samples of the objects in question (Figure 2(h)). Connected components that show similar sizes as the ones in the samples are then removed from Figure 2(g) in order to generate the final cleaning result (Figure 2(i)).

3.3   Road Layer Vectorization

Once the road layer has been cleaned, we employ our previously described technique for automatic generation of road geometry [Chiang et al., 2008] and subsequently convert the road geometry to road vector data automatically [Chiang and Knoblock, 2011]. Figure 2(j) shows the road vectorization results (without manual post-processing) consisting of 1-pixel wide road centerlines.

In this road vectorization example, the horizontal map grid line is not removed during the cleaning process and the vectorization result thus contains a portion of these grid lines. Additional operators would be needed or manual post-processing (manually edit the road vector data) would have to be done to remove such elements. Also some broken road lines can be observed, which indicates the need to refine the procedure or to manually edit the final data layer. Such post-processing steps are generally needed for both semi- and fully- automatic approaches to process maps of limited image quality.

4   Experiments

In this section our experiments are described in which the proposed approach is tested for extracting road vector data from a historical USGS topographic map that covers the city of St. Jose, California.[3,4] Figure 3(a) shows the original map tile (2283 × 2608 pixels). We compared the interactive recognition technique with a completely manual map digitization process by (i) the required manual processing time and (ii) the accuracy of extracted road vector data. The required manual processing time for our approach includes the time for user labeling and manual post-processing. We use Esri ArcMap[5] for both our manual post-processing step and the compared manual digitization work.

Given the test map tile, a user first specified the number of desired map layers. Then the segmented map with separated color layer was generated based on CIS (Figure 3(b)). The user-specified number of desired map layers was 4 in this case: black, red, blue and white (background). Within the segmented map, the user selected 1 sample area of roads and 2 sample areas of noise objects to generate a cleaned road layer. Figure 4(a) shows the extracted road layer with some of the remaining non-road pixels, and Figure 4(b) shows the cleaned result after removing these noise pixels. Some of the broken road lines were also eliminated, accidentally. The cleaned road layer was then automatically converted to a set of road vector line features. Finally, the user manually edited the road vector data (e.g., recover the broken lines) to achieve a complete road vectorization result.

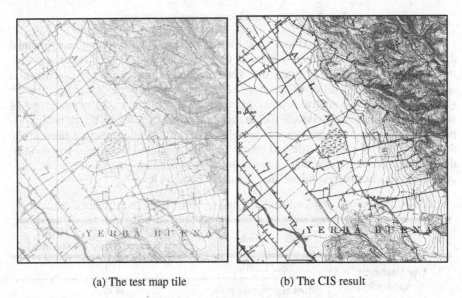

(a) The test map tile   (b) The CIS result

Fig. 3. The test map tile and intermediate results

---

[3] USGS Topographic Maps: Map page, San Jose, California (San Jose Quadrangle); edition of 1899 (reprint 1926), engraved in July 1897 by USGS; scale: 1/62,500

[4] The detailed information for obtaining the test map and the ground truth can be found on: http://www.isi.edu/integration/data/maps/ prj_map_extract_data.html

[5] http://www.esri.com/

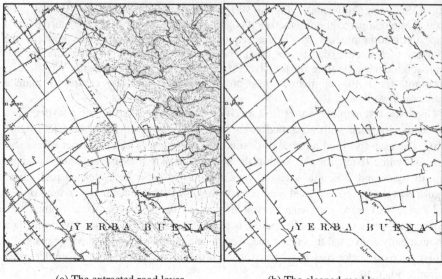

(a) The extracted road layer   (b) The cleaned road layer

Fig. 4. The test map tile and intermediate results

Table 1 shows the required user time for our approach and the completely manual digitization. Our approach required a total of 50 minutes and 33 seconds to vectorize the road network from the test map tile. The computing time for road-layer-extraction was 3 seconds, for road-layer-cleaning 52 seconds, and for road vectorization 56 seconds. In contrast, complete manual digitization required 1 hour, 21 minutes, and 24 seconds. Our approach reduced the digitization time by *38%*. The manual post-processing time in our approach was mainly spent with creating missing lines in the top-right corner of the map tile and connecting broken lines. The completely manual digitization required more than 1 hour because manual tracing of the exact road centerlines requires precise mouse movement on the pixel level.

Table 1. Comparison of the required user time for road vectorization from the test map

Methods	Task	Manual Work Time (Hours: Minutes: Seconds)
Our Interactive Approach	User labeling	0:0:33
	Manual post-processing	0:49:52
Completely Manual Approach	Manual Digitization	01:21:24

We also compared the extracted road vector data from the two approaches based on the completeness, correctness, quality, redundancy, and the root-mean-square (RMS) difference (the average distance between the extracted lines and the ground truth) [Heipke et al., 1997; Chiang and Knoblock, 2011]. We use the manual digitization results as ground truth to compute the described metrics from the road vector data generated by our interactive approach.

Table 2. Accuracy of the extracted road vector data from our interactive approach using the manual digitization results as the ground truth

Road Buffer	Completeness	Correctness	Redundancy	RMS
1 pixel	99.9%	100%	0.054%	0.152 pixels
2 pixels	100%	100%	0.14%	0.152 pixels

The completeness is the length of true positives divided by the sum of the lengths of true positives and false negatives, and the optimum is 100%. The correctness is the length of true positives divided by the sum of the lengths of true positives and false positives, and the optimum is 100%. The redundancy is the length of matched extraction minus the length of matched reference. The redundancy shows the percentage of the matched ground truth that is redundant (i.e., more than one true positive line matched to one ground-truth line), and the optimum is 0. The RMS difference is the average distance between the extracted lines and the ground truth, which represents the geometrical accuracy of the extracted road vector data. To identify the length of the true positives, false negatives, and matched ground truth, we used buffer widths of 1 and 2 pixels. This means that a correctly extracted line is no farther than 1 or 2 pixels from the ground truth.

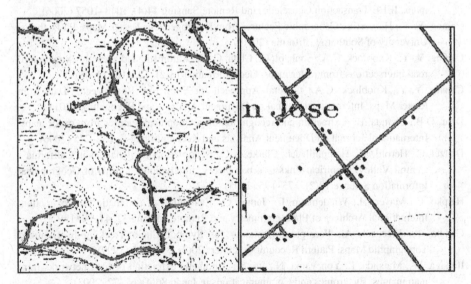

Fig. 5. Samples of our road vectorization results

Table 2 shows the accuracy of our extracted road vector data using the manual digitization results as the ground truth. Our approach generated accurate results (high completeness and correctness) at both 1-pixel and 2-pixel buffer sizes. In addition, our results contain very few redundant road lines and are very close to the ground truth regarding their geometry (i.e., low RMS). Figure 5 shows details of portions of the final road vector data from our approach on top of the extracted raster black layer. Note that the resultant road vector data are very close to the original road centerlines.

5   Conclusions and Future Work

We presented an efficient and robust approach for graphics recognition from historical raster maps. We showed that this approach minimizes the required user intervention and reduces the manual digitization time for road vectorization from a historical USGS topographic map by 38%. The presented technique shows high potential for robust extraction of cartographic information from historical maps of low graphical quality and opens unique opportunities for "spatio-historical" research in various fields.

We plan to improve our graphics recognition technique by further refining and constraining the final region-growing step in the CIS to reduce the number of noise objects in the CIS result. Moreover, we plan to incorporate connectivity and additional geometry constraints in the image-cleaning-by-example step to further reduce the required manual processing time.

References

Chen, Y., Wang, R., Qian, J.: Extracting contour lines from common-conditioned topographic maps. IEEE Transaction Geoscienceand Remote Sensing 44(4), 1048–1057 (2006)

Chiang, Y.-Y.: Harvesting Geographic Features from Heterogeneous Raster Maps. Ph.D. thesis, University of Southern California (2010)

Chiang, Y.-Y., Knoblock, C.A., Shahabi, C., Chen, C.-C.: Automatic and accurate extraction of road intersections from raster maps. GeoInformatica 13(2), 121–157 (2008)

Chiang, Y.-Y., Knoblock, C.A.: General Approach for Extracting Road Vector Data from Raster Maps. International Journal on Document Analysis and Recognition (2011)

Dhar, D.B., Chanda, B.: Extraction and recognition of geographical features from paper maps. International Journal on Document Analysis and Recognition 8(4), 232–245 (2006)

Dietzel, C., Herold, M., Hemphill, J.J., Clarke, K.C.: Spatio-temporal dynamics in California's Central Valley: Empirical links to urban theory. International Journal of Geographical Information Science 19(2), 175–195 (2005)

Heipke, C., Mayer, H., Wiedemann, C., Jamet, O.: Evaluation of automatic road extraction. International Archives of Photogrammetry and Remote Sensing 32, 47–56 (1997)

Gamba, P., Mecocci, A.: Perceptual Grouping for Symbol Chain Tracking in Digitized Topographic Maps. Pattern Recognition Letters 20(4), 355–365 (1999)

Itonaga, W., Matsuda, I., Yoneyama, N., Ito, S.: Automatic extraction of road networks from map images. Electronics and Communications in Japan 86(4), 62–72 (2003)

Knoblock, C.A., Chen, C., Chiang, Y.-Y., Goel, A., Michelson, M., Shahabi, C.: A General Approach to Discovering, Registering, and Extracting Features from Raster Maps. In: Proceedings of the Document Recognition and Retrieval XVII of SPIE-IS&T Electronic Imaging, vol. 7534 (2010)

Kozak, J., Estreguil, C., Troll, M.: Forest cover changes in the northern Carpathians in the 20th century: a slow transition. Journal of Land Use Science 2(2), 127–146 (2007)

Leyk, S.: Segmentation of Colour Layers in Historical Maps Based on Hierarchical Colour Sampling. In: Ogier, J.-M., Liu, W., Lladós, J. (eds.) GREC 2009. LNCS, vol. 6020, pp. 231–241. Springer, Heidelberg (2010)

Leyk, S., Boesch, R.: Colors of the Past: Color Image Segmentation in Historical Topographic Maps Based on Homogeneity. GeoInformatica 14(1), 1–21 (2010)

Leyk, S., Boesch, R.: Extracting Composite Cartographic Area Features in Low-Quality Maps. Cartography and Geographical Information Science 36(1), 71–79 (2009)

Petit, C.C., Lambin, E.F.: Impact of data integration technique on historical land-use/land-cover change: Comparing historical maps with remote sensing data in the Belgian Ardennes. Landscape Ecology 17(2), 117–132 (2002)

Raveaux, R., Burie, J.-C., Ogier, J.-M.: Object extraction from colour cadastral maps. In: Proceedings of the IAPR Document Analysis Systems, pp. 506–514 (2008)

On the Use of Geometric Matching for Both: Isolated Symbol Recognition and Symbol Spotting

Nibal Nayef and Thomas M. Breuel

Technical University Kaiserslautern, Germany
nnayef@iupr.com, tmb@informatik.uni-kl.de

Abstract. Symbol recognition is important in many applications such as the automated interpretation of line drawings and retrieval-by-content search engines. This paper presents the use of geometric matching for symbol recognition under similarity transformations. We incorporate this matching approach in a complete symbol recognition/spotting system, which consists of denoising, symbol representation and recognition. The proposed system works for both isolated recognition and spotting symbols in context. For denoising, we use an adaptive preprocessing algorithm. For symbol representation, pixels and/or vectorial primitives can be used, then the recognition is done via geometric matching. When applied on the datasets of GREC'05 and GREC'11 symbol recognition contests, the system has performed significantly better than other statistical or structural methods.

Keywords: Symbol Recognition, Symbol Spotting, Geometric Matching.

1   Introduction

Graphics recognition is a challenging problem in the field of document image analysis. It deals with graphical entities that appear in line drawings such as architectural and electrical symbols. The localization and recognition of such symbols are important for retrieval applications among others. Much valuable work has been done on the recognition of isolated symbols, and the number of methods for recognizing symbols in context is increasing. However, the solutions proposed so far have not reached to the point where they can be reliably used in real world applications like automatic analysis of technical drawings or query based retrieval in a digital library.

In this paper, we present the usage of geometric matching techniques for recognizing symbols both isolated and in context. The system starts by applying an adaptive preprocessing algorithm inspired by the work in [14] for denoising. After that, for symbol or line drawing representation, either pixels or vectorial primitives can be used as features. For matching a pair of images – a query with a database image –, the geometric matching framework of [1] is used.

Y.-B. Kwon and J.-M. Ogier (Eds.): GREC, LNCS 7423, pp. 36–48, 2013.

The authors have used similar techniques in a previous preliminary work [7] for symbol spotting. In this paper, we largely extend our previous work as follows.

- The geometric matching framework is generalized to deal with vectorial primitives such as lines and arcs, not only pixels. This gives the flexibility to use either a statistical or a structural representation for symbols. It also speeds up the matching since the number of features as lines and arcs is much smaller than in the pixel representation.
- The geometric matching framework is improved to deal with very similar shapes. This is done by assigning penalties to the non-matched features, which helps – for example – in recognizing symbols whose shapes are subsets of other symbols' shapes.
- An adaptive preprocessing module is added to the system to deal with different noise types including clean images.
- Large-scale experiments and benchmarks have been carried out for both isolated symbol recognition and symbol spotting.

The rest of the paper is organized as follows: Section 2 presents the related work. Section 3 describes the proposed recognition system. Section 4 presents the performance evaluation, and Section 5 concludes the paper.

2   Related Work

Isolated symbol recognition approaches can be classified into structural [2], [5], [15], statistical [6], [12], [13], [16] and hybrid [3], [11] approaches. We review here the ones that use geometric techniques, whether for feature extraction or for matching and recognition.

Coustaty et. al. [2] used an adapted Hough transform to extract the segments of the symbol, and arrange them in a topological graph as a structural signature of the symbols, and then, Galois Lattice classifier is used for recognition. Min et. al. [6] presented a pixel distribution based method, and a similarity measure called bipartite transformation distance. In their system, the symbols are aligned by their angular distributions to achieve rotation invariance. They also presented a denoising algorithm to deal with different noise types before applying the recognition system. Wong et. al. [12] computed descriptors of symbols from a modified Hough transform, which makes them invariant to scale and rotation, after that, those descriptors were compared to find matching symbols.

In general, the methods in the structural approach rely on vectorial signatures of the symbols, so the preprocessing and primitives extraction greatly affect the matching results. The statistical approaches are more popular, but they are sensitive to noise. More importantly, most of the methods from both approaches are designed to recognize segmented (isolated) symbols, they cannot recognize symbols in context.

As for spotting approaches, they usually find regions of interest in the drawings and describe them using various descriptors, and then index them based on the query symbol. The regions could be described in various ways: based on vectorial primitives as in Rusinol et. al. [10], or on graphs as in Qureshi et. al. [9] and Locteau et. al. [4] or on local shape contexts [8]. Different indexing techniques were used in those works as hashing and inverted file structures.

The scheme followed in these spotting methods is unrelated to our proposed matching framework, since our proposed algorithm searches for matching symbols in an image whether it contains an isolated symbol or a complete line drawing, without identifying or locating regions of interest first.

3   Description of the Recognition System

3.1   Adaptive Preprocessing and Feature Points

Although independent of the actual matching; preprocessing has an important effect on matching results, specially when the problem has extremely different noise types. As a preprocessing module, we use a largely modified version of the adaptive noise reduction algorithm by Zhang et. al. [14].

Zhang's algorithm [14] is based on the assessment of noise distributions and line widths, and then, according to this automatic assessment, different median and morphological filters are applied on an image. Inspired by the idea of the assesment of the image noise to automatically infer the noise type, we develop our adaptive preprocessing algorithm. It is called "adaptive" since it automatically adapts to the noise type and deals with it accordingly.

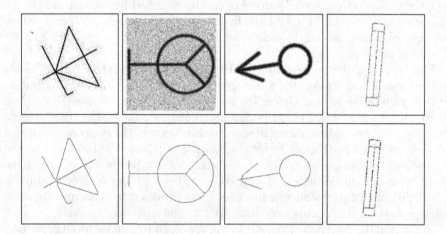

Fig. 1. Preprocessing; input: images in the first row, output: corresponding images in the second row

In many cases, the noise components are large, and its density distribution is higher than foreground symbols. Hence, instead of using actual median filters, we simply remove the small connected components that are smaller than a certain size. This size is adaptively and automatically determined based on noise distribution. This operation has the same effect as a median filter, but it removes noise components of different sizes with the same filter template.

Moreover, a smoothing step is needed to get better results in the subsequent feature extraction step, so we apply a Gaussian smoothing step followed by binarization. This operation is also adaptive based on the previously mentioned criteria. Fig. 1 shows the results of applying the preprocessing algorithm on different cases from the GREC'05 dataset.

For getting the feature points; equidistant points or line segments are sampled along the edges. Those feature points are the geometric primitives used as input for matching.

3.2   Recognition Using Geometric Matching

Geometric matching is concerned about simultaneously finding the pose and the correspondences between two sets of feature points using geometric relations. The two sets of features are usually extracted from two images. An example of such matching is shown in Fig. 2. In this section, we show how we use geometric matching to solve the problems of symbol recognition and symbol spotting.

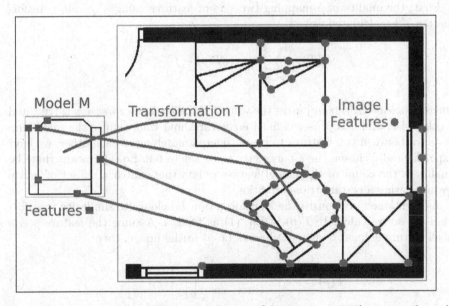

Fig. 2. Geometric matching: The model features (blue square points) are transformed by a certain transformation T (green curve) to match a subset of image features (red circle points). This matching gives us the correspondences between the two feature sets. For clarity of showing, we show only few feature points along the edges, and how some of them match.

Geometric Matching. First we define the problem of matching a pair of images: the model which is an isolated query symbol, and the image (an image of an isolated symbol or an image of a complete line drawing). This definition is adapted from [1].

Assume that the images have been preprocessed, so, the model M and the image I are defined as two sets of features. The features could be pixels, line segments or arcs. The matching solution is defined for any kind of geometrically parameterized features. The model $M = p_1, p_2, ..., p_m$ has m features, and the image $I = f_1, f_2, ..., f_n$ has n features.

A certain instance of the query symbol M can be inside the image I, but in that image, this symbol instance can be transformed with a certain transformation T which belongs to similarity transformations, so the symbol in the image can be a translated, rotated and/or scaled version of the query symbol M. Further more, the symbol instance inside image I could be surrounded by lots of clutter, for example, in non-isolated symbols, or complete line drawings, a certain symbol occupies just a small region within an image, the clutter in this case is the connecting lines and the other symbols in the image.

The goal is to find the transformation T_{max} that maps a **maximal subset** of the model features to **maximal subset(s)** of image features, with minimal error as defined by some error function.

First, the quality of a mapping two sets of features using a certain transformation T is calculated as:

$$Q(T) = \sum_{p \in M} \max_{f \in I} \lfloor \|T(p) - f\| < \epsilon \rfloor . \tag{1}$$

where $\lfloor boolean\ expression \rfloor$ gives the value 1 if the *boolean expression* is true, and 0 otherwise, and ϵ is a user-defined error threshold that defines the maximum distance between two features to be considered matching to each other, we have experimentally chosen the ϵ parameter to be set to 6.0. Eq. (1) means that the quality is the count of the model feature points that match a subset of image features using a certain transformation.

As mentioned previously, the transformation T belongs to similarity transformations, so we calculate $T(p)$ in Eq. (1) as follows. Assume the feature p is a pixel feature defined by its coordinates (x, y) in the image, then:

$$T(p) = s * \begin{bmatrix} \cos \alpha & \sin \alpha \\ -\sin \alpha & \cos \alpha \end{bmatrix} \begin{bmatrix} x \\ y \end{bmatrix} + \begin{bmatrix} dx \\ dy \end{bmatrix} . \tag{2}$$

where s is the scale parameter, α is the rotation angle, and dx, dy are the translation parameters in the horizontal and vertical directions respectively.

Similarly, assume that the feature p is a line segment feature defined by the coordinates of its two end points (x_1, y_1) and (x_2, y_2), in order to transform this line segment with a certain transformation T, we simply apply Eq. (2) on each of the two end points.

We want to find T_{max} among all transformations T_{all} that maximizes this quality of match function for a certain matching problem:

$$T_{max}(M, I, \epsilon) = arg \max_{T \in T_{all}} Q(T; M, I, \epsilon) . \qquad (3)$$

Finding T_{max} in Eq. (3) can be achieved using a search algorithm. The search is done in the 4D transformation space (2D translations, rotation and scale). We have set the transformation space parameters as follows: $dx \in [-dm_x, di_x]$, $dy \in [-dm_y, di_y]$, $\alpha \in [0, 2\pi]$ and $s \in [0.5, 3.0]$, where dm_x is the horizontal dimension of the model and dm_y is the vertical dimension of the model, and similarly di_x and di_y are the horizontal and vertical dimensions of the image respectively.

For each of the possible transformations in the search space, the algorithm transforms the model features M using that possible transformation T, and then calculates the quality of mapping those transformed model features to a subset(s) of the image features I using Eq. (1). The transformation that achieves the maximum quality of mapping is the transformation T_{max} that we are looking for according to Eq. (3).

Of course, a full search is not possible, so we use the branch and bound search algorithm described in our previous work [7]. The search algorithm can recognize/spot multiple instances of the query in an image as follows: once the algorithm finds one T_{max} result, it proceeds to find the next best mapping with the next T_{max}, until it stops according to a user-defined minimum quality of mapping. For example, if the model M has m features, the user can define the minimum quality of mapping to be 75% of the model features, this means at least 75% of the model M will always be matched to each of the model instances that exist in the image I. If the algorithm does not find any mapping that achieves the minimum quality, it will announce that there are no instances of the model inside the image. We have set the minimum quality parameter to 70% of the model features.

Penalizing Non-matched Features. In this subsection, we show how the recognition accuracy of our geometric matching framework can be improved by dealing with the problem of symbols that are very similar to each other.

Assume that we want to recognize the symbol in Fig. 3(a), so we will match it against the different available library symbols, among those symbols, there are some symbols that are very similar to each other like the two symbols in Fig. 3(b) and Fig. 3(d). Since the geometric matching aligns the points of the model on the points of the image, the test symbol in Fig. 3(a), will match both images in Fig. 3(b) and Fig. 3(d) with the same quality of match. The matching results are marked in red in Fig. 3(c) and Fig. 3(e). It is clear that the same number of model features were matched to both images, simply because the shape of symbol (b) is a subset of the shape of symbol (d). This might cause the problem of recognizing the test symbol in Fig. 3(a) to be the symbol in Fig. 3(d) instead of what it truely is (Fig. 3(b)).

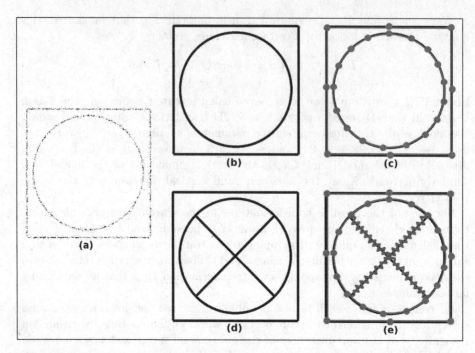

Fig. 3. Matching similar symbols shapes: (a) query test symbol (b) library symbol-1 (c) result of matching (red) the query symbol in "a" to the library symbol-1 (d) library symbol-2 (e) result of matching (red) the query symbol in "a" to the library symbol-2, some features (blue zig-zag) are not matched, because they do not exist in the query

We solve this problem by adding a quality value for each of the image features. This quality is calculated as the number of model points matched with this feature. This means, after the matching is done, we examine the model-image feature correspondences found by the algorithm. For each image feature, if it does not have a certain minimum number of model points matched with it, the quality of the overall match is penalized. This results in a higher quality of matching for the correct symbol. This is illustrated in Fig. 3(e), the image features marked with a zig-zag blue line, were not matched to any of the model points, we call those features the "non-matched features".

Assume the features marked with zig-zag blue in Fig. 3(e) are represented as 4 line segments, that means there are 4 non-matched features in the found match, the score of the whole match will be penalized by a certain amount. The penalty is calculated as follows. Each of the non-matched features has a feature size, in the case of line segments, the size is the length of the line segment, so for each non-matched feature we subtract half the feature size from the overall quality of match.

Note that the problem of similar shapes, does not arise in the following case: if the symbol we want to recognize is the same as the symbol in Fig. 3(d), then the quality of matching it to Fig. 3(d) will be higher than matching it to Fig. 3(b).

That is because each extra matching feature increases the overall quality of match.

The penalizing procedure easily generalizes to the non-isolated cases as follows. Having a number of candidate matching regions in a line drawing, we apply the same penalizing procedure by examining the features that are inside the region of a match.

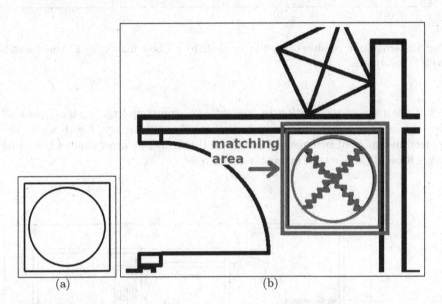

Fig. 4. Penalizing non-matched features for non-isolated cases (spotting): (a) query symbol (b) The algorithm finds the matching region (marked in green) with the feature correspondences, some of the features inside the region match to the query (marked in red), and some features do not match (marked in blue zig-zag lines), this match will be penalized

This is illustrated in Fig. 4. It is important to mention that we only examine the features that are inside the matching area (the bounding box that includes the matched features). That means we do not penalize the non-matched features that are outside this area. This is important for this procedure to work on non-isolated symbols, so the background and the lines connected to a symbol will not play any role in this penalization procedure.

3.3   Recognition

For the case of isolated recognition, the task is to recognize a certain query symbol. The query symbol is matched against a predefined set of library symbols. The query symbol is recognized to be the one that achieves the highest matching score among the library symbols. Fig. 5 shows a query symbol and its three best matches.

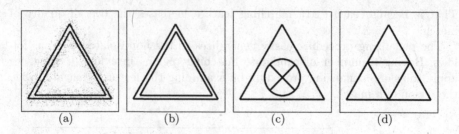

Fig. 5. Recognition results: (a) A test symbol (b) 1st best match (c) 2nd best match (d) 3rd best match

For the case of recognition in context –i.e. spotting–, the system spots all the regions that match the query symbol in all the drawings. Fig. 6 shows the spotted instances of two query symbols. In the figure, we draw shaded bounding boxes around the spotted instances of the query.

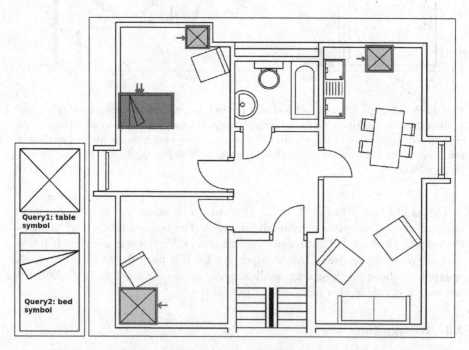

Fig. 6. Recognition results: (a) query symbol (b) spotting output

4 Performance Evaluation

4.1 The Datasets

We have used the publicly available GREC'05[1] and the GREC'11-contests datasets[2] for evaluation. Both datasets have a symbol library of 150 symbols segmented from architectural and electrical drawings. The symbols are composed of lines and circular arcs.

The test images in GREC'05 dataset are for isolated recognition, and they are degraded with 6 different noise types and different transformation (rotation and/or scaling).

The GREC'11 dataset has tests for both the isolated recognition and the spotting. In the isolated recognition tests, the test images are also transformed and degraded. There are 3 noise types with up to 25 levels of degradation in each type, the noise types simulate real world noise (due to scanning or otherwise).

The spotting training sets in GREC'11 dataset have 20 architectural drawings and 20 electrical drawings, also corrupted by 3 different noise types. The task is to spot query symbols in these drawings. There are 16 architectural and 21 electrical queries, we use only a subset of them.

4.2 Experimental Results

We present first the isolated recognition performance. We have evaluated our system on *all* of the tests of GREC'05 dataset, and also a random subset of the GREC'11 tests. Tables 1 and 2 show the results of testing with GREC'05 and GREC'11 datasets respectively. The recognition accuracy metric is used for evaluation.

Table 1. ISOLATED recognition results on all the tests of GREC'05 dataset (6000 images). The results are divided according to the degradation and transformation models used in the test images.

	noise1	noise2	noise3	noise4	noise5	noise6
no transformation	100	100	100	98.2	91.0	96.2
rotation	98.0	99.0	97.2	98.7	94.0	73.7
scaling	98.5	96.5	96.0	94.0	87.5	58.5
rotation+scaling	97.0	91.5	92.0	92.0	72.5	41.5

In general, the recognition accuracies decrease with scaling more than with rotation, because the scaled down versions of the models are severely corrupted even with simple degradation models, and they do not have much information about the symbol at the first place. Examples of such images are shown in Fig 7, those images are hard to recognize even by humans.

---

[1] http://iapr-tc10.univ-lr.fr/index.php/symbolrecognitionhome
[2] http://symbcontestgrec05.loria.fr/

Table 2. ISOLATED recognition results on GREC'11 dataset. N is the number of test images in each different case, total=3150.

Noise type (no transformation)	noise A (N=750)	noise B (N=750)	noise C (N=750)
Recognition accuracy %	98.6	94.0	97.0
Transformation & random degradation	rotation (N=300)	scaling (N=300)	rotation & scaling (N=300)
Recognition accuracy %	97.0	96.4	97.0

Fig. 7. Examples of scaled down corrupted images. The system fails to recognize those symbols.

Fig. 8 shows that the system scales well as the number of models increases. The scalability test is applied on the GREC'05 dataset.

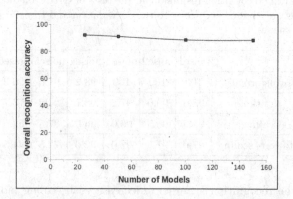

Fig. 8. Recognition system scalability

Table 3 shows the spotting performance of the system. Each of the recall and precision values is the average of spotting a number of different queries in all the drawings. As for the running time for matching a pair of images – both isolated and in context –, it ranges from a fraction of a second to few seconds.

Table 3. SPOTTING results on GREC'11 training datasets. Average recall and precision for 14 queries in 20 electrical drawings, and for 12 queries in 20 architectural drawings

Dataset	Noise type	# of instances of queried symbols	average Recall	average Precision
architectural	random	366	98.1	98.9
electrical	random	223	98.7	94.1

Table 4 shows a comparison with previous methods for both recognition and spotting. The comparison is shown for the methods that use the same datasets. Note that the methods that have higher overall accuracy than our method, have used a much smaller set of models and test images, also with simpler noise types and only a subset of the transformations.

Table 4. Comparison with previous methods. Note that some methods have used different numbers of models and test images, with different noise types and transformations.

Isolated Symbol Recognition - only for GREC'05 dataset					
Method	Accuracy	Models	Dataset - no. of tests	Noise	Transform
Our method	90.1	25 - 150	GREC'05 - 6000	Yes (all types)	Yes
Min et. al [6]	83.3	25 - 150	GREC'05 - 6000	Yes (all types)	No
Zhang et. al [16]	82.8	25 - 150	GREC'05 - 6000	Yes (all types)	Only rotation
Luqman et. al [5]	94.5	20 - 100	GREC'05 - 40	Yes (their own noise)	No
Wong et. al. [12]	94.0	25	GREC'05 - 100	yes (random)	Yes (random)
Symbol Spotting - for GREC'11 and similar datasets					
Method	Recall	Precision	Dataset (architectural)		Noise
Our method	98.1	98.9	12 queries, 20 drawings (8 backgrounds)		Yes
Nguyen et. al [8]	88.0	70.0	6 queries, 15 drawings		No

5   Conclusions and Future Work

The proposed system provides a practical and highly accurate solution for both isolated and non-isolated symbol recognition. The paper has shown that the use of geometric matching techniques can solve symbol recognition in context with interfering strokes, and can also perform competitively on isolated recognition tasks. The paper has also shown that adaptive preprocessing can be an important part of symbol recognition methods, specially in the case of extreme variability in images noise.

The methods that the system uses can be a basis for future work on applications like symbol retrieval and automatic analysis of line drawings. For example, using a set of known models, the spotting method can be used to spot symbols off-line, and then for on-line retrieval, the previously spotted symbols can be quickly indexed and retrieved.

References

1. Breuel, T.M.: Implementation techniques for geometric branch-and-bound matching methods. CVIU 90(3), 258–294 (2003)
2. Coustaty, M., Guillas, S., Visani, M., Bertet, K., Ogier, J.-M.: On the Joint Use of a Structural Signature and a Galois Lattice Classifier for Symbol Recognition. In: Liu, W., Lladós, J., Ogier, J.-M. (eds.) GREC 2007. LNCS, vol. 5046, pp. 61–70. Springer, Heidelberg (2008)
3. Locteau, H., Adam, S., Trupin, É., Labiche, J., Héroux, P.: Symbol Recognition Combining Vectorial and Statistical Features. In: Liu, W., Lladós, J. (eds.) GREC 2005. LNCS, vol. 3926, pp. 76–87. Springer, Heidelberg (2006)
4. Locteau, H., Adam, S., Trupin, E., Labiche, J., Heroux, P.: Symbol spotting using full visibility graph representation. In: GREC, pp. 1–7 (2007)
5. Luqman, M.M., Brouard, T., Ramel, J.: Graphic symbol recognition using graph based signature and bayesian network classifier. In: ICDAR, pp. 1325–1329 (2009)
6. Min, F., Zhang, W., Wenyin, L.: Symbol Recognition Using Bipartite Transformation Distance and Angular Distribution Alignment. In: Liu, W., Lladós, J. (eds.) GREC 2005. LNCS, vol. 3926, pp. 398–407. Springer, Heidelberg (2006)
7. Nayef, N., Breuel, T.M.: Graphical symbol retrieval using a branch and bound algorithm. In: ICIP, pp. 2153–2156 (2010)
8. Nguyen, T., Tabbone, S., Boucher, A.: A symbol spotting approach based on the vector model and a visual vocabulary. In: ICDAR, pp. 708–712 (2009)
9. Qureshi, R.J., Ramel, J.-Y., Barret, D., Cardot, H.: Spotting Symbols in Line Drawing Images Using Graph Representations. In: Liu, W., Lladós, J., Ogier, J.-M. (eds.) GREC 2007. LNCS, vol. 5046, pp. 91–103. Springer, Heidelberg (2008)
10. Rusiñol, M., Lladós, J., Sánchez, G.: Symbol spotting in vectorized technical drawings through a lookup table of region strings. Pattern Analysis and Applications 13(3), 321–331 (2010)
11. Su, F., Lu, T., Yang, R.: Symbol recognition combining vectorial and pixel-level features for line drawings. In: 20th International Conference on Pattern Recognition (ICPR), pp. 1892–1895 (2010)
12. Wong, A., Bishop, W.: Robust invariant descriptor for symbol-based image recognition and retrieval. In: IEEE Int. Conf. on Semantic Computing, pp. 637–644 (2007)
13. Yang, S.: Symbol recognition via statistical integration of pixel-level constraint histograms: A new descriptor. PAMI 27(2), 278–281 (2005)
14. Zhang, J., Zhang, W., Wenyin, L.: Adaptive Noise Reduction for Engineering Drawings Based on Primitives and Noise Assessment. In: Liu, W., Lladós, J. (eds.) GREC 2005. LNCS, vol. 3926, pp. 140–150. Springer, Heidelberg (2006)
15. Zhang, W., Wenyin, L.: A new vectorial signature for quick symbol indexing, filtering and recognition. In: ICDAR, pp. 536–540 (2007)
16. Zhang, W., Wenyin, L., Zhang, K.: Symbol recognition with kernel density matching. PAMI 28(12), 2020–2024 (2006)

Classification of Administrative Document Images by Logo Identification

Marçal Rusiñol[1], Vincent Poulain D'Andecy[2], Dimosthenis Karatzas[1], and Josep Lladós[1]

[1] Computer Vision Center, Dept. Ciències de la Computació
Edifici O, UAB, 08193 Bellaterra, Spain
{marcal,dimos,josep}@cvc.uab.cat
[2] ITESOFT Parc d'Andron, Le Séquoia
30470 Aimargues, France
vincent.poulaindandecy@itesoft.com

Abstract. This paper is focused on the categorization of administrative document images (such as invoices) based on the recognition of the supplier's graphical logo. Two different methods are proposed, the first one uses a bag-of-visual-words model whereas the second one tries to locate logo images described by the blurred shape model descriptor within documents by a sliding-window technique. Preliminar results are reported with a dataset of real administrative documents.

Keywords: Administrative Document Classification, Logo Recognition, Logo Spotting.

1 Introduction

Companies deal with large amount of paper documents in daily workflows. Incoming mail is received and has to be forwarded to the correspondent addressee. The cost of manually processing (opening, sorting, internal delivery, data typing, archiving) incoming documents represents an important quantity of money if we consider the daily amount of documents received by large companies.

The Document Image Analysis and Recognition (DIAR) field has devoted, since its early years, many research efforts to deal with these kind of document images. As an example, Viola and collaborators presented in [6] a system aiming to automatically route incoming faxes to the correspondent recipient. However, most of the systems only process typewritten information making the assumption that the provider information is printed and well recognized by the OCR engine.

In many cases, some graphic elements that are present in the documents convey a lot of important information. For instance, if a company receives a document containing the logo of a bank, usually this document should be forwarded to the accounting department, whereas if the document contains the logo of a computer supplier, it is quite probable that the document should be addressed to the IT department. The recognition of such graphic elements can help to introduce contextual information to overcome the semantic gap between

Y.-B. Kwon and J.-M. Ogier (Eds.): GREC, LNCS 7423, pp. 49–58, 2013.

the simple recognition of characters and the derived actions to perform brought by the document understanding. In this paper we use the presence of logo images in order to categorize the incoming document as belonging to a certain supplier.

ADAO (Administrative Document Automate Optimization) is an FP7 Marie-Curie Industry-Academia Partnerships and Pathways (IAPP) project between the French company ITESOFT and the Computer Vision Center (UAB) in Spain, which is focused on key document analysis techniques involved in a document workflow management. Within this project, one of the tasks is centered on the categorization of document images based on trademark identification. In this paper we report the obtained results for this specific task. Two different methods have been proposed, the first one uses a bag-of-visual-words (BOVW) model whereas the second one tries to locate logo images described by the blurred shape model (BSM) descriptor within documents by a sliding-window technique.

The remainder of this paper is organized as follows: We detail in Section 2 the bag-of-visual-words model and in Section 3 the sliding window approach. Section 4 presents the experimental setup. Finally, the conclusions and a short discussion can be found in Section 5.

2   Bag-of-Visual-Words Classification

This first method is based on the work we presented in [5]. In the proposed approach, the bag-of-words model is translated to the visual domain by the use of local descriptors over interest points. Documents are thus categorized based on the presence of visual features coming from a certain graphical logo. We can see an overview of the presented method in Figure 1.

Logos are represented by a local descriptor applied to a set of previously extracted keypoints. The interest points are computed by using the Harris-Laplace detector presented in [4]. A given logo L_i is then represented by its n_i feature points description:

$$L_i = \{(x_k, y_k, s_k, F_k)\}, \text{ for } k \in \{1...n_i\}$$

where x_k and y_k are the x- and y-position, and s_k the scale of the kth key-point. F_k corresponds to the local description of the region represented by the key-point. In this case, we use the SIFT local descriptors presented in [3]. The same notation applies when the key-points and the feature vectors are computed over a complete document D_j. The matching between a keypoint from the complete document and the ones of the logo model is computed by using the two first nearest neighbors:

$$N_1(L_i, D_j^q) = \min_k (F_q - F_k)$$

$$N_2(L_i, D_j^q) = \min_{k \neq \arg\min(N_1(L_i, D_j^q))} (F_q - F_k) \tag{1}$$

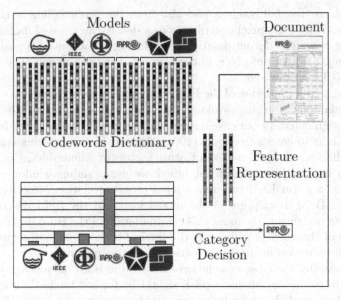

Fig. 1. Bag-of-visual-words model overview

Then the matching score is determined as the ratio between these two neighbors:

$$M(L_i, D_j^q) = \frac{N_1(L_i, D_j^q)}{N_2(L_i, D_j^q)} \qquad (2)$$

If the matching score M is lower than a certain threshold t this means that the keypoint is representative enough to be considered. By setting a quite conservative threshold ($t = 0.6$ in our experiments) we guarantee that the appearance of false positives is minimized since only really relevant matches are considered as such. That is, two keypoint descriptors are matched only if the ratio between the first and the second nearest neighbor is below a certain threshold. When a word in the dictionary belonging to a class C and a feature vector from the document are matched we accumulate a vote for the documents category C. After all the features of the document are processed, the class accumulating more evidences is the one selected as the document class.

3   Sliding Window over BSM Descriptors

The second method uses a sliding window framework together with the blurred shape model (BSM) descriptor [1] to categorize the incoming documents and locate the position of the logo.

The BSM descriptor spatially encodes the probability of appearance of the shape pixels and their context information in the following way: The image is divided in a grid of $n \times n$ equal-sized subregions, and each bin receives votes from the pixels that fall inside it and also from the pixels falling in the neighboring bins. Thus, each pixel contributes to a density measure of its bin and its neighboring ones. The output descriptor is a histogram where each position corresponds to the amount of pixels in the context of the sub-region. The resulting histogram is L1-normalized.

In the original formulation of the BSM descriptor, pixel density was computed over a regular $n \times n$ grid, provoking that the shapes to compare have to be previously segmented. In our case we reformulate the BSM descriptor by forcing the spatial bins to have a fixed size (100x100 pixels in our experimental setup). Images of different size will result in feature vectors of different lengths. In order to locate a logo within a document image we use a sliding-window approach computed as a normalized two-dimensional cross-correlation (described in [2]) between the BSM description of the model logo and the BSM description of the complete document. By using this reformulation of the BSM descriptor, the chosen size of the buckets will define the level of blurring and subsequently the information reduction for both the logos and the documents.

As the result of the cross correlation between the BSM models and the BSM descriptor from the document, a peak should be formed in the location where there is a high probability to find a something similar to the given logo. This process is repeated for each logo in the knowledge database, and the peak having the highest response would be the best match between a certain zone of the document and the logo model, thus representing the most plausible class C of the document.

In order to increase the robustness of the method, we want to give the same importance to match "black" pixels and to match "white" pixels. To do so, the normalized cross correlation is computed for both the BSM description and the inverse of the BSM descriptions. In the final step, the probability maps coming from both normalized cross correlations are combined by multiplying them to get rid of the background noise.

One of the advantages of this method is that from the obtained probability maps, we can have not only the class of the document but also the location within the document where the most feasible logo is found. We can see an example of the whole procedure in Figure 2.

4   Experimental Results

4.1   Dataset

The selected dataset consists of 3337 TIF binary images of scanned invoices. From this collection, 204 different document classes identifying the invoice supplier have been determined. The ground-truthing protocol was the following. We first define with an annotation tool as many bounding boxes as logos in the document.

Segmenting a logo is somehow subjective and there are many cases where it is difficult to determine what a logo is. We followed these rules to produce the groundtruth:

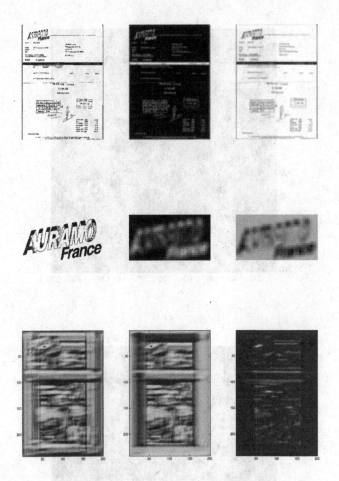

Fig. 2. Original images and BSM descriptors of the documents (first row) and logo models (second row). Probability maps for the BSM, the inverse BSM and the final combination of both are given in the third row.

- If there is some text close to the logo (usually the address), we tried not to select this text as a part of the logo.
- In some documents multiple logos might appear, we define a bounding box for each of them.
- If in the document we find multiple logos which are close to each other but are clearly of different nature, we try to define a separate bounding box for each of them.
- For the documents that do not contain any kind of graphical logos, we select the address as the logo of the document (see Figure 4). We keep track of these particular documents that do not contain any graphical logo.

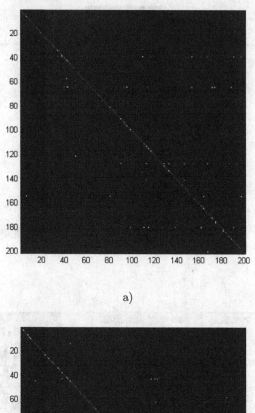

a)

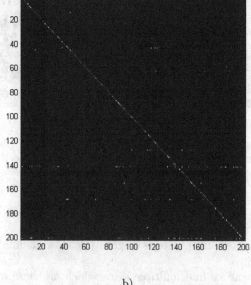

b)

Fig. 3. Confusion matrices for the a) BOVW and b) BSM methods when using 200 models

Finally, the annotation tool returns an XML like file with the same name as the image file defining the location of the bounding box and the label for each of the bounding boxes.

4.2 Results

We present in Table 1 the results of the document classification for the two presented methods when considering a different amount of model logos. In this experiment, only the subset of the 3337 document images that correspond to these particular logos is used.

Table 1. Document classification

Dataset	BOVW	BSM
50 models / 902 documents	88.11	92.84
100 models / 1832 documents	90.45	89.79
200 models / 3295 documents	87.07	78.36

During the analysis of our results we realized that there were some logo designs that introduced much more noise when using them as a cue to categorize documents than others. These logo designs were the responsible for obtaining better performances in the BOVW scenario when considering 100 models that when considering 50 models. We can see this effect in the confusion matrices presented in Figure 3. Looking in detail at those logo designs we realized that most of the classes where we obtained poor performances corresponded at mostly-textual logos. We can see an example of these logo designs that we have in our dataset in Figure 4.

It is obvious that trying to recognize this kind of logo designs from a graphical point of view does not make much sense. We run an additional experiment with a reduced model dataset where we just included logos having a graphic-rich design. Some examples of these graphic-rich logo designs can be seen in Figure 5. The obtained results with these models are shown in Table 2.

Table 2. Document classification with only graphical logos

Dataset	BOVW	BSM
50 graphical models	87.86	99.55

We can see that the BSM method outperforms the BOVW method in this case. The BSM method is also much cheaper to compute than the BOVW. However,

Fig. 4. Example of mostly-textual logos we have in the dataset

Fig. 5. Example of graphic-rich logos we have in the dataset

how these methods would scale when considering a larger amount of model logos is still an unanswered question that needs to be further investigated.

Another important issue is that with the BOVW model, all the spatial information is lost and we just obtain the category of the document as output of the system, whereas with the proposed approach based on cross-correlations over the BSM descriptors, not only we obtain the class of the input document but also the position of the logo in the document. In Figure 6 we show a screenshot of our classification demo software where we can see for an incoming document image, its recognized logo with its corresponding location in the original image.

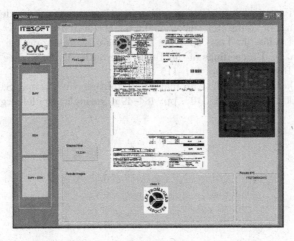

Fig. 6. Example of the logo localization when using the BSM descriptor

5   Conclusion

In this paper we have presented and compared a couple of methodologies aiming to perform document classification in terms of the presence of a given logo image. The obtained results are encouraging even if they are reported in a low-scale scenario. It has been shown that to take into account graphical information can be very useful for document classification, at least for disambiguation in the cases where the answer of the main administrative document classifier has low confidence.

Acknowledgment. This work has been supported by the European 7th framework project FP7-PEOPLE-2008-IAPP: 230653 ADAO. The work has been partially supported as well by the Spanish Ministry of Education and Science under projects RYC-2009-05031, TIN2011-24631, TIN2009-14633-C03-03, Consolider Ingenio 2010: MIPRCV (CSD200700018) and the grant 2009-SGR-1434 of the Generalitat de Catalunya.

References

1. Escalera, S., Fornés, A., Pujol, O., Escudero, A., Radeva, P.: Circular blurred shape model for symbol spotting in documents. In: Proceedings of the IEEE International Conference on Image Processing, pp. 2005–2008 (2009)
2. Lewis, J.P.: Fast normalized cross-correlation. In: Vision Interface, vol. 10, pp. 120–123 (1995)
3. Lowe, D.G.: Distinctive image features from scale-invariant keypoints. International Journal of Computer Vision 60(2), 91–110 (2004)

4. Mikolajczyk, K., Schmid, C.: Scale & affine invariant interest point detectors. International Journal of Computer Vision 60(1), 63–86 (2004)
5. Rusiñol, M., Lladós, J.: Logo spotting by a bag-of-words approach for document categorization. In: Proceedings of the Tenth International Conference on Document Analysis and Recognition, pp. 111–115 (2009)
6. Viola, P., Rinker, J., Law, M.: Automatic Fax Routing. In: Marinai, S., Dengel, A.R. (eds.) DAS 2004. LNCS, vol. 3163, pp. 484–495. Springer, Heidelberg (2004)

Symbol Recognition in Natural Scenes by Shape Matching across Multi-scale Segmentations

Ruimin Guan[1], Su Yang[1], and Yuanyuan Wang[2]

[1] Computer College of Computer Science and Technology
Fudan University
[2] Department of Electronic Engineering
Fudan University
{09210240012,suyang,yywang}@fudan.edu.cn

Abstract. Symbol recognition in natural scenes plays an important role in a variety of applications such as driver assistance and environment awareness. We propose a solution including 3 phases: (1) Image segmentation, (2) component-level shape matching, and (3) structure matching. To improve the robustness, we alter the parameters to obtain image segmentation at multiple scales and perform component-level template matching across the image segmentation results obtained at all scales. By means of such exhaustive search across all possible segmentations, the chance to obtain finely matched components is increased. Some initial experimental results are obtained, which are encouraging.

Keywords: symbol recognition, shape matching, image segmentation, component, part structure.

1 Introduction

Although symbol recognition is a well-studied problem in graphics recognition community, symbol recognition in natural scenes via camera has been receiving increasingly much attention recently. It plays an important role in a variety of applications such as driver assistance [1-3] and environment awareness [4]. This is a more challenging research topic than recognition of symbols in scanned images because symbols are embedded in natural scenes, which makes it difficult to distinguish them from the complex backgrounds. This accounts for why it is an open problem so far. The representative solutions for camera-based symbol recognition can be sorted into the following categories: (1) Perform image segmentation at first and then shape matching or classification on the segmented results [1,2]. (2) Detect candidate blocks with adaboost based machine learning and then classify the detected regions using a classifier [3]. (3) Apply symbol spotting to recognize and locate symbols in backgrounds directly [4]. Although a great deal of effort has been made, there are yet some problems with the above solutions. For adaboost based solution, the problem is that the performance is subject to much what kind of training data can be obtained for learning and the detected candidate blocks usually contain a portion of background,

Y.-B. Kwon and J.-M. Ogier (Eds.): GREC, LNCS 7423, pp. 59–68, 2013.

which may perturb the subsequent classification. For symbol spotting based solution, the present techniques are mostly vector-based methods focused on classical graphics recognition, which are in general not robust due to the error-prone vectorization, especially for camera-based recognition. For image segmentation based solution, it is known that machine-rendered segmentation is not always consistent with human perception and cognition. As the parameter of an algorithm changes, in general, the image segmentation results also vary, which makes the segmentation results unreliable for further recognition. To improve the robustness, in this study, we alter the parameters to obtain image segmentation at multiple scales and perform component-level template matching across the image segmentation results obtained at all scales. By means of such exhaustive search across all possible segmentations, the chance to obtain finely matched components is increased. The proposed method is composed of the following parts: (1) Group the image pixels into a couple of regions using an image segmentation method developed by us, where we try different parameters to obtain all possible image segmentations; (2) Compute the similarity between every component in every template and every segmented region obtained in the first phase. For each component in a given template, rank the matched regions in the natural scene image of interest according to the similarity and select 50 candidates with top ranks. (3) Make final decision based on the spatial constraints among components, where the gathering of the candidate regions satisfies the spatial constraints imposed by the components in the template under consideration will be preserved. We experiment with the data used in [7]. In the experiments, the object components can be correctly recognized and located in the corresponding natural scene images, which can validate our approach.

2   The Proposed Method

For the template of every traffic sign, it is usually composed of a couple of components and every component consists of a couple of pixels with similar color, that is, they possess similar RGB values. This makes it possible to group the pixels from a given component into one cluster via RGB value based clustering. Once the pixels composing a component can be segmented, then, the following processing can be simplified as classical shape matching. In this study, we solve the RGB value based clustering as follows: (1) we transfer the raster image into a binary mask according to whether the color of a pixel is consistent with those of its surroundings, where such a pixel is referred to as a foreground pixel. (2) We group the foreground pixels in the binary mask into a couple of regions, every of which is composed of connected pixels and isolated from the other regions. Note that, however, the clusters obtained as such are usually not satisfied. (3) We refine the previously obtained regions through region growing so as to achieve final image segmentation. Once the final image segmentation is reached, the segmented regions are matched against the components contained in every template. There are many good methods to realize the shape matching as mentioned above, for instance, shape context [5]. We run such shape matching based only on edge points. Since matching shape contexts is complex, we make use of a scheme for statistical integration of shape contexts as the statistical integration method applied in [6]. With regard to each component from the models, we preserve the 50 top ranked regions in terms of similarity as candidates following the shape matching. Note that a pre-defined threshold is applied to filter out pseudo candidates the similarity between which and the matched components is too low. As such, we obtain many candidate regions. Then, the task becomes assembling the candidate regions to satisfy the topological constraints imposed by the corresponding model/template, which also functions to remove pseudo candidate regions. For this sake, we first obtain the matched component in the image corresponding to the largest component in the template. It is known that the other components in the template should be enclosed in the largest component. Accordingly, we filter out the components that do not satisfy such inclusion relation with the largest component in the image. Finally, shape matching is run again over the whole shape formed by the collage of the largest components and the other inclusive components, which can be regarded as object-level shape matching. The flowchart is shown in Fig. 1. Note that the segmentation result is subject to the parameters applied in the previously mentioned binary masking and region growing steps. Here, we make use of such a scheme that we change the parameters across multiple levels to cover all possible segmentations for the sake of obtaining right profiles of the components, which is essential for the subsequent shape matching.

The above steps are summarized into three phases: (1) Image segmentation, (2) component-level shape matching, and (3) structure matching. In the following, we will present the algorithm in detail.

2.1   Image Segmentation

The image segmentation is composed of the following steps:

(1) Color consistence indicator: For every pixel P_i, compute 3 values similar to the standard deviation in its 3×3 neighborhood in RGB space, denoted as (VR_i, VG_i, VB_i). The computation of VR_i is as follows:

$$VR_i = \mathrm{int}\left(\sqrt{\frac{\sum\limits_{P_q \in r(P_i)}[R(P_q)]^2}{t} - \left[\frac{\sum\limits_{P_q \in r(P_i)}[R(P_q)]}{t}\right]^2}\right) \tag{1}$$

where $r(P_i)$ represents the 3×3 neighbor of P_i, t the number of pixels in $r(P_i)$, and $R(P_q)$ the red channel of P_q. VR_i indicates whether the red-channel color of P_i is consistent with that of its neighbors. VG_i and VB_i can be computed similarly. Note that lower VR_i corresponds with higher color consistence in terms of red. So are VG_i and VB_i.

(2) Binary masking: If $VR_i < T_1(R) \wedge VG_i < T_1(G) \wedge VB_i < T_1(B)$, where $T_1 = [T_1(R), T_1(G), T_1(B)]$ represents the RGB threshold, then, P_i is regarded as an interior point in a region since its color is consistent with its surround pixels. As different T_1 leads to different segmentation, here, we try T_1 at multiple levels to obtain all possible segmentations so as to guarantee that there exists reasonable segmentation for every component. The detailed implementation is as follows: (1) We compute the color consistence value for each pixel in the input image, that is, $\{VR_i, VG_i, VB_{il}$

i=1,2,...,N], where N is the number of all pixels in the input image. (2) We pick the pixels that possess higher color consistence value in each channel. For the red channel, $T_1(R)$ is set to be the value that can reject $(1-p) \times N$ pixels with lower color consistence values while preserve $p \times N$ pixels with higher color consistence value in terms of red. $T_1(G)$ and $T_1(B)$ are set similarly, which is also controlled by the value of p. Hereafter, we can obtain different T_1 by selecting p from {30%,...,90%}. When p=30%, it means that 70%$\times$N pixels with the lower color consistence values will be filtered out and the remaining 30%$\times$N pixels will be granted as the foreground pixels to undergo subsequent processing. An illustrative example is shown in Fig. 2 and Fig. 3. Fig. 2 is the original image and Fig. 3 is one case of binary masking of it with a specific T_1 determined by p=30%.

(3) Regions formed by connected pixels: Group the points in the binary mask, which is the foreground pixel, into a couple of regions based on the connectivity among pixels, where such regions are denoted as C={C_j | j=1,2,....,K},K is the number of regions.

(4) Region growing: The regions obtained in the former step are usually coarse and not comparable to the corresponding components in the templates. So, we run region growing to refine the image segmentation obtained previously. The detailed implementation is: For every region $C_j \in C$, calculate the average RGB values. Then, let it grow through the following procedure: For every pixel contained in C_j, if the RGB color of any of its 8 neighbors is close to the average RGB color of C_j, then, update C_j by including such neighbor, where the color similarity is computed as: If $|r-R|<T_2 \wedge |g-G|<T_2 \wedge |b-B|<T_2$, then the two RGB vectors (r,g,b) and (R,G,B) are regarded as close to each other in terms of color. T_2 must be between 0 and 255. Each of them may be used. Fig. 4 shows the regions clustered with T_2=20.

A couple of possible image segmentations can be obtained by running the above steps with different T_1 and T_2. All the segmented regions will be used as the input in the next phase, say, shape matching. Two image segmentation results with different T_1 and T_2 are shown in Fig. 5 and Fig. 6, respectively. In the two figures, different colors are used to mark different regions segmented. Note that each component of the corresponding template can be found in either of the two figures. This example shows why we make use of different T_1 and T_2 to produce all possible segmentations. We experimentally confirmed that $T_2 \in \{t \times 10 | t \in \{1,2,3,4,5,6,7,8,9\}\}$ can lead to satisfactory segmentations while promise reasonable computational time.

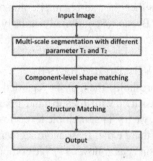

Fig. 1. The flow chart of the algorithm

Fig. 2. Original image

Fig. 3. Binary mask of fig.2:p=0.3   **Fig. 4.** Region growing: T$_2$=20

Fig. 5. Segmentation 1: p=0.3,T$_2$=20   **Fig. 6.** Segmentation 2: p=0.3; T$_2$=40

Fig. 7. Model 1,2,3   **Fig. 8.** Segmentation: p=0.61,T$_2$=100

Fig. 9. The most 50 similar regions for each component   **Fig. 10.** The filtered candidates with T$_3$ = 0.02

2.2   Template Preprocessing

Template segmentation should be performed prior to shape matching. The template segmentation is weakly affected by T$_1$ and T$_2$. The reason is: The background of templates is simple. Besides, the RGB difference across different components in a template is remarkable, so the selection of T$_1$ and T$_2$ does not affect the segmentation result of a given template obviously. Since we perform image segmentation on the raster images across multiple levels by setting different values for (T$_1$, T$_2$), there must exist one pair of parameter values that can generate similar image segmentation to that of template. The experiment confirms this. The results shown in Fig. 7 and Fig. 8 are obtained by setting p=0.61 and T_2=100. Fig. 7 shows the models. Fig. 8 shows the segmentation result of Fig. 7. For each template, we sort all the components according to its size in descending order. The reason is: the reliability in detecting a component increases with its size. Except for the shape context features, moreover, we compute the height, the length, and the number of pixels of every component for excluding obviously erroneous candidates.

2.3   Component-Level Shape Matching

Note that both the image and the template are segmented based on color consistence such that the shape matching is performed on image regions and template regions with consistent color inside, which are referred to as components in this study. Prior to compute the distance between two components, we compute the shape signature for each component at first. For each pair (T_1, T_2), we can get a couple of segmented regions. The detailed computation of shape matching between two regions is as follows:

(1) We first get the edge of every region by means of the following computation: If more than 2 pixels in the 4 neighborhoods around a pixel are not foreground pixels, then, such pixel is regarded as edge point.

(2) Compute the shape context descriptor for each edge point of each region [5]. The bin number of the shape context descriptor is 5×72 with 5° for every angle bin.

(3) Regarding each region, we apply the method referred to as statistical integration [6] to the shape contexts in association with every edge pixel in this region to obtain an overall descriptor. To avoid rotation interference, we rotate each template component with 5° each time and the rotation covers 5°×{0,1,2...,11}, which leads to 12 instances. Then, we computeχ^2 distance between every region segmented from the raster image and each instance of a given template component. The distance between the input region and the template component is defined as the minimum one among 12 possible cases. For each component in a given template, rank the matched regions in the natural scene image of interest and select 50 candidates with top ranks for further processing. In order to make the matching faster, here, we do not apply standard shape context matching and instead use the statistical integration scheme to produce a compressed descriptor for matching. To avoid that the 50 top ranked candidates are redundant regions, if a newly detected region overlaps mostly with any existing top-ranked candidate, we only preserve the one with shorter distance to the corresponding template component. For the 50 candidates obtained previously, we only preserve the ones the χ^2 distances of which to the corresponding template components are smaller than a threshold T_3 =0.02. Fig. 9 illustrates an example of the 50 candidates of each component and Fig. 10 shows the remained candidates following the above filtering.

(4) Furthermore, we run standard shape context matching for the component with the largest size in the template to the matched ones in the raster image for the sake of verification. If the matching score is less than a predefined threshold T_4=0.105, then, the subsequent structure matching is conducted since we regard that the matching between the template and the raster image is possible in such a case. Fig. 11 and Fig. 12 show the effect of such matching.

Fig. 11. The matched regions against the largest component in template

Fig. 12. The remained candidates in Fig. 11 with filtering via $T_4 = 0.105$

2.4   Structure Matching

In general, for every template, we should induce the spatial relations among components and check whether such relations hold for the corresponding components in raster images. In this initial study, we only make use of the inclusion relation between two components for further filtering due to the specific structure of traffic signs. We first check which components are enclosed by the largest component. Only the enclosed components are preserved to undergo the following verification. For every preserved component, we perform shape matching again to compute the distance between the collage of the largest component and the enclosed component and that of the template, which can be regarded as object-level shape matching based on statistical integration of shape contexts. Only when the distance is smaller than a threshold $T_5=0.8$ and the area of the object is consistent with that of the template, such a component is preserved as final output. Fig. 13 and Fig. 14 illustrate an example of the object level shape matching and the final output, respectively.

Fig. 13. Result of object-level matching with $T_5 = 0.8$

Fig. 14. Final output

3   Experiments

We use the data provided in [7] to do some initial experiments to validate the proposed method. The final results are shown in Fig. 15, where if a model appears in a corresponding image, we use the symbol "√" to mark it while we use the mark "×" to represent that no such model appears in a given image. The binary mask of the identified objects in the corresponding raster images are shown in Fig. 15. We can see that all the traffic signs can be correctly identified in the corresponding images and no false alarm appears. This means that both the precision and recall rate is 100%, which is equal to the performance reported in [7].

Image#	Model 1	Model 2	Model 3	Image#	Model 1	Model 2	Model 3
1	×	√	√	25	√	×	×
2	×	√	×	26	√	×	×
3	×	√	×	27	√	×	×
4	×	√	×	28	√	×	×
5	×	√	×	29	√	×	√
6	×	√	×	30	√		√
7	×	√	×	31	√	×	√
8	×	√	×	32	√	×	×
9	×	√	×	33	×	×	√
10	×	√	×	34	×	×	√

Fig. 15. Experimental results

Fig. 15. (*Continued*)

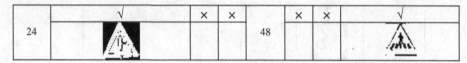

| 24 | | √ | | × | × | | × | × | 48 | | √ |

Fig. 15. (*Continued*)

4   Conclusions

We propose a method for symbol recognition in natural scenes. The method is experimentally validated. The effectiveness of the proposed algorithm has been experimentally confirmed. The standpoint of this method is that we apply different parameters to yield many possible segmented regions, which guarantee the performance of subsequent shape matching.

Acknowledgment. This work is supported by 973 Program (grant No. 2010CB731401), Natural Science Foundation of China (grant No. 61071133), Major Program of Natural Science Foundation of China (grant No. 91024011), Ministry of Industry and Information Technology of China (grant No. 2010ZX01042-002-003-004), and Science and Technology Commission of Shanghai Municipality (grant No. 09JC1401500, 08DZ2271800, and 09DZ2272800).

References

1. Maldonado Bascón, S., Acevedo Rodríguez, J., Lafuente Arroyo, S., Fernndez Caballero, A., López-Ferreras, F.: An optimization on pictogram identification for the road-sign recognition task using SVMs. Computer Vision and Image Understanding 114, 373–383 (2010)
2. Nguwi, Y.Y., Kouzani, A.Z.: Detection and classification of road signs in natural environments. Neural Computing and Applications 17, 265–289 (2008)
3. Baró, X., Escalera, S., Vitrià, J., Pujol, O., Radeva, P.: Traffic Sign Recognition Using Evolutionary Adaboost Detection and Forest-ECOC Classification. IEEE Transactions on Intelligent Transportation Systems 10(1), 113–126 (2009)
4. Rusinol, M., Llados, J., Dosch, P.: Camera-based graphical symbol detection. In: 9th International Conference on Document Analysis and Recognition, vol. 2, pp. 884–888. IEEE Press (2007), doi:10.1109/ICDAR.2007.4377042
5. Belongie, S., Malik, J., Puzicha, J.: Shape Matching and Object Recognition Using Shape Contexts. IEEE Transactions on Pattern Analysis and Machine Intelligence 24(4), 509–522 (2002)
6. Yang, S.: Symbol recognition via statistical integration of pixel-level constraint histograms: A new descriptor. IEEE Transactions on Pattern Analysis and Machine Intelligence 27(2), 278–281 (2005)
7. Grigorescu, C., Petkov, N.: Distance sets for shape filters and shape recognition. IEEE Trans. on Image Processing 12(10), 1274–1286 (2003)

Building a Symbol Library from Technical Drawings by Identifying Repeating Patterns

Nibal Nayef and Thomas M. Breuel

Technical University Kaiserslautern, Germany
nnayef@iupr.com, tmb@informatik.uni-kl.de

Abstract. This paper describes a novel approach for extracting a library of symbols from a large collection of line drawings. This symbol library is a compact and indexable representation of the line drawings. Such a representation is important for efficient symbol retrieval. The proposed approach first identifies the candidate patterns in all images, and then it clusters the similar ones together to create a set of clusters. A representative pattern is chosen from each cluster, and these representative patterns form a library of symbols. We have tested our approach on a database of line drawings, and it achieved high accuracy in capturing and representing the contents of the line drawings.

Keywords: Repeating patterns, Statistical grouping, Shapes clustering, Symbol library, Content analysis.

1 Introduction

A large number of documents contain technical line drawings, such as architectural floor plans, electronic circuit diagrams etc. The users are interested in retrieving specific symbols in a database of drawings. To perform such tasks, the automated content analysis of line drawings is required. Such analysis is essential in applications like retrieval search engines and digital libraries. To this end, we present in this paper our work on analyzing the contents of line drawings and representing them in an indexable representation.

When analyzing images, one finds that they contain objects that consist of components, repetitions of these components in a set of images usually imply that these components are meaningful parts of objects. Hence, identifying those components and clustering the similar ones together, results in a much smaller and a more meaningful representation of a dataset than the images themselves.

This work discusses a method to extract a library of symbols from a large collection of line drawings. This symbol library is a compact and indexable representation of the complete dataset, which can be used for the development of efficient symbol retrieval systems. The symbol library consists of clusters of symbols patterns from the dataset. The symbols patterns are found using a statistical grouping algorithm introduced by the authors in [8], and the clusters are then formed by clustering the similar symbols patterns. The clustering is based

Y.-B. Kwon and J.-M. Ogier (Eds.): GREC, LNCS 7423, pp. 69–78, 2013.

on geometric matching, which matches the symbols patterns under translation, rotation and scaling.

We show that the method is highly accurate in capturing the contents of the database and in representing it. For capturing the contents of the line drawings, we measure the ability of the algorithm to find all the symbols (or symbols patterns) that appear in the line drawings, and for representing the database as a symbol library, we measure the ability of the proposed clustering algorithm to create the correct clusters of similar symbol patterns.

Figure 1 illustrates the input and output of the proposed method, from a collection of drawings as in Figure 1(a), we get a set of clusters' representatives as shown in Figure 1(b), each representative is a symbol part up to a complete symbol, and each cluster contains all the symbols parts that are similar to each other. We call the set of clusters' representatives a *symbol library*. Using such a library, symbol retrieval becomes straightforward and fast – the retrieval itself is **not** a part of this work though–.

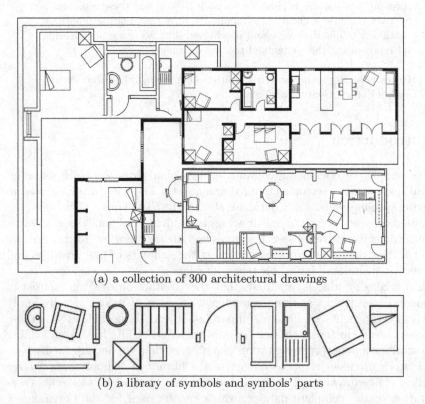

(a) a collection of 300 architectural drawings

(b) a library of symbols and symbols' parts

Fig. 1. Actual results of the proposed method: building a symbol library as in (b) from a collection of architectural drawings as in (a). For clarity of showing, only some drawings are shown, and only a part of the symbol library.

The rest of this paper is organized as follows: Section 2 discusses the related work, Section 3 presents the overall proposed approach. Section 4 presents the experimental results, and in Section 5 we conclude the paper.

2   Related Work

The notion of repeating patterns or visually similar parts in images has been introduced in the literature, but not for complicated line drawings that contain many non-isolated symbols along with connecting background lines.

Most of the works in the literature deal with repetitions within one image. Tuytelaars et. al. [12] presented a Hough transform-based geometric framework for the detection of regular repetitions of planar patterns under perspective skew. Schaffalitzky et. al [11] proposed a RANSAC-based technique for finding the repetitions within a scene. Leung et. al. [6] proposed to find the repeating patterns by matching the neighboring patches in an image under affine transformation using a registration technique. The work of Sanchez et. al [10] discussed using repetitive structured patterns to recognize textured symbols, where they automatically infer an attributed context-sensitive graph grammar to model and recognize a given textured symbol.

Some works have introduced the concept of utilizing repeating patterns across images for retrieval but not in the context of line drawings. A recent work by Doubek et. al. [5] discussed image retrieval using repeating patterns. In their work, the patterns could be found using any of the previously mentioned methods, and then the patterns are described by an invariant descriptor, then matched across images. Another related concept is clustering the visually similar parts in the famous bag-of-(visual)-words approach [2]. This approach is widely used in the field of object recognition and content-based image retrieval. The bag-of-words approach is based on extracting image patches around key points, and coding these patches by transformations-invariant feature descriptors, then clustering the similar descriptors together, this creates a code book for the images parts, and this code book can be later used for object retrieval.

Our approach is conceptually similar to both Doubek et. al. [5] and the works that apply the bag of words approach, however, it uses totally different techniques for each step, since we are dealing with shapes and line drawings. The approach in this paper, applies the concept of repeating patterns to line drawings for the same purpose as the bag-of-words approach. The purpose is creating an indexable representation of a database of images, so that it can be used later for fast retrieval. To the best of our knowledge, there are no published works that utilize repetitions in a database of line drawings.

Our approach has a number of advantages. First, it finds the repetitions in a database of images rather than in individual images as some of the mentioned approaches do. Second, it handles the cases when patterns are not adjacent in an image, or when they are rotated and/or scaled. Third, for finding the patterns, our approach uses a grouping technique [8] that proved to be efficient in extracting meaningful symbol parts from the background. This is advantageous to the methods that use patches or grid regions to extract the patterns. Using patches does not work well for line drawings because the line patterns in a drawing are very similar, which makes the extracted patches not discriminative enough.

3   The Method

In this section, we discuss the two main modules of our approach. The first module deals with extracting a set of patterns from all images, it includes pre-processing and identifying the symbols patterns. The set of patterns is a set of meaningful symbols' parts extracted from the line drawings. The second module takes these patterns and clusters the similar ones together, it uses a geometric matching algorithm as a clustering technique.

3.1   Identifying Symbols Parts via Grouping

The method starts by simple preprocessing of the images of the dataset. First, morphological edge detection is applied, which outputs thin inner and outer contours of the objects in the images. Then a vectorization step is performed by sampling line segments along the contours. We use these line segments as input to the next step that identifies the symbols parts. We call this next step *grouping*, because it groups sets of line segments together to form patterns. The grouping technique has been introduced by the authors in [8].

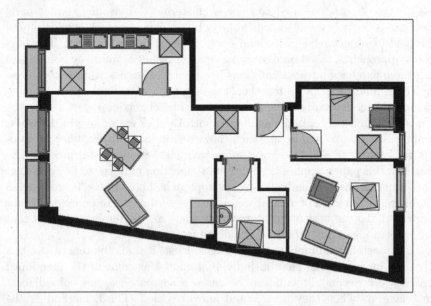

Fig. 2. The found **patterns** of a line drawing (adjacent different patterns have different shading). We draw red bounding boxes around the patterns found by the algorithm.

We apply the grouping procedure on each preprocessed image, and output a set of patterns, where each pattern is a set of line segments. Those patterns correspond mostly to meaningful parts of the symbols of the line drawings. The grouping technique is based on statistical grouping of line segments. It groups a set of line segments together based on non-accidental properties such as convexity. We have shown in [8] that this kind of statistical grouping provides a high probability to capture the symbols parts.

Figure 2 shows the output of the grouping procedure applied on a line drawing. The shaded parts are the patterns – or the symbols parts – found by the procedure. In the figure, red bounding boxes are drawn around the patterns found by the grouping procedure, we also use different shading for adjacent patterns. We define a *pattern* as the set of all the line segments that are inside a group including the segments that constitute the group itself (In Figure 2, this corresponds to all the line segments that lie inside a red bounding box). It is clear that the found patterns of an input image are meaningful parts of symbols up to complete symbols.

For each pattern, we also need to keep information about where this pattern can be found, like which image it comes from and its location in that image.

3.2   Clustering the Patterns via Geometric Matching

Having a list of patterns from all the images of the database, we need to find the repeating – or highly similar – patterns and put them together. Matching the patterns together is done using geometric matching. The patterns that correspond to the same part of a symbol could be rotated or scaled. Recall that each pattern is a set of line segments, so, using the geometric matching algorithm in [1], two patterns can be matched under similarity transformation. Since we are looking for repeating patterns, a pattern is accepted as a matching pattern only if it matches >75% of the other pattern's segments. This is an experimentally-set threshold for clustering the similar patterns together. The following is the clustering algorithm.

- *clusters*: an initially empty list of lists
- *patterns*: list of all patterns, marked "false" meaning they do not belong to any cluster yet.
- for each pattern p of the patterns list
  - if p does not belong to any cluster:
    * add p to *clusters*
    * use the geometric matching algorithm from [1] to match p with each of all other marked "false" patterns
    * add the accepted matches of p to the list of *clusters[p]* with their information
    * mark the accepted matches of p as "true"
  - else: (p already belongs to some cluster):
    * skip p
- End

This clustering results in a set of different clusters of patterns. The number of clusters is much smaller than the total number of patterns extracted from all images, hence, this set is a compact representation of the database. Figure 3 shows some of the resulting clusters. We select a cluster representative – i.e. a pattern – from each cluster, the set of the clusters' representatives composes a symbol library.

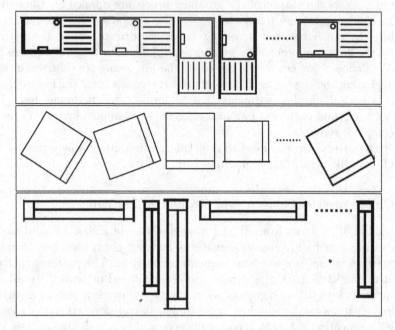

Fig. 3. Clusters: Example clusters of patterns

In this algorithm, there is no need to specify the number of clusters beforehand, the geometric matching step will control the output number of clusters, based on the mentioned acceptance criterion (a pattern should match at least >75% of the other pattern).

It is worth mentioning that the order in which the patterns are examined for clustering, does not affect the results. This is because the geometric matching algorithm [1] we use for matching two patterns will give the same matching score if we match pattern a to patterns b and c or if we match pattern b to patterns a and c, or any other random order.

We should also mention that we do not use soft clustering. That means, in our algorithm, the patterns that are matched with a certain pattern are **not** considered for matching with other patterns. This does not cause problems because we consider the pattern that is currently being matched as the cluster center, or -strictly speaking- the cluster representative, and we match it to the other patterns using a strict acceptance criterion, so, it can be assumed that the matched patterns do not belong to any other cluster. In case of false matching, extra clusters will be formed. It would be useful to investigate how soft clustering or other clustering variants can be used with the proposed algorithm to improve our clustering algorithm.

4   Experiments and Evaluation

4.1   The Dataset

In this section we present the evaluation of the approach on a dataset of architectural drawings. The dataset is a set of 300 images taken from the dataset generated in [3] and in [4], the dataset is a standard dataset in the community of graphics recognition, and it is publicly available[1]. The images are synthesized documents that imitate real complete floor plans with sizes ranging from 2M to 7M pixels. Subsets of this dataset have been used for the current GREC'11 symbol spotting contest, and by researchers for symbol spotting in [9] and [7].

4.2   Evaluation

Here we evaluate the ability of the proposed algorithm to capture the contents of the line drawings, and also its ability to represent those contents compactly as a symbol library. As mentioned previously, using the symbol library for symbol retrieval is not a part of this work, but is a part of a future work.

The performance of the clustering depends on the output of the grouping algorithm, since the patterns found by grouping are the input to the clustering algorithm. We have evaluated the performance of our grouping algorithm on the same dataset in our previous work in [8], where we evaluated the ability of the grouping to find all the parts of the symbols i.e. not missing any parts (recall). Also, whether the found parts are actually relevant symbol parts, not just random segments from different symbols or the background (precision). The grouping algorithm achieved 98.8% recall and 97.3% precision [8].

Now, we present the evaluation of the clustering algorithm. The clustering procedure involves finding the repeating patterns and putting them together. To evaluate the clustering performance, we **adapt** the recall and precision metrics to repeating patterns as follows:

- **cluster recall**: the number of the patterns in the cluster that are similar to the cluster representative divided by the number of all occurrences of that pattern in the dataset.
- **cluster precision**: the number of the patterns in the cluster that are similar to the cluster representative divided by the total number of patterns in the cluster.

Table 1 summarizes the results.

---

[1] http://mathieu.delalandre.free.fr/projects/sesyd/index.html

Table 1. Results of applying the **CLUSTERING** method to **300** document images of architectural drawings. The provided recall and precision values are the average values for all the formed clusters.

Number of patterns to be clustered		**13780**
Number of the formed clusters		**30**
All Clusters	Avg. Recall	Avg. Precision
	95%	**96.5%**

In Table 1, the "patterns to be clustered", are the patterns found by the grouping module. In some cases, the grouping outputs some irrelevant patterns – non-meaningful symbols' parts –, those irrelevant patterns do not affect the accuracy of the clustering, they only affect the run time, since the clustering procedure has to perform extra matching operations, and also few extra clusters of irrelevant symbols' parts will be formed. Figure 4 shows an example of an extra irrelevant cluster. However, the "recall" of the grouping output which is related to the missing symbols or the missing parts of symbols, affects the "recall" value of the clustering, since the parts missing from the grouping output stay missing from the clusters too.

As Table 1 shows, the clustering module has placed the repeating symbols in clusters with high accuracy. The errors come from unsuccessful matchings. Figure 5 shows an example of a false matching.

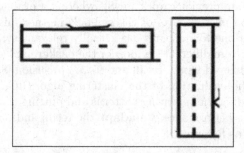

Fig. 4. An example of a cluster that contains irrelevant patterns. Irrelevant patterns are patterns that do not correspond to symbols or parts of symbols.

The running time required to form the clusters is 45 min. on average per forming 1 cluster on a 2.80GHz CPU. This can be significantly improved by speeding up the matching step. However, the running time is still reasonable given the large number of patterns to be clustered (13780) and the achieved high accuracy. The clustering step is to be carried out offline.

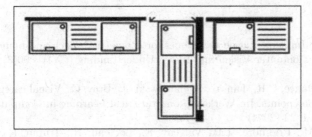

Fig. 5. An example of a cluster that contains a false match. The third symbol (the false match) is very similar to the other symbols that were correctly matched.

4.3   Discussion

In the following, we discuss the importance of clustering the repeating patterns for representing datasets compactly. In a certain application domain like architectural floor plans or electric circuits, there is a defined small set of symbols, which is used to draw the technical line drawings. For example, in the dataset we used for evaluation in this work, only 16 different symbols were used, those symbols appear many times in many of the drawings. The total number of symbols that appear in all the drawings is 6987, and they appear within the drawings connected to other symbols and lines, which means they have to be searched for and located.

Using our proposed approach, we build a library of 30 clusters that contains these symbols and all their repeating instances, along with their location information in the dataset. This library makes the potential applications of fast symbol retrieval from the dataset easy as follows: if we want to retrieve a specific query symbol in this dataset, we only need to match this query to the 30 clusters' representatives, and the best matching cluster will be retrieved. Without the symbol library, we would need to search all the documents in the dataset for a query symbol using a symbol spotting method.

In summary, our proposed approach can be considered as a content analysis method, where a database of document images is processed offline, to get another representation that can later be used for online retrieval.

5   Conclusions and Future Work

This paper has described a novel approach for analyzing the contents of technical line drawings, and has shown some interesting results. Finding the repeating patterns has proved to be an effective way of compactly representing a dataset of technical image documents. The paper also showed the use of feature grouping for extracting meaningful visual patterns. Moreover, the use of geometric matching as a clustering method produced good results for comparing the symbols. Future work includes incorporating the proposed approach in a large-scale symbol retrieval system.

References

1. Breuel, T.M.: Implementation techniques for geometric branch-and-bound matching methods. Computer Vision and Image Understanding (CVIU) 90(3), 258–294 (2003)
2. Csurka, G., Dance, C.R., Fan, L., Willamowski, J., Bray, C.: Visual categorization with bags of keypoints. In: Workshop on Statistical Learning in Computer Vision (ECCV), pp. 1–22 (2004)
3. Delalandre, M., Pridmore, T.P., Valveny, E., Locteau, H., Trupin, É.: Building Synthetic Graphical Documents for Performance Evaluation. In: Liu, W., Lladós, J., Ogier, J.-M. (eds.) GREC 2007. LNCS, vol. 5046, pp. 288–298. Springer, Heidelberg (2008)
4. Delalandre, M., Valveny, E., Pridmore, T., Karatzas, D.: Generation of synthetic documents for performance evaluation of symbol recognition and spotting systems. IJDAR 13(3), 187–207 (2010)
5. Doubek, P., Matas, J., Perdoch, M., Chum, O.: Image matching and retrieval by repetitive patterns. In: ICPR, pp. 3195–3198 (2010)
6. Leung, T., Malik, J.: Detecting, Localizing and Grouping Repeated Scene Elements From an Image. In: Buxton, B.F., Cipolla, R. (eds.) ECCV 1996. LNCS, vol. 1064, pp. 546–555. Springer, Heidelberg (1996)
7. Luqman, M.M., Brouard, T., Ramel, J., Llodos, J.: A content spotting system for line drawing graphic document images. In: ICPR, pp. 3420–3423 (2010)
8. Nayef, N., Breuel, T.M.: Statistical grouping for segmenting symbols parts from line drawings, with application to symbol spotting. In: ICDAR, pp. 364–368 (2011)
9. Nguyen, T., Tabbone, S., Boucher, A.: A symbol spotting approach based on the vector model and a visual vocabulary. In: ICDAR, pp. 708–712 (2009)
10. Sánchez, G., Lladós, J.: A graph grammar to recognize textured symbols. In: ICDAR, pp. 465–469 (2001)
11. Schaffalitzky, F., Zisserman, A.: Geometric Grouping of Repeated Elements within Images. In: Forsyth, D., Mundy, J.L., Di Gesú, V., Cipolla, R. (eds.) Shape, Contour, and Grouping 1999. LNCS, vol. 1681, pp. 165–181. Springer, Heidelberg (1999)
12. Tuytelaars, T., Turina, A., Gool, L.V.: Non-combinatorial detection of regular repetitions under perspective skew. PAMI 25(4), 418–432 (2003)

Notation-Invariant Patch-Based Wall Detector in Architectural Floor Plans

Lluís-Pere de las Heras, Joan Mas, Gemma Sánchez, and Ernest Valveny

Computer Vision Center - Universitat Autònoma de Barcelona
Campus UAB, 08193 Bellatera, Barcelona, Spain
{lpheras,joan.mas,gemma.sanchez,ernest.valveny}@cvc.uab.es
http://www.cvc.uab.cat

Abstract. Architectural floor plans exhibit a large variability in notation. Therefore, segmenting and identifying the elements of any kind of
plan becomes a challenging task for approaches based on grouping structural primitives obtained by vectorization. Recently, a patch-based segmentation method working at pixel level and relying on the construction
of a visual vocabulary has been proposed in [1], showing its adaptability
to different notations by automatically learning the visual appearance of
the elements in each different notation. This paper presents an evolution
of that previous work, after analyzing and testing several alternatives for
each of the different steps of the method: Firstly, an automatic plan-size
normalization process is done. Secondly we evaluate different features to
obtain the description of every patch. Thirdly, we train an SVM classifier to obtain the category of every patch instead of constructing a
visual vocabulary. These variations of the method have been tested for
wall detection on two datasets of architectural floor plans with different notations. After studying in deep each of the steps in the process
pipeline, we are able to find the best system configuration, which highly
outperforms the results on wall segmentation obtained by the original
paper.

Keywords: graphics recognition, floor plan interpretation, patch-based
segmentation.

1 Introduction

Floor plan interpretation is an active research topic inside the graphical document analysis field. One of the main reasons is that most of the architectural
projects involve the reutilization or modification of previous designs. Therefore,
automatic floor plan interpretation becomes an actual need to be able to reuse
existing designs and retrieve any kind of information of interest. In this direction,
several works exist as those proposed by Dosch *et al.* [2] — for printed floor plans
— and Juchmes *et al.* [3] — for sketched floor plans — which aim to construct
the 3D representation of the buildings modeled in the floor plans. The authors
also proposed in [4] a complete interpretation system using a syntactic model to
interpret structurally, hierarchically and semantically this kind of documents.

Y.-B. Kwon and J.-M. Ogier (Eds.): GREC, LNCS 7423, pp. 79–88, 2013.
© Springer-Verlag Berlin Heidelberg 2013

However, floor plan interpretation is still a non-solved problem. The non-existence of a standard notation creates a large variability in building models. Thus, building entities as walls, doors, rooms, dimensions, areas, etc. are modeled differently in distinct plans. On top of that, existing floor plan interpretation approaches are based on vectorizing the images in order to extract the basic linear components. Interpretation is done by applying a set of rules that permit to group this basic components into high-level entities (walls, doors, etc.). Thus, these methods need to completely reformulate the segmentation process to deal with every different notation. This is the case of the recent approaches presented by Macé *et al.* in [5] for room segmentation in floor plans, and Ahmed *et al.* in [6] for a complete interpretation of floor plans. Both approaches assume a priori knowledge of the graphical structure of the walls.

With the aim of solving this problem, the authors proposed in [1] a wall segmentation approach capable to deal with plans having completely different notations. This technique, which is a bag-of-patches approach, is based on recent works on patch-based image segmentation and object localization [7, 8]. A grid of patches is defined using three different topologies over the learning images. Then, feature vectors are extracted from every patch and clustered into a codebook. After that, and using the ground-truth information, a probability of belonging to each class of objects is assigned to every word. In the testing phase, each patch is assigned to the nearest word in the dictionary, inheriting the class probabilities of the word. In order to test it for wall segmentation, this approach is tested in floor plans with different resolutions and wall notations. As the visual appearance of every class of objects under each different notation is automatically learned by the codebook and the probability distribution of patches, the method can be easily adapted to work with several notations by just providing a set of learning images.

In this paper we study the impact of introducing some modifications to the original patch-based detector for walls. Firstly, as floor plans could be found with different sizes and resolutions, an unsupervised image size normalization is applied over all the images in the dataset. Secondly, we evaluate different descriptors extracted from the patches (image pixels, PCA and Blurred Shape Model [9]) in order to analyze their suitability for different datasets and compare their influence in the global performance of the system. Thirdly, instead of clustering these feature vectors to build a codebook of patches, we train a Support Vector Machine classifier that permits to directly classify every patch into one floor plan object class. These modifications are introduced to the original method and have been tested over the same two datasets used in [1] in order to evaluate their benefits and disadvantages. All in all, as a result of this study, the best system configuration is found, which considerably outperforms the results obtained by the original approach.

The rest of the paper is organized as follows. In section 2 we describe all the steps of the proposed approach. Section 3 is devoted to explain the experimental setup and in section 4 we show the results of the application of the method. Finally, section 5 concludes the paper.

2   Methodology

The pipeline of the system is shown in figure 1. First, some standard image processing techniques are applied. Then, a grid is placed over the image and some features are extracted for every patch of the grid. In the learning step, a ground-truth of patch descriptors is used to train a classifier. Finally, in the testing, input image pixel categorization will rely on patch classification. All these steps are described in the remainder of this section.

2.1   Image Preprocessing

In [1], all the dataset images are first binarized by applying the well-known approach proposed by Otsu in [10]. Then, textual information is removed using the text-graphic separation algorithm presented in [11]. In addition to that, in this paper we propose a new pre-processing step to normalize images in terms of resolution and line thickness.

Images in a given dataset can be at different resolutions and therefore, the line thickness can vary from one image to another. This would result in a larger variability in the visual appearance of the regular patches. To avoid it, an automatic line-thickness normalization is applied to all documents. This process consists in creating a histogram accounting for the length of the sequences of consecutive black pixels in the horizontal direction for each document. The histogram maxima corresponds to the thickness of the thinnest lines in the document. Then, all the images are resized using a bilinear interpolation method in order to achieve the same line width. Hence, the thickness of the walls becomes similar for all plans, and thus, the relative size of patches is similar for each floor plan.

2.2   Grid Creation

As introduced before, a rigid grid is placed over the images where every cell defines a regular patch. Each patch allows to capture local redundancy of neighboring pixels which later can be modeled by different description approaches. We have used two different rigid grid topologies – those that performed better in [1] – forming squared patches over the images: *Non-overlapped regular grid* and *Overlapped regular grid*.

Non-overlapped Regular Grid: This grid is composed of squared non-overlapped patches directly defined over the image. The main advantage of this topology is its simplicity and its cheap computation cost. However, since each pixel of the image belongs to only one patch, final pixel class assignment will be only affected by its patch label, while sometimes one patch can contain pixels from different categories. Moreover final assignment of pixel category will strongly depend on how patches fall into the image.

Overlapped Regular Grid: In order to avoid the strong dependence on the grid location over the image, we have also defined a squared patched grid, but with overlapping. In this grid, each pixel belongs to several patches according to the parameter ϕ_{ov}, which specifies in pixels, the separation between patch neighbor centers. Therefore, final class assignment of a pixel is weighted up between the class probabilities of all its patches. This process is explained in section 2.5. The main advantage of this topology is that images are defined by more patches, thus object boundaries would be better segmented. On the other hand, for the same reason, pixel-level classification is more costly with respect to a non-overlapped grid.

2.3 Feature Extraction

Once the desired grid is created, a patch-descriptor is calculated to represent every patch that contains at least one black pixel. Hence, since white patches are considered as *background*, they are ruled out in the learning step due to computational reasons. We have used three patch-descriptors to analyze the impact of feature extraction in the global performance of the system.

- **PID: Pixel Intensity Descriptor:** This simple descriptor is formed by concatenating the raw pixels of the patch in a row-wise manner.
- **PCA: Principle Component Analysis:** PCA is calculated over the row-wise vectors of all patches. The 95% of the discriminative information of the patches is maintained meanwhile the dimensionality is highly reduced.
- **BSM: Blurred Shape Model:** BSM is a shape descriptor introduced by Escalera et al. in [9] that has been successfully applied to different graphics recognition applications. The patch is divided in $n \times n$ equal-sized subregions (*BSMreg*) where each subregion receives votes from the points in it, and also from the points in the neighboring subregions. Each point contributes with a weight according to the distance between the point and the subregion centroid. The final description is a vector formed by concatenating the number of weighted votes received by each subregion.

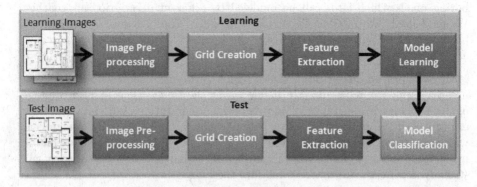

Fig. 1. Process pipeline

2.4 Model Learning

In [1], a vocabulary of visual words is created by clustering similar patch-descriptors. Later, the likelihood of each word belonging to every class is learned from the training-set. Thus, each visual-word in the codebook has a probability of belonging to each of the classes. In the testing, each patch-descriptor of the input image is compared with all the words in the codebook and hard-assigned to the closest one, inheriting its class probabilities defined for such word.

Contrarily, to enhance the system velocity in testing time, which is a critical issue in [1], here we train support vectors to discriminate between classes. This process starts by choosing a previously specified number N of labeled instances, selected randomly from the two classes of objects to segment, $C = \{Wall, Background\}$, $N/2$ patches for each class. Then, a support vector machine (SVM) using the LIBSVM [12] implementation with a Gaussian RBF Kernel is trained on the labeled patches. The Radial Basis Function used is defined as

$$K(pd_i, pd_j) = e^{-\gamma \|pd_i - pd_j\|^2}, \tag{1}$$

where pd_i and pd_j are patch-descriptors and $\gamma \in \mathbb{R}_+$ is a the RBF width parameter selected by cross-validation.

2.5 Model Classification

The earliest steps in the final classification process – from patch to pixel classification – are equal to those in the learning phase, as it can be seen in figure 1.

Firstly, every test image is preprocessed as explained in section 2.1. Secondly, features are extracted from patches in the manner it is described in sections 2.2 and 2.3. Thirdly, each patch-descriptor is classified using the SVM model trained in the learning phase. Finally, as in [1], final pixel classification will depend on the grid topology used to describe the input images.

In the case of the non-overlapped grid, every pixel in the image is contained in a single patch. Thus, pixels are directly categorized with the same label than their respective patches have obtained by SVM classification.

Distinctively, when an overlapped grid is used, pixels belong to several patches. Then, the classification of each pixel would depend on the several patches that contain that pixel, which allows to add contextual information in this process. Therefore, not only a classification label for each patch is needed, but also a confidence score for each class. In order to obtain a degree of classification confidence for each input patch, the probability estimation implemented in LIBSVM is used. In such a way, we can assign to every pixel a definite number of classification probabilities per object category $P(c_i|pd)$, one for each patch pd that the pixel px belongs to. Then, the final classification of a pixel can be seen as a combination of classifiers problem. Adapting the Mean Rule presented in the theoretical framework for combining classifiers proposed by Kittler et al. in [13], every pixel is finally classified to class c_i according to:

$$C(px) = \arg\max_i mean(P(c_i|pd)), \forall pd \mid px \in pd. \tag{2}$$

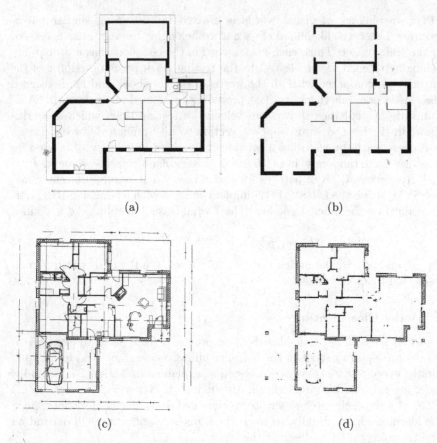

(a)

(b)

(c)

(d)

Fig. 2. Qualitative results for wall segmentation in both datasets. (a) and (c) Plan examples of *Dataset-1* and *Dataset-2* respectively. (b) and (d) walls segmented using the best system configuration for each dataset.

3   Experiments

Even though wall detection is a fundamental process in floor plan interpretation, it can not be found in the literature any work that gives a quantitative evaluation of this task. Moreover, the lack of public datasets in architectural drawings provoke that the performance of our approach could only be compared with our previous work in [1].

In this section we describe the experimental setup used to evaluate the results obtained by our approach. Firstly, the datasets used for wall segmentation are presented. Finally, the evaluation protocol followed to evaluate the performance of our system is explicated.

3.1   Floor Plan Dataset

In order to evaluate our approach, we use the two datasets used in [1]. Both collections were specifically created to perform wall segmentation and they contain plans with complete different graphical notations and resolutions. They were manually labeled for the classes *Wall* and *Background*. These datasets will be made publicly available soon. Actually, they have already been used to perform floor plan interpretation in [6].

- **Dataset-1** is a collection of 90 real architectural floor plan drawings of high resolution, see figure 2a. Both, interior and exterior walls are modeled by black lines of different thickness. The dataset is split in two subsets: the validation-set and test-set. The former contains 30 plans and is used for parameter validation, e.g. patch-size or number of learning samples, using a 5-fold cross-validation. The test-set contains the rest of the plans, and using a 10-fold cross-validation is used to evaluate our system.
- **Dataset-2** contains 10 real floor plans documents at low-resolution, see figure 2c. The notation for walls varies whether they are exterior or interior. Exterior walls are modeled with hatched lines meanwhile interiors are modeled with dotted lines. Our intention is to confirm whether the system is capable to segment walls in plans with a completely different graphical convention. Due to the small amount of plans in this dataset – only 10 – all the documents have been used for training and testing following a Leave-One Out strategy. Moreover, these plans contain images at different resolutions which allows us to evaluate the performance of the system by introducing the wall thickness normalization methodology explained in section 2.1.

3.2   Evaluation Protocol

The protocol chosen for evaluating our system is completely the same used in [1]. We evaluate our method at pixel level but only considering in the score those pixels which are black in the original binary image, as only black pixels convey relevant information for segmentation. All the results in the experiments are expressed using the Jaccard Index *JI*. This index takes values between 0 and 1 and the higher it is, the better segmentation is performed.

$$JI = \frac{TruePos}{(TruePos + FalsePos + FalseNeg)}. \tag{3}$$

4   Results and Discussion

In essence, our system is influenced by two general parameters: the grid topology (GT), and the method used to describe patches (D). In the first case, table 1 shows that overlapping grid behaves better than the non-ovelapped. The main reason is that using overlapping patches, pixels which belong to wall boundaries are better represented and therefore, more respected. Contrarily, using

Table 1. System behavior regarding grid topology in dataset-2

Dataset	GT	PS	D	LS	ϕ_o	JI
Dataset-2	Non-overlapped	15×15	PCA	1000	-	0.7316
Dataset-2	Overlapped	15×15	PCA	1000	3	**0.7981**

Table 2. System behavior regarding descriptor in dataset-2

Dataset	GT	PS	D	LS	JI
Dataset-2	Non-overlapped	15×15	PID	7500	0.7206
Dataset-2	Non-overlapped	15×15	PCA	7500	0.7316
Dataset-2	Non-overlapped	15×15	BSM_8	7500	**0.7441**

a non-overlapped grid, some boundaries are lost because pixels in these areas can easily fall into patches which mostly represent background. In the case of patch-descriptors, table 2 shows the performance of the system using different approaches to describe patches. BSM, that can be seen as a local blurring of the image in each patch, describés walls better, and also it can characterize better high intra-class variability, as it is the case for walls in dataset-2. In addition to that, as it can be seen in table 3, the proposed image normalization process improves the global performance of the system because it reduces the large variability in patch appearance when plans have different resolutions. Lastly,it is worth saying that the number of subregions selected while using BSM descriptor (BSMreg), the size of the patches (PS), the number of overlapped pixels (ϕ_o) in the overlapped-grid, and the SVM learning samples (LS) have been learned experimentally in the system validation process.

Up to this point, we have proved that the best system configuration includes the image-size normalization, an overlapping grid and BSM as patch-descriptor. The next step is to analyze the behavior of the system –in its best configuration– when different classification strategies are used. With this aim, table 4 shows the best system performances using SVM classifier (SVM-WD) and vocabulary based classifier ([1]+iNorm+BSM). Both methods are compared with the baseline approach proposed in [1].

According to the results, SVM-WD performs very similar to the baseline method in both datasets, and closely to the [1]+iNorm+BSM in dataset-1.

Table 3. System behavior regarding image normalization in dataset-2

Dataset	GT	PS	D	LS	JI
Dataset-2	Non-overlapped	15×15	BSM_8	7500	0.7357
Normalized Dataset-2	Non-overlapped	15×15	BSM_8	7500	**0.7441**

Table 4. Best wall-segmentation results for (SVM-WD) and [1] $+iNorm+BSM$ using the best system configurations. Both systems are compared with the baseline approach ([1]). DS is the codebook size used in [1].

Method	Dataset	GT	PS	D	LS	DS	ϕ_o	*JI*
[1]	*Dataset-1*	Overlapped	8×8	PCA	-	100	4	**0.9673**
	Dataset-2	Overlapped	20×20	PCA	-	2000	5	**0.8241**
SVM-WD	*Dataset-1*	Overlapped	15×15	BSM_8	50000	-	3	**0.9667**
	Dataset-2	Overlapped	15×15	BSM_8	7500	-	3	**0.8233**
[1]$+iNorm+BSM$	*Dataset-1*	Overlapped	10×10	BSM_8	-	100	5	**0.9714**
	Dataset-2	Overlapped	18×18	BSM_{16}	-	2000	3	**0.8612**

Moreover, SVM-WD is three times faster in testing-time than using a vocabulary-based classifier. This yields to consider the use of SVM as a good alternative when datasets obey to the same characteristics as dataset-1. On the other hand, [1]+iNorm+BSM highly outperforms the SVM-WD for the challenging dataset-2 (from 0.82 to 0.86) and slightly improve the classification in dataset-1. This concludes that a vocabulary based classifier must be used when performance is more critical than time, as it is usually the case of floor plan interpretation methods.

5 Conclusion

This paper presents a notation-invariant method to detect and segment walls in floor plans. This approach, which is an evolution of the previous wall detector presented by the authors in [1], is a statistical patch-based detector that escapes from the traditional structural techniques based on vectorization. For that reason, our method only needs to be retrained for every new notation, instead of being reformulated as the majority of the state-of-the-art techniques do.

Three different alternatives from our previous work are analyzed. Firstly, since floor plans can be found at different resolutions, an unsupervised pre-process to normalize the size of all input images is applied. Secondly, after dividing the images into patches following two different strategies – squared-rigid grid and overlapped grid –, the influence that different patch-description techniques have into the global system performance is studied. The patch descriptors tested are PID, PCA and BSM, being BSM that one that better encapsulates the information from patches. Finally, patch classification is performed by a Support Vector Machine. Experiments on two datasets with different notations show that using these alternatives – an SVM classifier along with image normalization and BSM features – yields to a very similar accuracy to the baseline approach presented in [1], but being a big deal faster in testing time. In addition have also proved that joining the vocabulary-based classification used in [1] with the image normalization and BSM features as presented in this paper leads to the best configuration of the system, which highly outperforms the results of the original paper.

Acknowledgment. This work has been partially supported by the Spanish projects TIN2009-14633-C03-03, TIN2011-24631, a CONSOLIDER-INGENIO 2010(CSD2007-00018), an Eureka project TSI-020400-2011-50 and by a research grant of the Universitat Autonoma de Barcelona (471-02-1/2010).

References

[1] de las Heras, L., Mas, J., Sánchez, G., Valveny, E.: Wall Patch-Based Segmentation in Architectural Floor. In: Int. Conf. on Document Analysis and Recognition, pp. 1270–1274 (2011)

[2] Dosch, P., Tombre, K., AhSoon, C., Masini, G.: A complete system for the analysis of architectural drawings. International Journal on Document Analysis and Recognition 3(2), 102–116 (2000)

[3] Juchmes, J., Leclercq, P., Azar, S.: A Multi-Agent system for the Interpretation of Architectural Sketches. In: Eurographics Workshop on Sketch-Based Interfaces and Modeling, pp. 53–61 (2004)

[4] de las Heras, L.-P., Sánchez, G.: And-Or Graph Grammar for Architectural Floor Plan Representation, Learning and Recognition. A Semantic, Structural and Hierarchical Model. In: Vitrià, J., Sanches, J.M., Hernández, M. (eds.) IbPRIA 2011. LNCS, vol. 6669, pp. 17–24. Springer, Heidelberg (2011)

[5] Macé, S., Locteau, H., Valveny, E., Tabbone, S.: A system to detect rooms in architectural floor plan images. In: Proc. IAPR Int. Work. on Document Analysis Systems, pp. 167–174 (2010)

[6] Ahmed, S., Liwiki, M., Weber, M., Dengel, A.: Improved Automatic Analysis of Architectural Floor Plans. In: Int. Conf. on Document Analysis and Recognition, pp. 864–869 (2011)

[7] Larlus, D., Verbeej, J., Jurie, F.: Category Level Object Segmentation by Combining Bag-of-Words Models with Dirichlet Processes and Random Fields. Int. Journal on Computer Vision, 238–253 (2010)

[8] Burns, T.J., Corso, J.J.: Robust unsupervised segmentation of degraded document images with topic models. In: IEEE Conf. on Computer Vision and Pattern Recognition, pp. 1287–1294 (2009)

[9] Escalera, S., Fornés, A., Pujol, O., Radeva, P., Sánchez, G., Lladós, J.: Blurred Shape Model for Binary and Grey-level Symbol Recognition. Pattern Recognition Letters 30, 1424–1433 (2009)

[10] Otsu, N.: A threshold selection method from gray-level histogram. IEEE Trans. Syst. Man Cybern. 9, 62–66 (1979)

[11] Tombre, K., Tabbone, S., Pélissier, L., Lamiroy, B., Dosch, P.: Text/Graphics Separation Revisited. In: Document Analysis Systems V, pp. 615–620 (2002)

[12] Chang, C., Lin, C.: LIBSVM: A library for support vector machines. ACM Transactions on Intelligent Systems and Technology 2, 27 (2011)

[13] Kittler, J., Hatef, M., Duin, R.P.W., Matas, J.: On combining classifiers. IEEE Trans. Pattern Analysis and Machine Intelligence. 20, 226–239 (1998)

Interest of Syntactic Knowledge for On-Line Flowchart Recognition

Aurélie Lemaitre[1], Harold Mouchère[2], Jean Camillerapp[3],
and Bertrand Coüasnon[3]

[1] IRISA - Université de Rennes 2
Campus de Beaulieu 35042 Rennes Cedex, France
aurelie.lemaitre@irisa.fr
[2] IRCCyN/IVC - UMR CNRS 6597
Rue Christian Pauc - BP 50609 44306 Nantes Cedex 3, France
[3] IRISA - INSA
Campus de Beaulieu 35042 Rennes Cedex, France

Abstract. In this paper, we address the problem of segmentation and recognition of on-line *a posteriori* flowcharts. Flowcharts are bi-dimensional documents, in the sense that the order of writing is not defined. Some statistical approaches have been proposed in the literature to label and segment the flowcharts. However, as they are very well structured documents, we propose to introduce some structural and syntactic knowledge on flowcharts to improve their recognition. For this purpose, we have used an existing grammatical off-line method with on-line *a posteriori* signal. We apply this work on a freely available database. The results demonstrate the interest of structural knowledge on the context to improve the recognition.

Keywords: structured documents, flowcharts, symbol recognition, on-line analysis, grammatical analysis, segmentation.

1 Introduction

We work in the context of handwritten document recognition, and more particularly complex bi-dimensional documents such as schemes, plans, diagrams, flowcharts (example on figure 1).

These kinds of documents are *complex* as they are not only made of text but also of symbols, shapes, boxes... Consequently, the steps of segmentation and of structure analysis are essential before the handwriting recognition.

The *bi-dimensional* aspect of these documents is also very important for the recognition. Indeed, in these documents, the order of writing is not necessarily from left to right, nor from top to bottom. Consequently the order of reading and of analyzing the document must be adapted depending on the content of the document. For example, even if the main orientation of a flowchart is left to right or top to bottom, these diagrams will be read by following the arrows, which can have any orientation.

Y.-B. Kwon and J.-M. Ogier (Eds.): GREC, LNCS 7423, pp. 89–98, 2013.

The final objective of flowchart recognition is to produce a semantic analysis of its content. In this paper, we propose some first experiments: we focus our analysis to label each stroke of the flowchart and to group the strokes depending on the symbol they belong to. We work on the *a posteriori* analysis of on-line signal. These tasks present several challenges. First, the strokes represent either pieces of text or pieces of symbols, and confusion can occur between some strokes of text and some strokes of symbol. For example, a circular stroke could be the letter "o" or a circle shape, or even something else. The second challenge is to deal with the fact that most of the symbols are multi-strokes, and that the strokes of one symbol have not necessarily been written successively. To sum up, we are faced with two segmentation problems for the strokes: the confusion between symbols and text and the confusion between symbols.

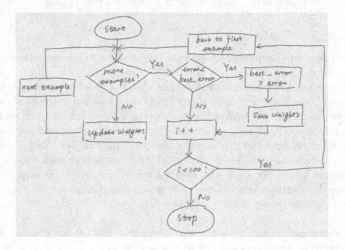

Fig. 1. Example of handwritten flowchart

Several methods have been proposed in the literature to deal with handwritten diagram recognition. However, one of the important limits of these methods is the difficulty to make the classification between strokes of text and of symbols. For example, Qi *et al.* [5] focus on diagrams that are only made of symbols. This is also a constraint mentioned by Feng *et al.* in [3]. As diagrams often contain both text and symbols, some authors assume that the user will explicitly choose a kind of writing, text or symbol, when drawing its diagram. For example, Tilak *et al.* [6] propose to add text on handwritten diagrams using a specific form. Yuan *et al.* [8] remove this constraint of separating text and symbol strokes, but impose symbols to be mono-stroke. This shows that the segmentation of strokes into text and symbols remains an open problem.

Concerning the flowcharts in particular, the existing methods are only based on statistical approaches. Thus, Yuan *et al.* [8] use a hybrid SVM-HMM for sketch recognition. Awal *et al.* [1] have also presented some work for flowchart recognition. Concerning the recognition of symbols, they apply two different methods: the separation of text and graphic symbols using a method based on entropy, and the recognition of symbols using TDNN or SVM after a step of stroke re-ordering. They also propose a global learning/recognition approach using dynamic programming and TDNN. However, these authors conclude that their statistical approach obtains limited results, due to the instability of stroke signal. Thus the introduction of structural knowledge could improve the recognition. This conclusion joins the work of Mace *et al.* [4] who use grammatical descriptions for the recognition of complex documents, such as electrical schemes.

In this paper, we propose to show that a structural method is particularly convenient for bi-dimensional complex handwritten documents. Thus, we present syntactic knowledge to describe the flowcharts is section 2. Then, we present how we have implemented this structural approach into an existing structural method (section 3). At last, we present in section 4 our experiments on a freely available database and demonstrate that our structural approach increases the recognition rates, by comparison with the statistical methods.

2 Syntactic Knowledge on Flowcharts

We first present the different symbols that compose a flowchart[1]. Then, we propose to express some syntactic knowledge on the organisation of the flowcharts, using a grammatical description. We conclude by the structural flexibility that is required by the analysis.

2.1 Existing Symbols

The flowcharts are used to describe algorithms or processes. They are made of different symbols such as circles, rectangles... Arrows are used to represent the control flow. Some text is present inside the symbols or close to the arrows. The figure 2 synthesizes the different kinds of symbols that can be found in our flowcharts.

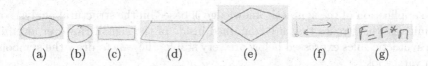

(a)   (b)   (c)   (d)   (e)   (f)   (g)

Fig. 2. Existing symbols on flowcharts: terminator, connection, process, data, decision, arrow, text

The terminator and the connection can be described as circular shapes, and more particularly oval or circles. The process, the data and the decision are described as specific quadrilaterals: rectangle, parallelogram and diamond. The arrows are made of a succession of line segments, possibly ended by a pointer.

---

[1] This work is applied to the database presented in [1].

2.2   Syntactic Rules

In this work, we propose some syntactic rules that enable the grammatical analysis of flowcharts. As a flowchart always begins by a connection or a terminator, we propose two ways to `StartDiagram`:

```
StartDiagram :: terminator, arrow, RestOfDiagram.
StartDiagram :: connection, arrow, RestOfDiagram.
```

These two rules call the analysis of the following symbols of the diagram, using `RestOfDiagram`.

Three kinds of symbols can continue a diagram: process, data, decision. They are followed by one or two arrows (for decision). So, these three rules recursively call `RestOfDiagram`.

```
RestOfDiagram :: process, arrow, RestOfDiagram.
RestOfDiagram :: data, arrow, RestOfDiagram.
RestOfDiagram :: decision,
                 arrow1, RestOfDiagram1,
                 arrow2, RestOfDiagram2.
```

The `RestOfDiagram` can also be the end of the diagram if we meet a terminator, a connection, or an element that has been seen before in the analysis, in the case of a loop.

```
RestOfDiagram :: terminator.
RestOfDiagram :: connection.
RestOfDiagram :: seenBeforeElement.
```

These rules that we have proposed simply describe the syntax of our flowcharts. We have realised a global description that ensures a global consistence in the recognition of the whole flowchart. We now detail some structural aspects of the analysis.

2.3   Structural Aspects

The application of the syntactic knowledge is based on the structural analysis of primitives: the strokes that are contained inside of the signal. However, even if the syntactic rules expressed below are very stable, the way to draw the symbols can vary a lot.

Firstly, we can mention the case of the arrows, presented in Figure 2(f). Indeed, the number of edges is not defined (often one, two or three ...). Moreover, the end pointer of the arrow has a varying shape, or can be nonexistent. Consequently the structural analysis must be flexible enough to deal with all these cases.

Secondly, we are faced with the fact that the diagram is not built from left to right nor from top to bottom. Consequently, when looking for the `RestOfDiagram`, we have to study the four directions after a symbol: right, left, top, bottom.

Thirdly, we must notice that each symbol can be composed of a varying number of strokes. For example, figure 3 shows that a rectangle can be made of 1, 3, 5 strokes. Here again, the structural analysis must be flexible enough to deal with all these cases.

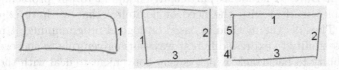

Fig. 3. Variable number of strokes for a rectangle: respectively 1,3,5

At last, the structural analysis must deal with the presence of text inside of the symbols. As presented on figure 4, the presence of text is not mandatory. The text can be on one or several lines and can overflow out of the symbols.

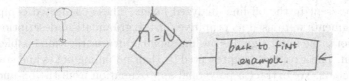

Fig. 4. Variable configurations of text inside of the symbols

As a conclusion, we can notice that the primitives that could be useful for symbol recognition (for example sides of a quadrilateral) are not always directly present in the on-line signal, and that the order of the strokes is not always relevant. Thanks to our grammatical structural approach, we will solve these local problems by using the relative positioning of the strokes in the image and ensure a global consistence of the recognition.

3 Implementation with a Grammar-Based Method

We have implemented our syntactic and structural description of flowcharts using an existing grammar-based method: DMOS.

3.1 Existing DMOS Method

The DMOS (Description and MOdification of the Segmentation) method [2] is a grammatical method for structured documents recognition. It is based on a grammatical language, EPF (Enhanced Position Formalism) that enables a syntactic and structural description of the content of a document. Once the description has been realized in EPF for a kind of document, the associated analyzer is automatically produced by a compilation step.

This method has been applied for the analysis of various kinds of documents: tabular, archive documents, mathematical formulae... and at a large scale (> 600,000 images). However, it had never been applied to on-line signal.

The use of DMOS method is particularly adapted to our problem. Indeed, DMOS enables to deal with the need of flexibility that we have exposed on section 2.3. Thus, as the method is based on logical programming, it naturally offers the possibility to express different ways for a given rule to succeed. It also offers the ability to backtrack, which is very convenient to deal with the various possible configurations of the diagram, and ensures that the final result of the recognition is globally consistent.

3.2   Adaptation to On-line Signal

Our first contribution has consisted in improving the existing DMOS method to make it treat on-line signal.

Thus, in the previous version of the method, the input signal was scanned images. We were extracting the connected components and the line segments that were present in the off-line analyzed image. These connected components and line segments were used as primitive for the grammatical description.

In our work, the input signal is on-line signal. Our contribution enables its interpretation. The strokes are represented by their bounding boxes and stands for the components. We extract a polygonal approximation from the on-line signal to compute the line segments, using the classical Ramer-Douglas-Peucker algorithm [7]. Consequently, our experience on scanned images with DMOS method can be used for on-line signal as the analysis is based on an homogeneous set of primitives.

3.3   Interest of Two Sets of Primitives

As our grammatical description is based on the combination of two kinds of primitives (strokes and line segments) (figure 5), it enables to deal with some difficulties previously presented. For example, the line segments are convenient to detect the sides of the quadrilaterals: the figure 5(b) shows that the rectangles are composed of four line segments, whatever the number of strokes that compose them. On the opposite, the segmentation using strokes (figure 5(c)) enables an easy description of the text, even when it overlaps the sides of the symbols.

3.4   Grammatical Description

Our work has consisted in expressing our syntactic and structural rules, presented on section 2, using the two sets of primitives. This has been realized thanks to the grammatical EPF language.

The rules presented on section 2 have been expressed using EPF formalism. For example, we present the translation of the first RestOfDiagram rule with EPF syntax.

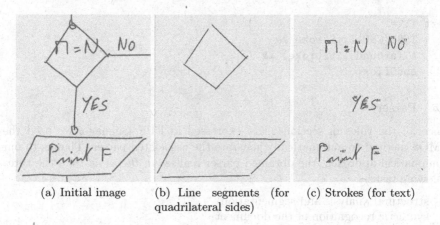

(a) Initial image	(b) Line segments (for quadrilateral sides)	(c) Strokes (for text)

Fig. 5. Primitives used for the grammatical analysis

```
restOfDiagram::=
    process P &&
    AT(aroundSymbol P) &&
    arrow A &&
    AT(otherArrowEnd A) &&
    restOfDiagram.
```

In EPF language, && is the concatenation operator. AT is the position operator. It indicates where to find the next item for the following analysis. For example, once the process P is found, we search around P for an arrow. The rules process and arrow are non-terminals.

We now detail the analysis of the process rule. It is made of a rectangle with text inside.

```
process P::=
    rectangle R &&
    AT(insideSymbole R) &&
    text T.
```

As we said above (see figure 5), we combine two kind of primitives for the description of a process. The rule rectangle is based on finding four consecutive sides S1, S2, S3, S4. We use the TERM_SEG operator to search terminals in line segments. On the opposite, the text uses the strokes (stored as connected components). Consequently, the text rule uses the TERM_CMP operator to find a terminal TxtStroke among all the stroke primitives.

```
rectangle R::=
    TERM_SEG noCondS S1 &&
    AT(end S1) && TERM_SEG S2 &&
    AT(end S2) && TERM_SEG S3 &&
    AT(end S3) && TERM_SEG S4.
```

```
text T:∵=
    TERM_CMP TxtStroke &&
    AT(around TxtStroke) &&
    endOfText.
```

3.5 Parser

Once all the rules of section 2 are expressed in EPF language, we used the DMOS method to automatically generate the associated parser. Thanks to our grammatical approach, the obtained parser realises *in the same time* the three following tasks:

- − structural analysis and segmentation,
- − syntactic recognition of the document,
- − labelling of strokes.

The analysis only succeed if we can find a global consistence for these three tasks. Consequently, the final structural segmentation is totally linked to the syntactic description.

This implementation enables to evaluate our approach on an existing database, and to show the interest of the syntactic knowledge for flowchart recognition.

4 Experimental Results

4.1 Database and Metrics

In order to evaluate our method, we have worked on the freely available database presented by Awal *et al.* in [1]. This database is made of handwritten flowcharts (example on figure 1), of various complexity (different patterns), that have been written by 31 writers using the Anoto pen technology. The table 1 summarizes the properties of the database. A ground truth is provided for each flowchart, containing the label for each stroke (one of the 7 classes presented on figure 2) and the segmentation of strokes into symbols. We notice that each stroke owns exactly one label.

Table 1. Properties of the database

	Writers	Patterns	Flowcharts	Strokes	Symbols
Validation set	31	14	248	23359	5541
Test set	15	14 other	171	15696	3792

The authors have identified two tasks: the labeling of each stroke and the correct segmentation and recognition of the symbols. A stroke is correctly labeled if the result label corresponds to the ground truth. A symbol is correctly segmented and recognized if the set of strokes corresponding to the symbol is exactly the same in the result and in the ground truth, and that the label of the symbol is correct.

4.2   First Results and Discussion

We have used the validation set to validate our grammatical description. We present the first results that we obtain on the test set in table 2.

Table 2. Our first results on the test set

Class	Correct stroke labeling	Correct symbol segmentation and recognition
Connection	80.0%	81.4%
Terminator	58.9%	70.3%
Data	84.7%	80.4%
Decision	84.0%	66.5%
Arrow	79.6%	68.9%
Process	85.7%	81.3%
Text	97.8%	71.7%
Total	**91.1%**	**72.4%**

We obtain a good recognition rate, 91.1% for the individual strokes. Indeed, thanks to our grammar, we are able to easily classify each stroke, depending on their position and their context. However, these first results show that the recognition at symbol level is weaker. Indeed, the metric is very strict and considers that a symbol is not recognized if only one small stroke is not joined to the segmentation. This is often the case in our analysis. Thus, we believe that, for this kind of documents, we should set up a metric that consider the syntax of the recognized symbols ("here is a connection") more than the presence of all the strokes.

We have also compared our results with the ones proposed by Awal *et al.* in [1], who use a statistical approach. The results in table 3 demonstrate the interest of the syntactic and structural knowledge for flowchart recognition. Thus, our method enables a big increase of non-text stroke and symbol recognition, thanks to the presence of context.

Table 3. Interest of our structural method for recognition

Method	Stroke labeling		Symbol recognition	
	Text	Non-text	Text	Non-text
Statistical [1]	73.9%	39.8%	71.9%	29.6%
Structural (ours)	**97.8%**	**80.6%**	**71.7%**	**72.8%**

5 Conclusion

In this paper, we have presented a way to use some syntactic knowledge for hand-written on-line flowchart recognition. We have proposed a grammatical description of this kind of document. This is particularly adapted to the bi-dimensional and structured properties of the flowcharts.

In our implementation, we have shown that the existing off-line method, DMOS, could be used for the analysis of on-line documents. We have used the EPF language to express the grammtical description of flowcharts. The ability to back-track, provided by DMOS method, and the verification of the global consistence provided by the structural description of the wall document enable to solve the local problems of segmentation, that are often met in the literature.

We have validated our work on an open database. Our first results show that our structural approach really increases the recognition rates of flowcharts, compared to the statistical methods (up to 50% of increase). In a future work, we are planning to mix our structural approach with the results obtained by the statistical methods in order to improve the recognition rate.

References

1. Awal, A.-M., Feng, G., Mouchère, H., Gaudin, C.V.: First Experiments on a new Online Handwritten Flowchart Database. In: Document Recognition and Retrieval XVIII, vol. 01, United States (2011)
2. Coüasnon, B.: DMOS, a generic document recognition method: Application to table structure analysis in a general and in a specific way. International Journal on Document Analysis and Recognition, IJDAR 8(2), 111–122 (2006)
3. Feng, G.H., Viard Gaudin, C., Sun, Z.X.: On-line hand-drawn electric circuit diagram recognition using 2D dynamic programming. Pattern Recognition 42(12), 3215–3223 (2009)
4. Macé, S., Anquetil, E.: Eager interpretation of on-line hand-drawn structured documents: The dali methodology. Pattern Recognition 42(12), 3202–3214 (2009)
5. Qi, Y., Szummer, M., Minka, T.P.: Diagram structure recognition by bayesian conditional random fields. In: CVPR, pp. II:191–II:196 (2005)
6. Tilak, G., Ananthakrishnan, K.: Sketchuml – sketch based approach to class diagrams. In: Proceedings of IUI (2009)
7. Urs, Ramer: An iterative procedure for the polygonal approximation of plane curves. Computer Graphics and Image Processing 1(3), 244–256 (1972)
8. Yuan, Z., Pan, H., Zhang, L.: A Novel Pen-Based Flowchart Recognition System for Programming Teaching. In: Leung, E.W.C., Wang, F.L., Miao, L., Zhao, J., Kleinberg, R.D. (eds.) WBL 2008. LNCS, vol. 5328, pp. 55–64. Springer, Heidelberg (2008)

A Recognition System for Online Handwritten Tibetan Characters

Long-Long Ma and Jian Wu

National Engineering Research Center of Fundamental Software
Institute of Software, Chinese Academy of Sciences
Beijing, P.R. China
{longlong,wujian}@iscas.ac.cn

Abstract. This paper describes a recognition system for online handwritten Tibetan characters using advanced techniques in character recognition. To eliminate noise points of handwriting trajectories, we introduce a de-noising approach by using dilation, erosion, thinning operators of the mathematical morphology. Selecting appropriate structuring elements, we can clear up large amounts of noises in the glyphs of the character. To enhance the recognition performance, we adopt three-stage classification strategy, where the top rank output classes by the baseline classifier are re-classified by similar character discrimination classifier. Experiments have been carried out on two databases MRG-OHTC and IIP-OHTC. Test results show the used recognition algorithm is effective and can be applied in pen-based mobile devices.

Keywords: online handwritten Tibetan character recognition, de-noising, pre-processing, three-stage classification.

1   Introduction

Tibetan is one of the most common written languages in China, especially in Xizang, Yunnan and Qinghai provinces. Tibetan language is still used by more than six million people. Research on Tibetan character, which will enable easier modernization of Tibetan culture and digitization of Tibetan document, is very important in theoretical value as well as in extensive application perspective.

Due to the increase of new pen input devices and pen applications, online handwritten character recognition is gaining renewed interest. However, compared to the existing research work on CJK (Chinese, Japanese and Korean) and Arabic, Online handwritten Tibetan character recognition (OHTCR) is a relatively unexplored field.

More research works focus on printed Tibetan character. Ding designed a novel and effective recognition method for multi-font printed Tibetan OCR [1]. Ngodrup proposed local self-adaptive binary algorithm and grid-based fuzzy stroke feature extraction to improve the recognition accuracy [2]. Masami used Euclidean distance with deferential weights to discriminate similar characters [3]. There is far little reported work on OHTCR. Wang [4],[5] combined HMM based on stroke type with

Y.-B. Kwon and J.-M. Ogier (Eds.): GREC, LNCS 7423, pp. 99–107, 2013.
© Springer-Verlag Berlin Heidelberg 2013

HMM based on the position relation between strokes to improve the recognition performance. We create an online handwritten Tibetan character database named MRG-OHTC and intend to publish the database [6].

This paper describes an online recognition system for handwritten Tibetan characters and reports our results using based-on de-noising approach and three-stage classification strategy. As for all handwritten recognition problem, handwritten Tibetan character recognition is difficult due to the wide variability of writing styles and the confusion between similar characters. The methods of online character recognition can be roughly grouped into two categories: statistical and structural [7]. Whereas structural matching is more relevant to human learning and perception, statistical methods are more computationally efficient. Taking advantage of learning from samples, statistical methods can give higher recognition accuracies.

We adopt a statistical classification scheme, wherein the recognition accuracy depends on the techniques of pre-processing, feature extraction, and classifier design. We use a de-noising approach to eliminate noise points of trajectories [8],[9]. Equidistance re-sampling, smoothing and nonlinear shape normalization are used in pre-processing step. The local stroke direction of character pattern is decomposed into direction maps, which are blurred and sub-sampled to obtain feature values [10],[15].

The confusion between similar characters is one of main reasons of lower recognition accuracy. The recently proposed LDA (linear discriminant analysis)-based compound distance [11] and the critical region analysis based pair discrimination [12] further improve the recognition accuracy. A logistic regression (LR) classifier is used to discriminate confusing characters and costs only small storage of extra parameters [13], compared to the method [11],[12]. To discriminate confusing characters, we use three-stage classification strategy, similar to the strategy in [13]. Firstly, candidate classes are selected with a coarse classifier according to the Euclidean distance (ED) to class means. Secondly, fine classification with the modified quadratic discriminant function (MQDF) [14] re-orders the candidate classes. Thirdly, the top rank candidate classes are re-classified by similar character discrimination classifier. Our experiments on two databases, MRG-OHTC and IIP-OHTC, demonstrate that similar character discrimination classifier can improve the recognition accuracy by about 3%.

The rest of this paper is organized as follows. Section 2 gives an overview of the recognition system. Section 3 describes a de-noising approach during pre-processing process and section 4 introduces three-stage classification strategy. Section 5 reports our experimental results and section 6 provides concluding remarks.

2   System Overview

The OHTCR system is shown diagrammatically in Fig. 1. The input pattern trajectory is composed of the coordinates of sampled pen-down points. To eliminate noise points and remove certain variations among character samples of the same class, we introduce a de-noising approach at pre-processing stage. For feature extraction, we use direction feature extraction method where the stroke direction is the one in origin pattern, not in normalized pattern. At three-stage classification process, we introduce similar character discrimination to reduce the recognition error from the confusion between similar characters.

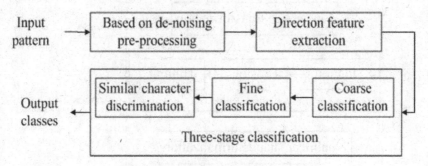

Fig. 1. Overview of the OHTCR system

3   Based on De-noising Pre-processing

Pre-processing is to regulate the pattern shape for reducing the within-class shape variation. Nonlinear shape normalization (NSN) is used to normalize shape variability [16]. However, the proportion of noise points in character point trajectories is magnified after NSN. Fig. 2 shows two examples. It's significant to eliminate these noises in order to make these characters be recognized accurately.

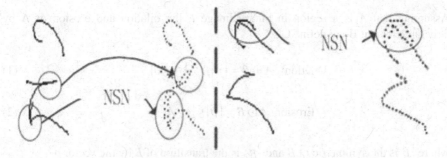

Fig. 2. Variation of noises after NSN

To eliminate these noise points, we introduce a de-noising method before NSN. The pre-processing process is illustrated in Fig. 3, where the de-noising step employs the operators (dilation, erosion and thinning) of mathematical morphology. Linear size transformation is to ensure that the character samples of the same class have approximately the same size. Re-sampling is purposed to reduce distance variation between two adjacent online points. We use Gaussian smoothing to reduce stroke variation in a small local region. We will take the image composed of trajectory points as the binary image.

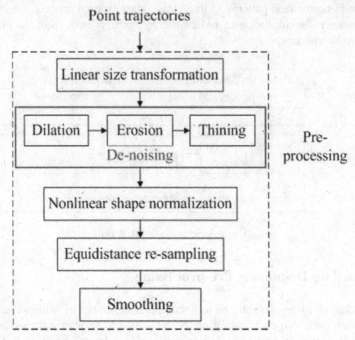

Fig. 3. Based on de-noising pre-processing flowchart

3.1   Dilation and Erosion

Assuming that A is a region in binary image I, the dilation and erosion of A by structure element B are defined as

$$\text{Dilation:} \quad A \oplus B = \{ p \,|\, \hat{B}_p \cap A \neq 0 \} \tag{1}$$

$$\text{Erosion:} \, A \ominus B = \{ p \,|\, B_p \subseteq A \} \tag{2}$$

where $\hat{B}$ is the symmetric of B and B_P is the transition of B by the vector p.

By dilation operation, some useless or re-written strokes can be connected to a component. Unlike offline recognition, online handwriting records stroke direction and point time sequences. According to point time information, we dilate trajectory binary image. For erosion operator, we use the same size structuring element (3×3 square, with the origin at its center) with that in dilation operator. Fig. 4(a)(b) gives the dilation and erosion results of origin pattern.

3.2   Thinning

After dilation and erosion operators, we get the images composed of the strokes with different pixel widths, which is shown in Fig 4(b). In order to regulate the transformed image, we use the thinning algorithm [17] to extract stroke skeleton. Finally the binary image consists of strokes with one pixel width. Compared to original pattern, we can see the noise points are removed from Fig. 4(c).

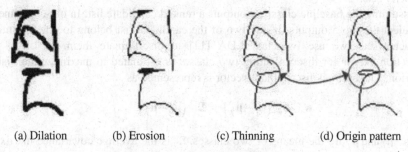

(a) Dilation   (b) Erosion   (c) Thinning   (d) Origin pattern

Fig. 4. An Example of the de-noising method

Fig. 5 gives the transformed image after pre-processing with or without the de-noising method. We can see the image (c) in shape is more similar to the corresponding real shape.

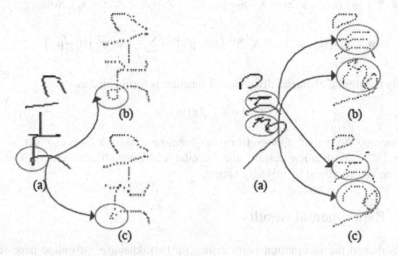

Fig. 5. (a) Origin trajectories image (b) the image after pre-processing without de-noising (c) the image after pre-processing with de-noising

4   Three-Stage Classification

After pre-processing and feature extraction of input pattern, the feature dimensionality is reduced by LDA. The coarse classifier gives some candidate classes according to the ED from the reduced vector, and the fine classifier (MQDF as the baseline classifier) reorders the candidate classes.

The similar character sets are built on the training dataset by 5-fold cross validation, i.e. rotationally using 4/5 for training the baseline classifier and the remaining 1/5 for validation. We use the selection criterion in [15] to get the similar character sets.

Assuming the baseline classifier outputs a ranked candidate list. In our experiment, we select the top 5 outputs. If any two of the candidate list belong to one of similar character sets, we use two-class LDA [11] to discriminate them. In LDA, the projection axis w for discriminating two classes is estimated to maximize the Fisher criterion. The optimal discriminant vector is represented as

$$\mathbf{w} = \mathbf{S}_w^{-1}\left(\mu_i - \mu_j\right) = \mathbf{\Sigma}_{ij}^{-1}\left(\mu_i - \mu_j\right) \tag{3}$$

where μ_i and μ_j are the means of two classes. $\mathbf{\Sigma}_{ij}$ is the average covariance matrix of two classes and can be rewritten as

$$\mathbf{\Sigma}_{ij} = \mathbf{\Psi}\mathbf{\Lambda}\mathbf{\Psi}^{\mathrm{T}} = \sum_{m=1}^{d}\lambda_m\psi_m\psi_m^{\mathrm{T}} \tag{4}$$

where $\mathbf{\Psi} = [\psi_1, \psi_2, \ldots, \psi_d]$ and $\mathbf{\Lambda} = diag[\lambda_1, \lambda_2, \ldots, \lambda_d]$ ($\lambda_1 \geq \lambda_2, \cdots, \lambda_d$). So

$$\mathbf{w} = \mathbf{\Sigma}_{ij}^{-1}\left(\mu_i - \mu_j\right) = \mathbf{\Psi}\mathbf{\Lambda}^{-1}\mathbf{\Psi}^{T}\left(\mu_i - \mu_j\right) = \sum_{n=1}^{d}\frac{1}{\lambda_n}\psi_n\psi_n^{T}\left(\mu_i - \mu_j\right) \tag{5}$$

Finally the similar character discriminant function is formulated as

$$f(x) = f_{LDA}(x) = w^T x \tag{6}$$

For the top N output classes from the baseline classifier, we can get at most N×(N-1)/2 classification results after similar character discrimination. The final decision is determined by majority voting.

5   Experimental Results

We evaluated the recognition performance on two databases of online handwritten Tibetan characters: MRG-OHTC and IIP-OHTC. The MRG-OHTC, collected by our research group, contains the handwritten samples of 910 characters, 130 samples each class. We choose the first 105 samples from each class for training, and the remaining 25 samples from each class for testing. The IIP-OHTC database, collected by northwest university for nationalities, contains 562 characters, 150 samples each class. We choose 120 samples per class for training and the remaining 30 samples per class for testing.

For each character pattern, we extract 512-dimensional directional features [10]. The 512-dimensional is reduced to 140-dimensional by LDA. The 140-dimensional projected vector is then fed to fine classification. The baseline classifier is the MQDF, with 40 principal eigenvectors for each class. Table 1 lists the recognition accuracy on two databases using the baseline classifier.

From Table 1 we can see the test accuracy is lower on two databases, and there is a big accuracy difference between top1 and top2, between top2 and top5. This mainly attributes to the confusion between similar characters. We use two-class LDA to further identify similar characters. The recognition accuracy is improved about 3%. Obviously, it is very challenging to present new algorithms for higher accuracy. Fig.6 shows the samples misrecognized by MQDF, but corrected by two-class LDA discrimination classifier. Fig.7 gives some examples with 5 candidate outputs, where correct results are labeled using red colors. We can see these five candidates are very similar in shape. The misrecognized results can't be corrected using the two-class LDA.

Table 1. Test Accuracy

	MRG-OHTC	MRG-OHTC
Top1	81.70%	77.01%
Top2	90.96%	88.99%
Top5	96.04%	95.79%

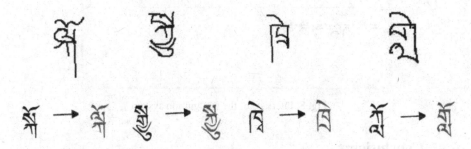

Fig. 6. Examples of misrecognized characers corrected by similar character discrimination

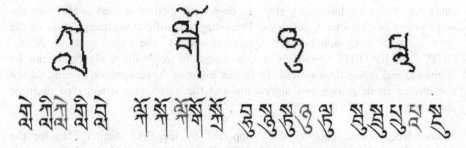

Fig. 7. Examples of the top 5 candidate outputs

Though the correct rate on two databases is lower, the accumulated recognition rate of the top 10 is higher than 97%. We apply the recognition algorithms to pen-based applications such as mobile phones. Fig.8 shows the interface of our recognition system, where the left sub-window displays the trajectories of handwriting, and the right sub-window gives the top ten recognition results. When the correct recognition result is selected, the character class is surrounded by red bounding box. The bottom sub-window gives the character string with correct outputs.

Fig. 8. Interface of the recognition system

6   Conclusion

In this paper, we describe a recognition system for online handwritten Tibetan character. At the pre-processing step, the de-noising method is used to eliminate the noise points of character trajectories. Three-stage classification strategy reduces the error from the confusion between similar characters. The experiments on MRG-OHTC and IIP-OHTC databases demonstrated the recognition algorithm can be applied to real recognition system. To further improve the recognition system, we are considering more recognition algorithms and the combining strategy of multiple classifiers.

Acknowledgements. This work is supported by the CAS Action Plan for the Development of Western China (No.KGCX2-YW-512) and National Science & Technology Major Project (No.2010ZX01036-001-002, 2010ZX01037-001-002). The authors would thank Professor Weilan Wang from Northwest University for Nationalities, for providing IIP-OHTC database.

References

1. Ding, X.Q., Wang, H.: Multi-font printed Tibetan OCR. In: Advance in Pattern Recognition, pp. 73–98 (2007)
2. Ngodrup, D.C.Z.: Study on printed Tibetan character recognition. In: Proc. AICI, pp. 280–285 (2010)
3. Masami, K., Yoshiyuki, K., Masayuki, K.: Character recognition of wooden blocked Tibetan similar manuscripts by using Eucliden distance with deferential weight. IPSJ SIGNotes Computer and Humanities, 13–18 (1996)
4. Liang, B., Wang, W.L., Qian, J.J.: Application of Hidden Markov Model in on-line Recognition of handwritten Tibetan characters. Journal of Microelectronics & Computer 26(4), 98–101 (2009) (in Chinese)
5. Wang, W.L., Ding, X.Q., Qi, K.Y.: Study on simlitude characters in Tibetan character recognition. Journal of Chinese Information Processing 16(4), 60–65 (2002) (in Chinese)
6. Ma, L.L., Liu, H.D., Wu, J.: MRG-OHTC database for online handwritten Tibetan character recognition. In: Proc. 11th ICDAR, pp. 207–211 (2011)
7. Liu, C.L., Jaeger, S., Nakagawa, M.: Online recognition of Chinese characters: the state-of-the-art. IEEE Trans. Pattern Anal. Mach. Intell. 26(2), 198–213 (2004)
8. Sun, Y., Liu, H.M., Rui, J.W., Wu, J.: De-noising approach for online handwriting character recognition based on mathematical morphology. Journal of Computer Science 36(10), 237–239 (2009) (in Chinese)
9. Sun, Y.: The study on online handwritten Tibetan character recognition. Master Thesis (2009) (in Chinese)
10. Hamanaka, M., Yamada, K., Tsukumo, J.: On-line Japanese character recognition experiments by an off-line method based on normalization-cooperated feature extraction. In: Proc. 3rd ICDAR, pp. 204–207 (1993)
11. Gao, T.F., Liu, C.L.: High accuracy handwritten Chinese character recognition using LDA-based compound distances. Pattern Recognition 41(11), 3442–3451 (2008)
12. Leung, K.C., Leung, C.H.: Recognition of handwritten Chinese characters by critical region analysis. Pattern Recognition 43(3), 949–961 (2010)
13. Zhou, X.D., Wang, D.H., Nakagawa, M., Liu, C.L.: Error reduction by confusing characters discrimination for online handwritten Japanese character recognition. In: Proc. 12th ICFHR, pp. 495–450 (2010)
14. Kimura, F., Takashina, K., Tsuruoka, S., Miyake, Y.: Modified quadratic discriminant functions and its application to Chinese character recognition. IEEE Trans. Pattern Anal. Mach. Intell. 9(1), 149–153 (1987)
15. Zhou, X.D., Liu, C.L., Nakagawa, M.: Online handwritten Japanese character string recognition using conditional random fields. In: Proc. 10th ICDAR, pp. 521–525 (2009)
16. Bai, Z.L., Huo, Q.: A study of nonlinear shape normalizaiton for online handwritten Chinese character recognition: dot density vs. line density equalization. In: Proc 18th ICPR, pp. 921–924 (2006)
17. Zhang, T.Y., Suen, C.Y.: A fast parallel algorithm for thinning digital pattern. Communicaition of the ACM 27(6), 236–239 (1984)
18. Kimura, F., Takashina, K., Tsuruoka, S., Miyake, Y.: Modified quadratic discriminant functions and its application to Chinese character recognition. IEEE Trans. Pattern Anal. Mach. Intell. 9(1), 149–153 (1987)

Incremental Learning for Interactive Sketch Recognition

Achraf Ghorbel[1], Abdullah Almaksour[2], Aurélie Lemaitre[2], and Eric Anquetil[1]

[1] INSA de Rennes
[2] Université Européenne de Bretagne, France
UMR IRISA, Campus de Beaulieu, F-35042 Rennes
Université Européenne de Bretagne, France
{achraf.ghorbel,abdullah.almaksour,aurelie.lemaitre,
eric.anquetil}@irisa.fr

Abstract. In this paper, we present the integration of a classifier, based on an incremental learning method, in an interactive sketch analyzer. The classifier recognizes the symbol with a degree of confidence. Sometimes the analyzer considers that the response is insufficient to make the right decision. The decision process then solicits the user to explicitly validate the right decision. The user associates the symbol to an existing class, to a newly created class or ignores this recognition. The classifier learns during the interpretation phase. We can thus have a method for auto-evolutionary interpretation of sketches. In fact, the user participation has a great impact to avoid error accumulation during the analysis. This paper demonstrates this integration in an interactive method based on a competitive breadth-first exploration of the analysis tree for interpreting the 2D architectural floor plans.

1 Introduction

In this paper, we are working on mapping technical paper documents, like architectural floor plans, to numerical ones. We aim at offering a complete, interactive and auto-evolving solution to unify paper document recognition and pen-based sketch interpretation (for instance: with Tablet PC).

At present, structured documents can be very complex. Faced with this complexity, the various existing methods [1] [2] [3] [4] keep a margin of error. Therefore, very often, an a posteriori verification phase will be necessary to ensure there is no recognition error. In this phase the user browses the document to correct the errors due to the interpretation.

To avoid the verification phase on the one hand, and avoid error accumulation during the analysis step on the other hand, we proposed an interactive method of analysis of off-line structured document where the decision process solicits the user if necessary. In our previous work [5], the role of user was limited to validate the right hypothesis and then unlock a situation where the decision process is not sure to make the right decision. In summary, the process can solicit the user to be sure to make the correct decision.

Y.-B. Kwon and J.-M. Ogier (Eds.): GREC, LNCS 7423, pp. 108–118, 2013.

Now, we want to exploit the solicitation of the user during the analysis not only to unlock a situation but also to improve the analysis process. In this context, we focus in this paper on improving the capacity of symbol recognition. In the sketch interpretation method, the symbol recognition is made by the classifier.

The classification systems can be generally categorized into two types: static and evolving systems. Static systems are trained in batch mode using a predefined learning dataset, while incremental learning algorithms are used to train evolving classifiers, like for our symbol recognition system. In incremental learning algorithms, new instances from existing classes can be progressively introduced to the system to improve its performance. Moreover, new unseen classes can be added to the system at any time by the incoming data.

In this work, we present the advantage of soliciting the user to improve the recognition capacity of the classifier by incremental learning. It is also able to dynamically add new classes.

The remaining of the paper is organized as follows. In the section 2, we introduce our existing interactive analysis method. Section 3 describes principles of the incremental classifier. The coupling of this incremental classifier with our interactive analysis of sketches is described in section 4. The rejection mechanism is explained in section 5. Experimental results are reported in section 6 and finally, section 7 concludes the paper.

2   Interactive Breadth-First Exploration

In this section, we summarize our interactive method of structured document interpretation (referred as IMISketch) [5] in which we propose to integrate our incremental classifier. This analyzer is based on the following characteristics:

- a priori structural knowledge of the document are expressed through a visual language based on production rules;
- a two-dimensional descending breadth-first analysis;
- a spatial contextual focus of the exploration to limit the combinatory;
- the uncertainty is formalized by the attribution of scores to each hypothesis represented by the tree analysis branch;
- if the ambiguities can not be resolved in the local context in an automatic manner, the user will be solicited by the analyzer to resolve the ambiguity.

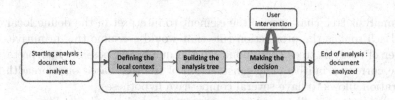

Fig. 1. Analysis process

These characteristics were chosen in order to ensure the best interactivity with the analysis system. This interactivity allows in particular to avoid a posteriori verification phase, which can become fastidious on complex documents. Indeed, the user participation, on the critical phases of the analysis of the document, has a great impact to avoid error accumulation during the analysis step and overcomes the combinatory due to the sketch complexity. Figure 1 shows the complete process of analysis and the relationship between the three parts of the analyzer.

The first step consists of extracting the necessary information from the structured document. This phase is generic and off-line and does not depend on the type of document to interpret. We have chosen to work only with line-segments, which represents the primitives of our analysis. The primitive recognition, depends on its neighbourhood in structured documents. The analyzer begins by defining a spatial contextual focus that aims to limit the combinatory exploration due to the breadth-first exploration of analysis tree. The structured document requires a two-dimensional context. This two-dimensional local context is defined for an analysis tree as the maximum distance between the elements of the root and the elements of any leaves.

Once the context is well defined, the analyzer goes to the second stage. In this stage, the analyzer explores all possible hypotheses of interpretation in the spatial context using a set of two-dimensional rules that describe the structure of the document. These production rules are described by the context-driven constraint multiset grammars (CD-CMG) [6]. Each primitive can be interpreted in several ways. Each node or leaf is the application of a production rule deduced from the previous node. Every leaf or node of the tree has a score calculated from both its local score and the score obtained from the preceding nodes. Every score determines the adequacy degree to validate a production. The score calculated by each production is due to preconditions and constraints of the rule production (Equation 1). The use of the square root is a normalization using a geometric average. The production score can also be deduced from a classifier. A score is associated with each branch (hypothesis). Equation 2 determines the degree of adequacy (score) of a hypothesis. |PS| is the number of production in the considered branch (referred as PS).

$$\rho_P = \sqrt{\mu_{preconditions} \cdot \mu_{constraints}} \tag{1}$$

$$\rho_{PS} = (\prod_{P_i \in PS} \rho_{P_i})^{\frac{1}{|PS|}} \tag{2}$$

Each analysis tree characterize the element to interpret in the define local context. Each root is the production rule that would consume this primitive. The number of analysis trees corresponds to the number of possible interpretations for the current primitive. The construction of the tree based on a breadth-first exploration allows to have several competitive hypotheses.

Once the tree is well constructed, we start the decision phase. The role of the decision process is to validate the right hypothesis among a set of competing hypotheses generated with a descending breadth first analysis.

Sometimes the decision process is not sure to make the right decision. In this case, it solicits the user. In practice, if the difference of scores between the top two branches is below a threshold of confidence and if these two branches are contradictory (at least one joint primitive is not consumed by the same rule production), the user intervention is required.

When the correct root is validated, other roots are put on hold and the new roots are either the sons of this root if exists, or the waiting roots otherwise and the analyzer go back to the first step (defining the local context step). The analysis is complete when no more production rule is applicable.

In the current state, the information provided by the user is only used to unlock situations. In this paper, we want to benefit more widely this information by learning continuously during the analysis. In this context, we propose to integrate an incremental classifier which uses information supplied by the user to improve its capabilities during the analysis.

3   Incremental Learning of a Fuzzy Inference System

The incremental learning algorithm is supposed to be supervised. The recognition of each data sample must be followed by a validation or a correction action in order to learn it. If the system answer is validated, the data sample will reinforce the system knowledge associated to its class. If an external correction signal is sent, the confusion between the (wrong) winner class and the true class is solved by the incremental learning algorithm. A third scenario may take place when the input data sample is declared as the first sample from a new unseen class. Our classification system is based on first-order Takagi-Sugeno (TS) fuzzy inference system[7]. It consists of a set of fuzzy rules of the following form:

$$\textbf{Rule}_i : \textbf{IF } x \textit{ is close to } P_i \textbf{THEN } y_i^1 = l_i^1(x), ..., y_i^k = l_i^k(x) \qquad (3)$$

where $x = \{x_1, x_2, ..., x_n\}$ is the input vector. It consists of a set of features values extracted from the symbol image. These features describe the symbol shape from different viewpoints. The estimation of these features is not the aim of the current paper; it will be the subject of a future paper. $l_i^m(x)$ is the linear consequent function of the rule i for the class m:

$$l_i^m(x) = \pi_i^m x = a_{i0}^m + a_{i1}^m x_1 + a_{i2}^m x_2 + ... + a_{in}^m x_n \qquad (4)$$

where n is the size of the input vector. a_{ij}^m is a coefficient value in the rule i between the score of class m and the feature j of the input vector. The Prototype P is defined by a center and a fuzzy zone of influence. To find the class of x, its membership degree $\beta_i(x)$ to each fuzzy prototype is first computed. After normalizing these membership degrees, the sum-product inference is used to compute the system output for each class:

$$y^m(x) = \sum_{i=1}^{r} \bar{\beta}_i(x) \, l_i^m(x) \qquad (5)$$

where r is the number of fuzzy rules in the system. The score of each class y^m is between 0 and 1. The higher is the score, the higher is the degree of confidence in that class to be associated to the given input. The winning class label is given by finding the maximal output and taking the corresponding class label as response:

$$class(\boldsymbol{x}) = y = argmax\ y^m(\boldsymbol{x}) \qquad m = 1, .., k \qquad (6)$$

The membership degree is computed by the prototype center $\boldsymbol{\mu}_i$ and its variance-covariance matrix A_i using the multivariate Cauchy probability distribution:

$$\beta_i(\boldsymbol{x}) = \frac{1}{2\pi\sqrt{|A_i|}} \left[1 + (\boldsymbol{x} - \boldsymbol{\mu}_i)^t A_i^{-1}(\boldsymbol{x} - \boldsymbol{\mu}_i)\right]^{-\frac{n+1}{2}} \qquad (7)$$

The incremental learning algorithm of our model consists of three different tasks: the creation of new rules, the adaptation of the existing rule's premises, and the tuning of the linear consequent parameters. These three tasks must be done in an online incremental mode and all the needed calculation must be completely recursive.

3.1 Incremental Clustering

When introducing a new training sample in an online learning mode, it will either reinforce the information contained in the previous data and represented by the current clustering, or bring enough information to form a new cluster or modify an existing one. The importance of a given sample in the clustering process can be evaluated by its *potential* value. The potential of a sample is defined as inverse of the sum of distances between a data sample and all the other data samples:

$$Pot_k(\boldsymbol{x}(k)) = \frac{1}{1 + \sum_{i=1}^{k-1} \|x(k) - x(i)\|^2} \qquad (8)$$

A recursive method for the calculation of the potential of a new sample was introduced in [8], which made this technique a promised solution for any incremental clustering problem. The recursive formula avoids memorizing the whole previous data but keeps - using few variables - the density distribution in the feature space based on the previous data:

$$P_k(\boldsymbol{x}(k)) = \frac{k - 1}{(k - 1)\alpha(k) + \gamma(k) - 2\zeta(k) + k - 1} \qquad (9)$$

where

$$\alpha(k) = \sum_{j=1}^{n} x_j^2(k) \qquad (10)$$

$$\gamma(k) = \gamma(k - 1) + \alpha(k - 1), \quad \gamma(1) = 0 \qquad (11)$$

$$\zeta(k) = \sum_{j=1}^{n} x_j(k)\eta_j(k), \quad \eta_j(k) = \eta_j(k - 1) + x_j(k - 1), \quad \eta_j(1) = 0 \qquad (12)$$

Introducing a new sample affects the potential values of the centers of the existing clusters, which can be recursively updated by:

$$P_k(\mu_i) = \frac{(k-1)P_{k-1}(\mu_i)}{k-2+P_{k-1}(\mu_i)+P_{k-1}(\mu_i)\sum_{j=1}^{n}\|\mu_i - x(k-1)\|_j^2} \tag{13}$$

If the potential of the new sample is higher than the potential of the existing centers then this sample will be a center of a new cluster and a new fuzzy rule will be formed in the case of our neuro-fuzzy model. So, the center of the new prototype $\mu_{r+1} = x_k$ and its covariance matrix $A_{r+1} = \epsilon I$, where I is the identity matrix of size n and ϵ is a problem-independent parameter and can generally be set to 10^{-2}.

3.2 Premise Adaptation

This adaptation process allows to incrementally update the prototype centers coordinates according to each new available learning data, and to recursively compute the prototype covariance matrices in order to give them the rotated hyper-elliptical form. For each new sample x_k, the center and the covariance matrix of the prototype that has the highest activation degree are updated.

The center coordination of the selected prototype is recalculated as follows:

$$\mu_i = (1 - \frac{1}{s_i+2})\mu_i + \frac{1}{s_i+2}(x_k - \mu_i) \tag{14}$$

where s_i represents the number of updates that have been already applied on this prototype. The covariance matrix is recursively computed as follows:

$$A_i = (1 - \frac{1}{s_i+2})A_i + \frac{1}{s_i+1}(x_k - \mu_i)(x_k - \mu_i)^t \tag{15}$$

For practical issues, since the membership degree can be calculated using only $A^{-1}(|A| = \frac{1}{|A^{-1}|})$, and in order to avoid any matrix inversion, we use an updating rule for A^{-1} directly:

$$A_i^{-1} = \frac{A_i^{-1}}{1-\alpha} - \frac{\alpha}{1-\alpha} \cdot \frac{(A_i^{-1}(x_k - \mu_i)) \cdot (A_i^{-1}(x_k - \mu_i))^t}{1+\alpha((x_k - \mu_i)^t A_i^{-1}(x_k - \mu_i))} \tag{16}$$

where $a = \frac{1}{s_i+1}$.

3.3 Linear Consequent Tuning

The tuning of the linear consequent parameters in a first-order TS model can be done by the weighted Recursive Least Square method (wRLS). Let Π_i be the linear consequent parameters of the rule i:

$$\Pi_i = \begin{bmatrix} \pi_i^1 & \pi_i^2 & ... & \pi_i^m \end{bmatrix}^t \tag{17}$$

where $\pi_i^c = [a_{i0}^c \ a_{i1}^c \ ...a_{in}^c]$. It can be recursively estimated as follows:

$$\Pi_i = \Pi_i + C_i\bar{\beta}_i(x_k)x_k(Y_k - x_k\Pi_i), \quad \Pi_{init} = 0 \tag{18}$$

$$C_i = C_i - \frac{\bar{\beta}_i(\boldsymbol{x}_k)C_i\boldsymbol{x}_k\boldsymbol{x}_k^tC_i}{1 + \bar{\beta}_i(\boldsymbol{x}_k)\boldsymbol{x}_k^tC_i\boldsymbol{x}_k}, \quad C_{init} = \Omega I \tag{19}$$

where Ω is a large positive number, and I is the identity matrix.

4   User Intervention in the Interactive Analysis Process

In this section, we present the possibilities offered by the introduction of a classifier based on incremental learning in our interactive sketch recognizer. In particular we detail when and how the user can interact with the incremental classifier.

During the analysis, each time the classifier is solicited to identify a symbol, the decision process uses the confident degree given by the classifier to make its decision. If the decision process considers that the confidence degree is sufficiently high to make the right decision, it validates the recognition. Otherwise, The decision process will solicit the user. The user is then in front of four possibilities (cf. Figure 2):

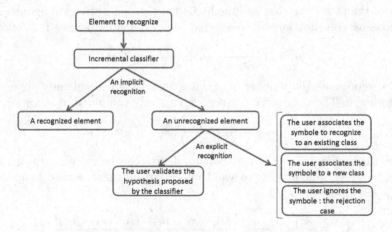

Fig. 2. Interaction scheme of symbol recognition

- The user validates the hypothesis proposed by the classifier in spite of the low degree of confidence given by the classifier. The classifier will enhance the model of this class.
- The user associates the symbol to recognize to other existing class in the classifier. The classifier will reduce the confusion between two classes.
- The user associates the symbol to a new class: the user considers that the symbol does not belong to an existing class. With this new information, the classifier will start to learn a new class of symbols.
- The user ignores the symbol to recognize: the rejection case. The user considers that the recognized symbol is an outlier (noise in the image). No action is done by the classifier.

With this interaction process, the classifier continuously learns to improve its interpretations. The more the analysis is going on, the more the classifier is accurate, the less the user is solicited. This incremental learning is able to deal with the recognition of new classes of symbols. It is a key point to absorb the great variability of symbols that can occur in a sketch.

Figure 3 shows a case where the user solicitation is judged necessary to interpret a handwritten architectural floor plan (Figure 4(a)). In this intervention the user is in front of the four possible actions described in section 4. The system presents an interface that contains the hypothesis given by the classifier, the other available classes of the classifier and a field where the user can add a new class. Figure 3(a) shows a case in which the user indicates that the symbol to recognize is a classical window. Figure 3(b) shows a case in which the user associates the symbol to a new class of windows (a sliding windows).

(a) The user associates the symbol to a 'Window'

(b) The user associates the symbol to a new class (sliding window).

Fig. 3. User interventions. Four possibilities exist. The user associates the set of primitives located in the bounding box 'O' to a right class.

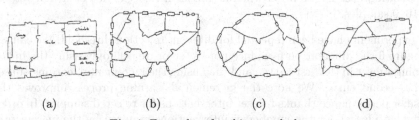

(a)   (b)   (c)   (d)

Fig. 4. Examples of architectural plans

The user participation has a great impact to avoid error accumulation during the analysis step. This solicitation allows the classifier to learn from confused recognized symbols. Adding a new symbol causes the creation of a new class in our classifier.

5   Confusion Reject

The purpose of the confusion rejection is to assess the reliability of the classifier by detecting patterns for which the classifier is likely to misclassify. These errors are near the decision boundaries because scores of at least two classes are nearly equal. Confusion reject can be realized by defining a reject zone on each side of decision boundaries. Each pattern within one of these zones is considered as potential error and is therefore rejected.

To formalize the confusion reject we use the notion of reliability functions. Here, the reliability function $\psi(X)$ represents the degree of confusion in classifying an sample X :

$$\psi(X) = (Sc_1(X) - Sc_2(X)/Sc_1(X) \tag{20}$$

where $Sc_1(X)$ is the score obtained for the best class and $Sc_2(X)$ is the score obtained for the second best class. A sample X is then rejected when the degree of confusion is below a specific threshold λ. The threshold value represents the width of the reject zones around decision boundaries.

6   Experimental Results

We analyze in this section the effect of our incremental learning approach on the evolution of the classification performance. This performance is measured by two values: error rate and rejection rate. We aim at reducing the recognition errors and minimizing as much as possible the number of user interventions. The entire dataset used in these experiments contains 1500 samples from three different classes (door, window, sliding window). Some examples of symbols are illustrated in Figure 5. We divide the dataset into three subsets:

- Initial learning subset: used to train the classifier in full-supervised manner, i.e. the label of each sample is given by the user. This subset contains 113 samples in our experiments.
- Evaluation subset: used to evaluate the classifier performance by measuring error and rejection rates. 378 samples are used in this subset.
- Incremental learning subset: used to improve the classifier performance by soliciting user intervention when a confusion reject is detected. It contains 1019 samples.

The experiments have been repeated for different rejection threshold. We can see in Figure 6 the different performance points (error, reject) only using the initial learning subset in the first curve , and then using the incremental learning subset in the second curve. We note the incremental learning process improves the classifier performance thanks to user interventions for rejected samples. In order to give an idea about the number of interventions required by the incremental learning process, we show in Figure 7 the evolution of error rate and rejection rate according to intervention numbers, for a specific rejection threshold value $\lambda = 0.5$. We notice that the estimated classifier error rate has been reduced by about 30% after 40 user interventions, and the estimated rejection rate has also been reduced by about 22%.

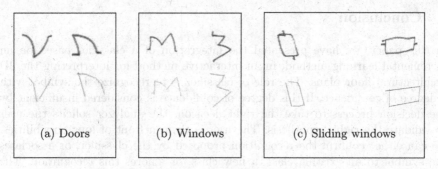

Fig. 5. Examples of symbols

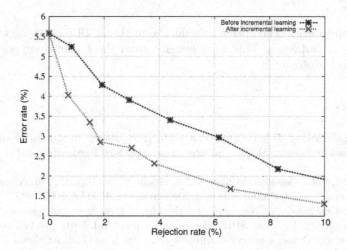

Fig. 6. Error/reject rates before and after the incremental learning process

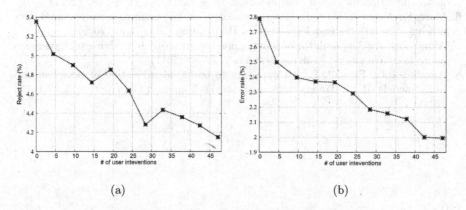

Fig. 7. Evolution of Error/Reject rates during the incremental learning process ($\lambda = 0.5$)

7   Conclusion

In this paper, we have presented the integration of a classifier based on an incremental learning method, in an interactive method for interpreting the 2D architectural floor plans. The role of classifier is to recognize the symbol with a degree of confidence. If this degree of confidence is considered insufficient by the decision process to take the right decision, the analyzer solicits the user to validate the right hypothesis. The user is then in front of four possibilities. He can either confirm the recognition proposed by the classifier, or associates the symbol to an existing class, a new class, or ignores this recognition. The classifier is incrementally learned during the analysis phase. This strategy offers an auto-evolutionary method for sketch interpretation.

Acknowledgment. The authors would like to thank all the people who took part in the experiments. This work benefits from the financial support of the ANR Project Mobisketch.

References

1. Chan, K.F., Yeung, D.Y.: An efficient syntactic approach to structural analysis of on-line handwritten mathematical expressions. Pattern Recognition 33(3), 375–384 (2000)
2. Fitzgerald, J.A., Geiselbrechtinger, F., Kechadi, T.: Mathpad: A fuzzy logic-based recognition system for handwritten mathematics. In: ICDAR 2007 (2007)
3. Mao, S., Rosenfeld, A., Kanungo, T.: Document structure analysis algorithms: a literature survey. In: Proc. SPIE Electronic Imaging, vol. 5010, pp. 197–207 (2003)
4. Coüasnon, B.: Dmos, a generic document recognition method: Application to table structure analysis in a general and in a specific way. In: IJDAR 2006, vol. 8(2) (2006)
5. Ghorbel, A., Macé, S., Lemaitre, A., Anquetil, E.: Interactive competitive breadth-first exploration for sketch interpretation. In: ICDAR, pp. 1195–1199 (2011)
6. Macé, S., Anquetil, E.: Eager interpretation of on-line hand-drawn structured documents: The dali methodology. Pattern Recognition, 3202–3214 (2009)
7. Almaksour, A., Anquetil, E.: Improving premise structure in evolving takagi-sugeno neuro-fuzzy classifiers. Evolving Systems 2, 25–33 (2011)
8. Angelov, P.P., Filev, D.P.: An approach to online identification of takagi-sugeno fuzzy models. IEEE Transactions on Systems, Man, and Cybernetics 34, 484–498 (2004)

Inconsistency-Driven Chemical Graph Construction in ChemInfty

Daniel Karzel[1], Koji Nakagawa[1], Akio Fujiyoshi[2], and Masakazu Suzuki[1]

[1] Faculty of Mathematics, Kyushu University, Fukuoka, Japan
karzel@math.kyushu-u.ac.jp, {kn,msuzuki}@kyudai.jp
[2] Faculty of Engineering, Ibaraki University, Ibaraki, Japan
fujiyosi@mx.ibaraki.ac.jp

Abstract. This paper proposes a new method of chemical graph construction which is implemented in the chemical structure recognition and correction system ChemInfty (www.inftyproject.org/en/ChemInfty/).

The system starts with recognizing the graphical elements of the chemical structure such as lines and characters. In the chemical graph construction phase the validity of the chemical graph is checked to detect inconsistencies. The graph construction starts with an empty chemical graph using only the graphical components. After a solving cycle the system returns a partially solved graph which can be checked for inconsistencies again. This results in a flexible, cycle based and inconsistency-driven graph construction. Furthermore the system introduces semi-automated correction allowing users to interact with the graph-construction cycles.

1 Introduction

Chemical structure recognition became one of the most focused targets in the area of graphics recognition throughout the last decade. Big database creation is in demand of technologies for retrieving data from chemical structure search services [1]. The recognition results just recently reached a practical level. An existing solution is the commercial software CLiDE [2]; tools in research are OSRA [3,4], chemoCR [5], chemReader [6], MolRec [7] and Imago [8].

This paper proposes a new method of chemical graph construction which is implemented in the chemical structure recognition and correction system ChemInfty [9]. The chemical structure recognition in ChemInfty is split into three Phases:

Phase 1: Recognition of the graphical components,
  1. Recognizing simple graphical components (e.g. characters, lines, ellipses),
  2. Recognizing advanced graphical components (e.g. triangular shapes, arrows).
Phase 2: Constructing the chemical graph from the graphical components,
  1. Detecting inconsistencies,
  2. Solving inconsistencies.

Y.-B. Kwon and J.-M. Ogier (Eds.): GREC, LNCS 7423, pp. 119–128, 2013.

Phase 3: Converting the result into a common chemical format.

Phase 1, the recognition of the graphical components, is described in a separated paper [10]. In order to export the chemical information the constructed chemical graph can be converted to common chemical formats such as SDF [11] or MRV [12] in Phase 3. The internally used chemical object format (COF, cf. Section 2) stores both graphical and chemical information. During the conversion only the chemical parts are converted to the common chemical format.

This paper focuses on Phase 2, the chemical graph construction in ChemInfty. The chemical graph construction is what separates the inconsistency-driven method from straightforward methods. Phase 2 builds on Phase 1, thus the recognition of the graphical elements has to be finished before the chemical graph construction can start. Currently Phase 2 assumes, that the graphical elements recognized in Phase 1 are correct thus the graphical elements don't change during the chemical graph construction in Phase 2. Since Phase 1 and Phase 2 are separated the recognition system used in Phase 1 can be replaced without affecting Phase 2; as long as the COF format is used for storing the graphical information.

Originally our inconsistency-driven graph construction approach started with the thought of detecting inconsistencies in partially solved graphs to point out problems in certain areas to the user. This was meant for improving the efficiency of the correction process. Once the inconsistency detection mechanism was developed the idea for automated solving of the found inconsistencies emerged. Through extending both the checking and solving functionality, the system was soon capable of solving the complete chemical structure starting from the graphical components.

In order to control the semi-automated correction and to visualize the construction process a user interface was created. Through the user-interface the user can start, pause and stop the automated correction as well as interfere in the correction process.

2   Chemical Object Format

Inconsistency-driven chemical structure recognition requires the data of the graphical elements of the structure as well as the chemical elements. For that purpose a new format (COF) was created. COF is based on the data serialization language YAML [13] and is thus easy to read and to understand. In COF the graphical elements of the image are referenced by the chemical elements of the formula via a referencing system. The format consists of three layers:

1. **Header Layer:** This layer includes file information, threshold information gathered by the graphical recognition and the validity status.
2. **Graphical Layer:** This layer includes the graphical elements (characters, lines and ellipses). These parts are generated in Phase 1 by the graphical recognition engine. Graphical elements include coordinates indicating their location.

3. **Chemical Layer:** This layer includes the chemical elements. Chemical elements can be classified in simple elements (e.g. atoms, bonds, containers, ...) and advanced elements (cf. Fig. 2). Each chemical element refers to its corresponding graphical elements. For example a chemical single bond element references one graphical line element (cf. Fig. 1), whereas a chemical double bond element references two graphical line elements. Nodes reference their characters. In Fig. 1 the chemical placeholder (R-Group) element "R" references the graphical character element "R". If a chemical element consists of two graphical characters (e.g. "Cl"), two graphical character elements ("C" and "l") are referenced.

```
(…) # header
                                                                    Layer
 graphical-parts:                                                     G
▶- { gid: 1, type: Line, begin: [51, 47], end: [96, 47] }
▶- { gid: 2, type: Char, begin: [103, 24], end: [138, 64], code: "H" }
▶- { gid: 3, type: Char, begin: [24, 22], end: [46, 66], code: "R" }
 chemical-parts:                                                    Layer
  molecules:                                                          C
   - mid: 1
     nodes:
       - node: { nid: 1, type: Placeholder, text: "R", char-gids: [3] }
       - node: { nid: 2, type: Atom, text: "H", char-gids: [2] }
     bonds:
       - bond: { bid: 1, type: Single, line-gids: [1], connection-nids: [1, 2]}
```

Fig. 1. COF example showing **R-H**

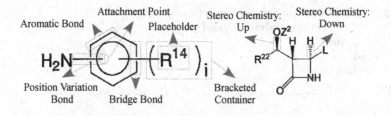

Fig. 2. Selection of advanced chemical elements

3 Chemical Graph Construction

The difference between straightforward methods and the inconsistency-driven method shall be defined formally. Let G be the graphical elements recognized from a raster image and C be a chemical graph composed of chemical elements. In straightforward methods the chemical graph construction is represented by Pseudocode 1.

Pseudocode 1. Straightforward Method

    Input: G, Graphical Information
    Output: C, Chemical Graph

    function StraightforwardMethod(g)
        $nds \leftarrow$ **DetectNodes**(g)
        $c \leftarrow$ **ConstructGraph**(nds)
        return c
    end

In comparison the inconsistency-driven chemical graph construction is represented by Pseudocode 2.

Pseudocode 2. Inconsistency-Driven Method

    Input: $\langle G, C_{in}\rangle$, Partially solved or empty chemical graph with graphical information
    Output: $\langle G, C_{out}\rangle$, Partially or completely solved chemical graph with graphical information

    function SolvingCycle($\langle g, cin\rangle$)
        $c \leftarrow cin$
        $ics \leftarrow$ **DetectInconsistencies**($\langle g, c\rangle$)
        while $ics \neq \{\}$ **and Solvable**(ics)
            $ic \leftarrow$ **GetNextInconsistency**(ics)
            $c \leftarrow$ **SolveInconsistency**($ic, \langle g, c\rangle$)
            $ics \leftarrow ics - \{ic\}$
            if StartNewSolvingCycle($ics, \langle g, c\rangle$)
                return SolvingCycle($\langle g, c\rangle$)
            end
        end
        return $\langle g, c\rangle$
    end

The pseudo codes point out that the output of straightforward methods is only the chemical graph whereas the inconstancy-driven method keeps the graphical information, allowing the system to accept partially solved chemical graphs as input. The graph construction can be stopped at any point and partially solved graphs ($\langle g, c\rangle$) can be saved in the COF format. The half-constructed graphs can be loaded again and the system can continue the construction at a different time. Furthermore the user can interact with the system. The user can pause the construction, interfere and later conclude the automated construction, resulting in a flexible, semi-automated process.

The inconsistency-driven graph construction is handled by the Solving Manager, which implements the function **SolvingCycle** of Pseudocode 2 in Java. In Phase 1 the graphical data is obtained. The graphical data and an empty chemical graph are passed to the Solving Manager in Phase 2 which constructs the chemical graph in cycles, resulting in the process: $\langle G, \{\} \rangle \to \langle G, C_1 \rangle \to \cdots \to \langle G, C_n \rangle$, where '$\to$' represents a state change of the chemical graph. One solving cycle includes certain steps represented by the functions:

DetectInconsistencies:

In this function inconsistencies are detected by a checking system using predefined rules. In our current implementation the system reports back to the user after a detection cycle. The user can then decide to use the automated, predefined system or to solve certain inconsistencies by hand. A detailed list of all inconsistencies can be found in our paper presented at GREC2011 [14].

Solvable:

Certain inconsistencies cannot be solved by the provided solution implementations. If the list only includes unsolvable inconsistencies the system stops and reports to the user.

GetNextInconsistency:

This function defines the solving strategy by ordering the inconsistencies. Depending on the order the behavior of the system can be significantly different.

SolveInconsistency:

In this function the next inconsistency, passed by GetNextInconsistency, is solved according to its corresponding solution. In the current implementation of our system the inconsistencies are sorted by type before solving. Each inconsistency type therefore needs a corresponding solution implementation. At the moment the system provides only one specific solution implementation for each inconsistency type. The order of the inconsistencies within the type does not matter.

StartNewSolvingCycle:

After certain inconsistency types are processed the system triggers a completely new solving cycle (including the detection of new inconsistencies). This mechanism allows the system to use the chemical information from partly constructed graphs.

The actual graph changes happen in **SolveInconsistency**. All other functions are mainly for controlling the behavior of the inconsistency-driven system. As the system can significantly change, if any of the solving cycle's functions changes, different solving strategies have to be discussed.

4 Solving Strategies

The solving strategy is decided by choosing branches in a search tree. In general there are three types of branches:

1. **Inconsistency solving order:** Depending on the order of inconsistencies passed to **SolveInconsistency** by **GetNextInconsistency**, the system can show different results. Note that the order has to be restricted by a set of rules in many cases, as some solving mechanisms build on others, making it impossible to solve certain inconsistencies without others being solved already.
2. **Many solutions for one inconsistency type:** By offering many solutions for one inconsistency type the system can choose solutions for certain scenarios thus the system gets more flexible. In order to realize such a mechanism a classification system is needed to define which solutions fit best for specific scenarios. Handling many solutions has to be implemented in the function **SolveInconsistency**.
3. **Invoking solving cycles or not:** One solving cycle includes detecting and solving inconsistencies. Detecting inconsistencies in partly solved graphs allows more advanced checks which can improve the accuracy. Chemical knowledge and rules can be used to define more accurate solutions. This branch is represented by **StartNewSolvingCycle**.

In our current implementation each inconsistency has a type which is used to sort the inconsistencies before solving. The order is defined hard coded for the time being. Furthermore the current implementation provides only one or no solution for each inconsistency type. Implementing many solutions for each inconsistency type is desired but complicated due to the dependencies between solutions. Certain solutions have to be processed after other solutions finished. This has to be considered once new solutions are added to the system. Not only the choosing mechanism for solutions, but also the order of the inconsistencies, defined by **GetNextInconsistency**, and the number of solving cycles may change.

The theoretical solving techniques described in [15] show more advanced methods than currently implemented in ChemInfty. The author classifies the problem (cadastral maps) into levels. According to these levels the inconsistencies detected are restricted to a certain context. For each level builders are specified. Builders can be improved by their frequency of correctly solved inconsistencies. As the problem presented in [15] is cadastral maps it differs from solving chemical formulae, however the theoretical concepts sound very promising for improving the ChemInfty system.

In order to control the behavior of the system by the user, and to easily add new solving rules, a description language may be useful. Approaches for rule definition in chemical structure recognition can be found in [16].

5   Example

The inconsistency-driven chemical graph construction shall be demonstrated on the small example used in Section 2. Two graphical characters (R and H) and one solid, graphical line are given (cf. Layer G in Fig. 1). These graphical parts do not change during the solving. Three states are defined:

State 1: State 1 is the starting scenario of the example. The formula was already partly solved by the user. The character "R" is already referenced by a placeholder (R-Group), as well as the line is referenced by a bond which connects to the placeholder, but the other side of the bond is unconnected (half connected bond). The character "H" has not been given a chemical meaning yet. Fig. 3 shows the COF representation of State 1.

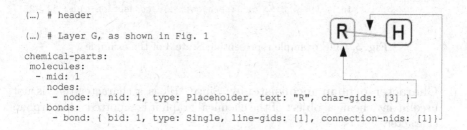

```
(…) # header

(…) # Layer G, as shown in Fig. 1

chemical-parts:
 molecules:
  - mid: 1
    nodes:
      - node: { nid: 1, type: Placeholder, text: "R", char-gids: [3] }
    bonds:
      - bond: { bid: 1, type: Single, line-gids: [1], connection-nids: [1] }
```

Fig. 3. COF example representing State 1 of the example

State 2: State 2 is reached after the first solving step. The character "H" is referenced by an atom but the bond is still in a half connected state. Fig. 4 shows the COF representation of State 2. The bold and underlined section indicates the changes between State 1 and State 2.

```
(…) # header

(…) # Layer G, as shown in Fig. 1

chemical-parts:
 molecules:
  - mid: 1
    nodes:
      - node: { nid: 1, type: Placeholder, text: "R", char-gids: [3] }
      - node: { nid: 2, type: Atom, text: "H", char-gids: [2] }
    bonds:
      - bond: { bid: 1, type: Single, line-gids: [1], connection-nids: [1] }
```

Fig. 4. COF example representing State 2 of the example

State 3: State 3 is reached after the second solving step; the formula is completely solved. The "H" atom was associated with the bond. Fig. 5 shows the COF representation of State 3. The bold and underlined section indicates the changes between State 2 and State 3.

For State 1 the initial inconsistency detection (**Inconsistency Detection 1**) will report two inconsistencies (A full list of all of the system's inconsistencies can be found in [14].):

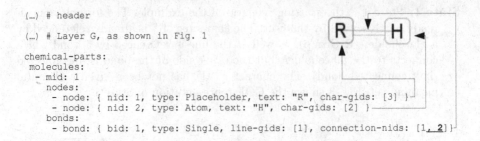

```
(…) # header

(…) # Layer G, as shown in Fig. 1

chemical-parts:
 molecules:
  - mid: 1
    nodes:
     - node: { nid: 1, type: Placeholder, text: "R", char-gids: [3] }
     - node: { nid: 2, type: Atom, text: "H", char-gids: [2] }
    bonds:
     - bond: { bid: 1, type: Single, line-gids: [1], connection-nids: [1, 2] }
```

Fig. 5. COF example representing State 3 of the example

1. **Character orphan inconsistency:** Since "H" is a character that is not used in any chemical object of the chemical graph it is reported as an orphan character.
2. **Bond connection inconsistency:** Since the bond does not have two nodes it is reported as inconsistent.

According to the solving strategy the system can now solve all inconsistencies in the same solving cycle or run another checking and solving cycle after a certain inconsistency type was solved completely. Let *Strategy A* be the strategy that solves all inconsistencies at once and *Strategy B* be the strategy that triggers a second solving cycle after Solving Cycle S1:

Solving Cycle S1: Solving Step S1.1
  – **Character orphan inconsistency solve:** The character is analyzed and the appropriate node-type is chosen. For H the appropriate node-type is a periodic atom. Once this inconsistency is solved the formula is in **State 2**.
Strategy A
  Solving Step S1.2
    – **Bond connection inconsistency solve:** The unconnected end of the bond is specified. A search for nodes in an area around the unconnected end point is performed. If a node can be found the node is associated with the bond. Otherwise a hidden carbon is created and then associated with the bond. After solving this inconsistency the formula is in **State 3**.
Strategy B
  Solving Cycle S2, Inconsistency Detection 2: A second inconsistency check is triggered after the character orphan inconsistency was solved. Two inconsistencies are reported:
    1. **Node hands inconsistency:** Since no bond is connected to H yet the valence electrons do not match the number of connection bonds thus the node hands check reports an inconsistency.
    2. **Bond connection inconsistency:** The bond connection inconsistency was not solved so it is reported again.

Solving Cycle S2: Solving Step S2.1
- **Node hands inconsistency solve:** The H-atom knows that it wants to have exactly one connection. The system detects th nearest bond to the H-atom and attaches it. After solving this inconsistency **State 3** is achieved.

Once **State 3** is achieved the formula is completely corrected thus the Solving Manager should terminate. If *Strategy A* is used all reported inconsistencies are solved once **State 3** is reached. The Solving Manager terminates because all inconsistencies were solved. If *Strategy B* is used there is still one inconsistency left, although the chemical graph is already completely solved. This happens because the solution for the node hands inconsistency, detected in **Inconsistency Detection 2**, solves the bond connection inconsistency as well. As the node hands inconsistency is solved first the bond connection inconsistency gets obsolete. The system has to define strategies for inconsistencies that were solved through other inconsistencies' solutions. There are three strategies for dealing with this problem:

1. The Solving Manager detects dependent inconsistencies while solving. This requires advanced inconsistency dependency management.
2. The bond connection inconsistency solve is triggered but aborted as the bond is already valid. (The current implementation is based on this strategy.)
3. Another inconsistency detection cycle is triggered to eliminate already solved inconsistencies.

6 Conclusion

This paper proposed the inconsistency-driven method of chemical graph construction starting from graphical objects. In order to show the practical usage of this method, a recognition engine using the presented method was developed by our project group. This engine was used to create a ground truth dataset of Japanese published patent applications from the year 2008. For 3381 chemical images of the Japanese published patents the graph construction, Phase 2, takes 548659 milliseconds on a 2.4 Intel Duo Core system running MacOSX Snow Leopard. Thus the average time to construct the chemical graph of one image, without taking the graphical recognition of Phase 1 in account, takes 162 milliseconds. The inconsistency-driven system of Phase 2, including the user interface that allows semi-automated correction, is implemented in Java.

The system introduces a cycle based, semi-automated correction process which allows the user to define flexible solving strategies. In order to offer more flexibility the solving strategy handling of the current system has to be extended.

The method of inconsistency-driven correction is not restricted to chemical-structure images, but can also be applied to images that include grammars or constraints such as room layouts, flow diagrams, class diagrams, electronic circuits, music scores, or maps.

Acknowledgements. This research was supported by the Adaptable and Seamless Technology Transfer Program through target-driven R&D, Japan Science and Technology Agency (JST, http://www.jst.go.jp/EN/). The software Marvin 5.5 (2011) and Instant JChem 5.5 (2011) from ChemAxon (http:// www.chemaxon.com) were used for proceeding this research.

References

1. CAS - Chemical Abstracts Service, http://www.cas.org/
2. Valko, A.T., Johnson, P.A.: CLiDE Pro: The Latest Generation of CLiDE, a Tool for Optical Chemical Structure Recognition. J. Chem. Inf. Model. 49(4), 780–787 (2009)
3. Filippov, I.V., Nicklaus, M.C.: Optical Structure Recognition Software To Recover Chemical Information: OSRA, An Open Source Solution. Journal of Chemical Information and Modeling 49(3), 740–743 (2009)
4. Filippov, I.V., Nicklaus, M.C.: Extracting Chemical Structure Information: Optical Structure Recognition Application. In: Pre-Proceedings of the 8th IAPR International Workshop on Graphics Recognition (GREC 2009), pp. 133–142 (2009)
5. Algorri, M.-E., Zimmermann, M., Hofmann-Apitius, M.: Automatic Recognition of Chemical Images. In: Eighth Mexican International Conference on Current Trends in Computer Science, pp. 41–46 (2007)
6. Park, J., Rosania, G.R., Shedden, K.A., Nguyen, M., Lyu, N., Saitou, K.: Automated extraction of chemical structure information from digital raster images. Chemistry Central Journal 3(4) (2009)
7. Sadawi, N.M., Sexton, A.P., Sorge, V.: Chemical Structure Recognition: A Rule Base Approach. In: 19th Document Recognition and Retrieval Conference, DRR 2012 (2012)
8. Imago, http://ggasoftware.com/opensource/imago
9. ChemInfty, http://www.inftyproject.org/en/ChemInfty
10. Fujiyoshi, A., Nakagawa, K., Suzuki, M.: Robust Method of Segmentation and Recognition of Chemical Structure Images in ChemInfty. In: Pre-Proceedings of the 9th IAPR International Workshop on Graphics Recognition, GREC 2011 (2011)
11. CTfile Formats, Symyx Solutions (June 2010), http://www.symyx.com/solutions/white_papers/ctfile_formats.jsp
12. ChemAxon, "Marvinsketch", http://www.chemaxon.com/products/marvin/marvinsketch/
13. Ben-Kiri, O., Evans, C., dt Net, I.: YAML Ain't Markup Language Version 1.1 (January 2005), http://yaml.org/spec/1.1
14. Karzel, D., Nakagawa, K., Fujiyoshi, A., Suzuki, M.: Inconsistency-Driven Chemical Graph Construction in ChemInfty. In: Pre-Proceedings of the 9th IAPR International Workshop on Graphics Recognition, GREC 2011 (2011)
15. Ogier, J.M., Mullot, R., Labiche, J., Lecourtier, Y.: Semantic Coherency: The Basis of an Image Interpretation Device - Application to the Cadastral Map Interpretation. IEEE Transactions on Systems, Man and Cybernetics - Part B: Cybernetics 30, 322–338 (2000)
16. Kral, P.: Chemical Structure Recognition via an expert system guided graph exploration. Master's thesis, Technical University Munich (2007)

Robust Frame and Text Extraction from Comic Books

Christophe Rigaud[1], Norbert Tsopze[1,2],
Jean-Christophe Burie[1], and Jean-Marc Ogier[1]

[1] Laboratory L3i, University of La Rochelle
Avenue Michel Crépeau 17042 La Rochelle, France
[2] LAMOCA - Department of Computer Science
University of Yaoundé I, BP 812 Yaoundé - Cameroon
{christophe.rigaud,norbert.tsopze,jcburie,jmogier}@univ-lr.fr

Abstract. Comic books constitute an important heritage in many countries. Nowadays, digitization allows to search directly from content instead of meta-data only (e.g. album title or author name). Few studies have been done in this direction. Only frame and speech balloon extraction have been experimented in the case of simple page structure. In fact, the page structure depends on the author which is why many different structures and drawings exist. Despite the differences, drawings have a common characteristic because of design process: they are all surrounded by a black line. In this paper, we propose to rely on this particularity of comic books to automatically extract frame and text using a connected-component labeling analysis. The approach is compared with some existing methods found in the literature and results are presented.

Keywords: comic books, comics frame extraction, comics text extraction, segmentation, connected-component labeling, k-means.

1 Introduction

Nowadays, comics represent an important heritage in many countries. Massive digitization campaigns have been carried out in order to enhance archives and contents. This work has been done by specific companies that index pages but not their content. If the "page only" limit could be exceeded then new usages of comics may become a reality such as the frame-per-frame reading [2,9] on mobile devices, the search of specific items by content based image retrieval from an large amount of albums and even content analysis from text. Such applications are currently possible with e-comics because they are designed with specific software and they can be indexed throughout the design process. The aim of our work is to process digitized comics in order to extract and analyse the content for full content search purpose. Full content search is requested by some cultural organisations such as the International City of Comics and Images [3] for specific object retrieval.

To enhance comic books, some works have been done recently but they are not robust enough to be industrialised. These works concern the segmentation of the frames, speech balloon and text (inside speech balloon). This paper proposes a method to automatically segment the frames and all the text contained in comics pages (not only text

Y.-B. Kwon and J.-M. Ogier (Eds.): GREC, LNCS 7423, pp. 129–138, 2013.
© Springer-Verlag Berlin Heidelberg 2013

included into speech balloon). The proposed method is based on connected-component labeling algorithm following by k-means [17] clustering and then filtering.

The paper is organised as follows. The section 2 presents the vocabulary of comics content. An overview of frame and text segmentation methods is given in section 3. Section 4 and 5 present respectively the proposed method and the experimentations. Finally, section 6 and 7 conclude this paper.

2   Comic Books

According to [14], there are three categories of comic books created respectively in America, Asia (manga) and Europe. In this paper, only the two first categories are considered because mangas are very different in terms of strokes, frames [18] and text [2]. A careful observation of the page content shows that the main characteristic of comics drawing is the black line that surround each element (or almost). Because of this feature, a connected-component (CC) based method is used in order to extract frame content from its edges. This algorithm has two advantages in our study. First, it is well adapted for frame segmentation as presented above. Second, it can be also used for text segmentation [7]. Moreover, using a single algorithm to segment a page is time saving.

Comic books relate stories drawn into albums. In traditional comics, pages are split up into strips separated by white gutter. A strip is a sequence of frames. A frame is a drawing generally in a box. Note that sometimes frame doesn't have box, in this case the reading and the segmentation become harder. Moreover, extended contents (e.g. speech balloons, characters, comics art) can overlap two frames or more [13]. All these particularities may punctually disturb the image processing.

Comics contain different types of text (handwriting or typewritten) depending on the nature of the message to read. Most of the text is inserted for speech purposes between characters and written into speech balloons. Other categories concern the narrative text and onomatopoeia. The onomatopoeias represent the sounds in a textual way or a sequence of symbols.

3   Existing Methods

3.1   Frame Segmentation

Frame segmentation has been mainly studied for reading comics on mobile device in order to display them frame by frame on a small screen. Here, our work concerns the indexing of a huge amount of albums that raises new issues in terms of variety of format, resolution and content.

Many segmentation methods have been studied to separate the background and the content as [9]. Most of them are based on white line cutting with Hough transform [6], recursive X-Y cut [8] or from gradient [16]. These methods doesn't handle empty area (case missing) [9] within a strip (figure 1a) or no full border frame (figure 1b). These issues have been corrected by connected-component approaches [1] but if some elements overlap (figure 1c), the frame segmentation process failed. The regions of interest (ROI) are often clustered by heuristic [2,13] relative to the page size that is width and height

(a) Missing frame [4]   (b) Partial box [4]   (c) Overlapping between three frames [12]

Fig. 1. Examples of specific frames

dependent. A sequence of N erosions following by N dilatations has been proposed by [13] for cutting overlapping elements but it is time consuming and the choice of N is unclear. [13] extracts the background of the pages by region growing algorithm, that is new in comparison with the binarisation applied by the other methods.

3.2   Text Segmentation

In comics, most of the text is part of speech balloons. It is probably the reason why it is the only type of text studied so far. Previous works extract text from speech balloon [18,1] or inversely speech balloon from text [13]. These approaches are really efficient but they suppose that text is written in black in a white balloon. We propose to enlarge this limitation: text background colour should be similar to page background.

4   Contribution

We propose a new method to extract frame and text area simultaneously from comics pages for indexation purpose. Our method processes page per page and begins by a pre-processing that binarise the page. Then, the ROI are defined as the set of the connected-component bounding boxes (rectangles). ROI are classified as "noise", "text" and "frame" depending to their sizes, topological relations, and for the text, spatial relations. Note that only speech and narrative texts are considered in this study because they aren't overlapped by object (e.g. line, drawing). The onomatopoeias will be studied in a future work. The originalities of this paper are frame segmentation, with or without box, and out-of-balloon text segmentation that can be extracted by CC algorithm.

4.1   Pre-processing

The aim of the pre-processing step is to separate background and content of the page in order to focus on the content later. Several processing are implemented in order to apply CC algorithm, and then, to extract the bounding boxes. It can be resumed as follows:

1. Grayscale conversion
2. Binarisation threshold computation

3. Image inversion depending on the threshold
4. Binarisation
5. Connected-component extraction

The first step consists in a grayscale conversion as given in [15]. Then, a binarisation (figure 2a) is applied with a threshold computed from the median value of the border page pixels. We assume that the border pixels of the page are representative of the page background. If the median value is closer to "black" gray levels than "white" gray levels, then, image inversion is applied and we redo the complete process in order to always get a white background at the end of this step. This pre-processing is more robust than [2] who assumes that the page is always white and uses a constant threshold. Binarisation is very important for the rest of the method because the background part won't be considered anymore. Then, CC algorithm is used to extract, from connected components, the bounding boxes of all the elements (sequence of black pixels) of the image (figure 2b).

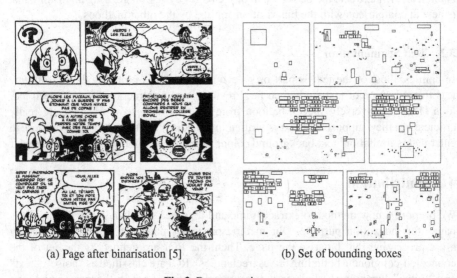

(a) Page after binarisation [5]   (b) Set of bounding boxes

Fig. 2. Pre-processing steps

4.2   ROI Classification

ROI are defined as the connected-component bounding boxes. We define a set of regions $R = \{R_1, R_2, ..., R_n\}$. The classification is performed on ROI heights with k-means algorithm. The number of expected classes is 3 according to our experiments on several comics. Classes are labelled as "frame" (the highest), "text" (the most numerous) and "noise" (few pixels height) as shown on figure 3. This classification is performed dynamically on each page that makes our method invariant to page format and resolution. Indeed, ROI height classification is not page size dependent unlike [13,2], and the number of pixels for each ROI is proportional to the page resolution (do not bias the classification). This method assumes that the page contains text with background brightness similar to page background otherwise the binarisation and thus the classification may fail.

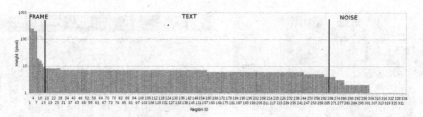

Fig. 3. Example of ROI classification on descendent histogram of the ROI height

Then, the variance of each class is computed to check the homogeneity of the ROI. If the variance of the "frame" class is high, a specific algorithm [13] is applied in order to improve the previous steps (binarisation and/or classification).

Example. Figure 4 shows the frame segmentation of a page containing two frames overlapped by a black arrow (figure 4a and 4b). As shown in figure 4c, these two frames are detected as only one single frame by the CC algorithm (the biggest bounding box in figure 4c and the region 1 in figure 4d). The histogram figure 4d (log scale) shows that the first ROI is much higher than the others within the "frame" class. The variance of the "frame" class is therefore much higher than the two other classes that may due to an issue from the binarisation step. To fix this issue, a specific algorithm proposed by [13] can be used. It consists in frame segmentation by region growing applied on page background (frames become black blocks) followed by a sequence of erosions and dilatations in order to "disconnect" the black blocks (removes small overlapping elements). Then we redo pre-processing and classification steps for the frames only.

Note that the gap between the frame 7 and 8 in figure 4d is due to some objects (e.g. the top left big interrogation mark in figure 2a) higher than a character height. These ROI will be removed by a topological filtering process as explained bellow section 4.3.

4.3   Filtering

After the classification stage, two filters are applied in order to remove false positive detection (region labelled mistakenly). The first filter is topological and keeps only the frames not fully contained in an other frame ($R_i \notin R_j \forall j, i \neq j$) (figure 5a and 5b).

The second filter merges all the "text" ROI closer than two times the median "text" class height to define text areas (figure 6). Sometimes, detected text areas do not contain text but many small elements as high as text (figure 7). Thus, a text/graphic separation method [11] is applied to remove areas without text. This method compares vertical and horizontal projected histogram of each text area.

(a) Page with an overlapping element [10]   (b) Zoom of the overlapping element [10]

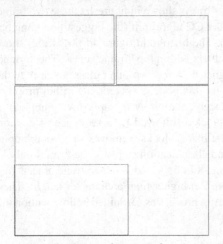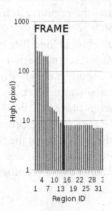

(c) Bounding boxes of connected-components   (d) Histogram zoomed on frames

Fig. 4. False positive frame detection

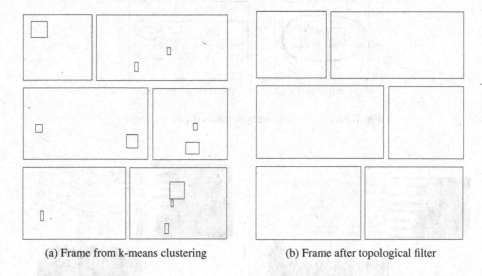

(a) Frame from k-means clustering   (b) Frame after topological filter

Fig. 5. Topological filtering of the frames

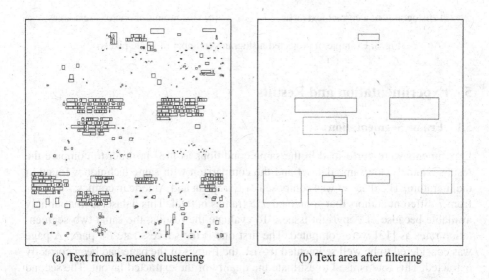

(a) Text from k-means clustering   (b) Text area after filtering

Fig. 6. Spatial filtering of text

Experimentally, we determined that to be a true text area, the variance of the horizontal projected histogram should be higher than the variance of the vertical projected histogram. The reason is that the horizontal projected histogram of a text area presents important variations due to the text and line spaces (figure 8a). This phenomenon isn't true for non-text areas (figure 8b).

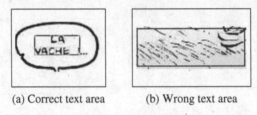

|(a) Correct text area | (b) Wrong text area|

Fig. 7. Example of text area detections (black rectangles)

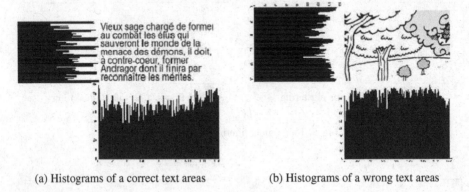

(a) Histograms of a correct text areas   (b) Histograms of a wrong text areas

Fig. 8. Example of projected histograms (number of white pixels)

5   Experimentation and Results

5.1   Frame Segmentation

Experiments were performed in the same conditions as [13] in order to compare the results. Namely, the same dataset and the comparison with same techniques found in the literature. The data set was composed of European and American comics: 42 pages from 7 different authors that contained 355 frames in total. This dataset is not publicly available because of copyright issues. To evaluate the results, the same two segmentation rates as [13] were computed. The first one is the success rate for page. A page was considered to be well segmented if ALL the frames of the page had been correctly extracted. This rate is used to estimate the quality of the extracted layout. The second is the success rate for frames. This rate gives the percentage of well extracted frames among the 355 frames of the data set.

Method	Tanaka [16]	Arai [1]	Ngo Ho [13]	Proposed method
Page (%)	42.8	47.6	64.3	66.7
Frame (%)	63.9	75.6	87.3	88.2

Fig. 9. Success rate comparison

In comparison with [1,13,16], the proposed method is more efficient for frame segmentation because we handle border-free frames. Moreover, this method is 60% faster than [13]. This approach is faster because a time consuming process (specific algorithms) is applied only if the page contains overlapping elements (section 4.2). Nevertheless, the frame success rate does not bias the text success rate because text areas are extracted from the whole page and not from frames.

5.2   Text Area Segmentation

Text areas were extracted (section 4.3) from the same data set mentioned above. In order to be more accurate, speech text areas and narrative text areas were distinguished, namely 435 and 79 text areas respectively for the whole data set. We define:

- TP: the areas labelled as text areas that contain only text (true positive)
- FN: the areas ignored that contain text (false negative)

The text areas that were segmented partially or in many parts are considered as "false negatives".

Text type	TP	FN
Speech (%)	78	22
Narrative (%)	53	47

Fig. 10. Success rates of the text areas

The results are encouraging for the speech text category because most of the 22% of FN are text plus extra parts that need specific process. An adapted filtering will be developed to improve the detection. The narrative text extraction is harder because of its lower contrast with background (no white or light background). Nevertheless, it is difficult to compare our method with other approaches because we do not look for speech balloon only but for every single text area in the page, and as far as we know this hasn't been studied before in comics processing.

6   Conclusion and Perspectives

A new method, to extract frames and texts simultaneously from comics, has been proposed and evaluated. The proposed approach is fast and especially robust to page format variations and border-free frames. Moreover, the method based on connected component analysis is able to extract all the text inside or outside the speech balloons.

The evaluation shows that more than 88% of the frames are correctly extracted. However, an effort has to be done to improve the results especially for large overlapping elements and narrative text extraction. The frame and text extraction was a first step. The main objective of our future work will be to analyse the content of the frame.

138   C. Rigaud et al.

Acknowledgement. This work was supported by the European Regional Development Fund, the region Poitou-Charentes (France), the General Council of Charente Maritime (France) and the town of La Rochelle (France).

References

1. Arai, K., Tolle, H.: Method for automatic e-comic scene frame extraction for reading comic on mobile devices. In: Seventh International Conference on Information Technology: New Generations, ITNG, pp. 370–375. IEEE Computer Society, Washington, DC (2010)
2. Arai, K., Tolle, H.: Method for real time text extraction of digital manga comic. International Journal of Image Processing (IJIP) 4(6), 669–676 (2011)
3. CIBDI: Cité internationale de la bande dessinées et de l'image, http://www.citebd.org
4. Cyb: La légende des Yaouanks. Studio Cyborga, Goven, France (2008)
5. Cyb: Bubblegôm. Studio Cyborga, Goven, France (2009)
6. Duda, R.O., Hart, P.E.: Use of the hough transformation to detect lines and curves in pictures. Commun. ACM 15, 11–15 (1972)
7. Fletcher, L., Kasturi, R.: A robust algorithm for text string separation from mixed text/graphics images. IEEE Transactions on Pattern Analysis and Machine Intelligence 10(6), 910–918 (1988)
8. Han, E., Kim, K., Yang, H., Jung, K.: Frame segmentation used mlp-based x-y recursive for mobile cartoon content. In: Proceedings of the 12th International Conference on Human-Computer Interaction: Intelligent Multimodal Interaction Environments, HCI 2007, pp. 872–881. Springer, Heidelberg (2007)
9. In, Y., Oie, T., Higuchi, M., Kawasaki, S., Koike, A., Murakami, H.: Fast frame decomposition and sorting by contour tracing for mobile phone comic images. Internatinal Journal of Systems Applications, Engineering and Development 5(2), 216–223 (2011)
10. Jolivet, O.: BostonPolice. Clair de Lune, Allauch (2010)
11. Khedekar, S., Ramanaprasad, V., Setlur, S., Govindaraju, V.: Text - image separation in devanagari documents. In: Proceedings of the Seventh International Conference on Document Analysis and Recognition, pp. 1265–1269 (August 2003)
12. Lamisseb: Les noeils Tome 1. Bac@BD, Valence, France (2011)
13. Ngo Ho, A.K., Burie, J.C., Ogier, J.M.: Comics page structure analysis based on automatic panel extraction. In: Nineth IAPR International Workshop on Graphics Recognition, GREC 2011, Seoul, Korea, September 15-16 (2011)
14. Ponsard, C., Fries, V.: An Accessible Viewer for Digital Comic Books. In: Miesenberger, K., Klaus, J., Zagler, W.L., Karshmer, A.I. (eds.) ICCHP 2008. LNCS, vol. 5105, pp. 569–577. Springer, Heidelberg (2008)
15. Pratt, K., Digital, W.: Digital image processing, 2nd edn. John Wiley & Sons, Inc., NY (1991)
16. Tanaka, T., Shoji, K., Toyama, F., Miyamichi, J.: Layout analysis of tree-structured scene frames in comic images. In: IJCAI 2007, pp. 2885–2890 (2007)
17. Tou, J., Gonzalez, R.: Pattern Recognition Principles. Addison-Wesley, USA (1974)
18. Yamada, M., Budiarto, R., Endo, M., Miyazaki, S.: Comic image decomposition for reading comics on cellular phones. IEICE Transactions 87-D(6), 1370–1376 (2004)

Unified Representation of Online and Offline Hand Drawn Graphics Using Bezier Curve Approximation

Jaehwa Park, Ho-Hyun Park, and Young-Bin Kwon

Dept of Computer Science and Engineering,
Chung-Ang University, Seoul Korea
{jaehwa,hohyun,ybkwon}@cau.ac.kr

Abstract. Integrating approaches in a unified system for the online and offline data type are seldom found, although the similar recognition alogirhtms are used for the two data stream. A practical solution which is able to represent online and offline hand drawn graphic messages simultaneously is presented. Freehand-sketched graphics captured by a digitizing tablet (online) or digital camera (offline) is approximated using the quadratic Bezier curve representation. A recursive architecture performing a piecewise curve approximation is proposed to represent pen strokes. As a primary unified tool for the online/offline symbol recognition system, a stroke ordering method which simulating online data of offline data is developed. The experimental results show good curve fitting and stroke generation ability of the proposed method, which can be applicable for practical real-time symbol recognition applications.

Keywords: Bezier Curve Approximation, Unified Symbol Recognition, Online Offline Unification.

1 Introduction

Recently, small mobile devices are becoming very popular and new data entry methods are highly required to ensure the user convenience. In the common user interface for the currently available mobile devices, the numeric keyboard for phone number entry is also used to enter the required symbol data. Symbols and signs are assigned to the numeric keyboards to enter the data. The number of symbols is greater than the number of keys used, however, for which reason plural symbols are assigned to one key. Therefore, a symbol selection process is required, and the method for such is more complicated than the use of a computer keyboard. Diverse methods have been introduced by device manufacturers, but symbol entry is not easy because there are too many keyboard arrays and entry methods depending on the devices.

To solve this problem, a handwriting recognition technology for symbol entry is being introduced to devices with touch pads. This method is suitable for small and light mobile devices because non-professionals can easily use it in a small space on the device. Also freehand sketched graphic messages are considered as a

Y.-B. Kwon and J.-M. Ogier (Eds.): GREC, LNCS 7423, pp. 139–148, 2013.

natural way to visualize ideas or messages that cannot be efficiently represented by speech or text. However, due to the physical limitations of small mobile devices, the conventional data entry methods for the desktop environment, such as keyboards and mouses, cannot be efficiently mounted. In small sized mobile devices, touch screen and camera are considered as primary input methods that can replace the traditional input devices.

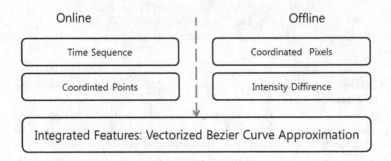

Fig. 1. Online and offline recognition approaches

It is expected that a user interface that uses both entry methods will soon be introduced, considering the rapid penetration of mobile communication devices equipped with digital cameras. Online and offline unified symbol recognition will become a part of the intelligent interface, which has not been yet integrated together with the existing numeric keyboard interface. In addition, in view of the diverse applications and contents demanded by mobile-communication-device users, the development of the online/offline unified recognition system will be a primary mean for the user interface to address diverse contents.

Although the similar recognition alogirhtms are used for the online and offline data in symbol recognition systems, unified approaches integrating in a unified system for the two data type are seldom found. In this paper, as a preliminary work for integrating online and offline recognition methods into a universal system, a practical representation method of online and offline hand drawing graphic messages simultaneously is presented.

The nature of data stream of freehand-sketched graphics, captured by a touch screen (online) or digital camera (offline) are different. Unlike in the online data, the lines extracted from an offline symbol image have unclear start and end points. If there are cross points among strokes, the stroke separations are much more difficult compared to online data. However, as shown in Fig. 1 those two type of data can be integrated into a unified format by i) simulate the time information in offline data and ii) re-ordering in unified rules cooperative to offline data in online data. A unified method is developed approximating graphics data into sequence of strokes which are represented in control points of the quadratic Bezier curve approximation.

A recursive architecture performing a piecewise curve approximation is proposed to represent pen strokes. To develop the online and offline graphics recognition system, a stroke ordering method which simulating online data of offline data is developed as shown in Fig. 2. The experimental results show good curve fitting and stroke generation ability of the proposed method, which can be applicable for practical real-time symbol recognition applications.

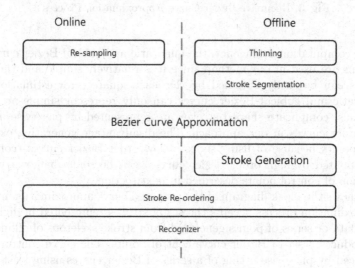

Fig. 2. Unified approach for online and offline universal recognition

2   Bezier Curve Approximation

A Bezier curve is defined using two anchor on-curve control points and at least an off-curve control point. The on-curve control points are the two end points of the curve actually located on the path of the curve, while the other off-curve control points define the gradient from the two end points, which are usually not located on the curve path. The off points control the shape of the curve. The curve is actually a blend of the off-curve control points [1].

The more off-curve control points a Bezier curve has, the more complicated shape can be represented; however the order of the mathematical curve equation becomes higher. The number of off-curve points determines the order of the Bezier Curve [2]. The approximation of hand-drawing strokes using high order Bezier curve reduces the number of on-curve points and produces more compact data representation. However, the approximation of high order curve equation usually requires large amount of computation since we don't have a clear solution but has trail-error approaches [3].

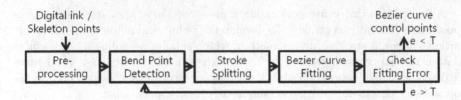

Fig. 3. Recursive Bezier Curve Approximation Process

For the computational efficiency, the quadratic and cubical Bezier curve representations are used in our method since it is relatively simple and the curve coefficients can be easily obtained by the least square error estimation. But the quadratic and cubical Bezier curves can only represent simple arc shape curves. Thus, complicate shaped strokes are represented by piecewise approximated Bezier curves in our approach. The disadvantage generating excessive on-curve points because of using series of low order Bezier curves (compared to approximated by high order Bezier curves) can be somewhat overcome by optimization of control points described in next section.

Fig. 3 shows the block diagram of the proposed curve approximation method. The approximation process accepts the set of strokes represented in digital ink of online data or series of points generated from stroke skeletons of offline data. and it produces a set of Bezier curve control points. The curve control points are produced by piecewise fitting of a series of Bezier curves using least square error approximation. This process has two independent sub-processing modules, preprocessing and curve approximation loop. The preprocessing is performed only once per given input set of stroke data, but the curve approximation routine operates recursively till the piecewise fitting results are satisfactory.

2.1   Digital Ink Preprocessing

The purpose of preprocessing is to extract sharp turning pen movement points so-called bending points; for example the sharp peak point of characters M or W. These bending points are generally difficult to handle for low order Bezier curve fitting. To minimize the burden of computation, the bending points are obtained based on curvature (tangent) estimation on each ink point before the curve fitting process. And the strokes that contain bending points are split into a set of smooth sub-strokes.

To minimize the effect of jitter noise erroneously being detected as bending points, a sliding window technique is used. The curvature on each point is estimated using the average of all curvatures obtained in the permissible window. It can minimize the chance of over-splitting caused by jitter of pen movements. The window size is given as a function of the perimeter and bounding box of each stroke.

An inward vector is defined as a transition from previous to current ink point and an outward vector is defined as a transition from the current to next ink point. The curvature angle is defined as the minimum angle between the inward and outward vectors. The difference between the inward and outward angles is assumed to be the curvature angle of the point. The final curvature angle is estimated by averaging of all the obtained curvature values between the corresponding pairs split by current point within the window. If the curvature angle is higher then a threshold, the curvature at the point is assume to be high.

A bending zone is established by a group of series points that have high curvature. Then the highest curvature point within the bending zone is assumed to be the bending point. The ink stroke between any two adjacent bending points is separated as a sub-stroke after all the bending points are detected. The curvature thresholds are determined in several values by the application to minimize the overhead of subsequent recursive curve approximation. If it is too low, the burden of recursive operation become large, otherwise it results in degradation of compression rate because of unnecessary over-splitting.

This problem can be solved if the curvatures along the line are calculated and if the slope differences between the two points are identified to determine the level of bending. If the window size is N_w and the center point for which the slope will be calculated is n, the value can be calculated as $N_w/2$. If n has been determined, the differences in Δx values between all the points from $n + 1$ to $n + (N_w/2)$ and n are summed up, and the resulting value is defined as Δx. In the same way, the differences in Δy values between all the points from $n + 1$ to $n + (N_w/2)$ and n are summed up, and the resulting value is defined as y. The value of $\Delta x/\Delta y$ is substituted in the inverse function of tangent, and the resulting value is defined as the negative slope at n.

The slope is calculated in the positive and negative directions from n. The slope difference at n is defined as the difference between the positive and negative slopes at n. As the slope difference for a point has been calculated, n is continuously increased by 1 to calculate the slope at each point, and the calculation ends when the entire window cannot be filled. After all the slope differences along a line are calculated, the process is also applied to other lines in the same way, to calculate the slope differences. Using the calculated slope differences, a line is divided into two pieces at a point where it is significantly bent.

2.2 Curve Fitting

For an ink stroke (or a sub-stroke), the minimum required curve-fitting condition (such as minimum number of ink points, size of bounding box, etc) is checked. If the ink stroke is determined to be eligible for the further processing, a quadratic Bezier curve approximation method is applied to find out the curve control points.

For a given ink sequence, a quadratic Bezier curve representation coefficients (usually coordinate of control points) are estimated which satisfy following conditions. i) The starting point of the estimated curve should be the same point of the first ink point of the stroke ink sequence. ii) The ending point of the estimated curve should be the same point of the last ink point of the stroke ink sequence. And iii) that has the Least Square Euclidean distance error between the actual ink points. The meditative parameter of Bezier curve representation (usually bounded in [0,1]) is estimated based on the proportional distance of each ink point on the perimeter from staring to end ink points [4].

Using the estimated curve control points, the fitting error between actual ink points and corresponding points of the approximated curve is calculated based on Euclidean distance measurement. If the fitting error is within acceptable range, $e < T$ where e and T denotes the curve fitting error and threshold respectively, the approximation is completed as shown in Fig. 3. Otherwise, new splitting points are determined using a relaxed curvature threshold as shown in the feedback path of Fig. 3.

The recursive curve fitting operation is applied to each newly split strokes till the error falls within tolerance or the size of split piece become smaller than the minimum size. Curve approximation function is controlled by two parameters: the minimum ink size and error tolerance. Both parameters control the accuracy of approximation and efficiency of compression.

The Bezier curve approximation of the entered stroke data is efficient for reducing the data size and removing the noise in the stroke (e.g., deviation and irregularity). The Bezier curve approximation was used to remove the unnecessary noise in symbol recognition, and to create the common features for online and offline recognizer [5].

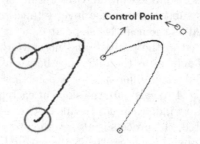

Fig. 4. Bezier curve approximation

Let $p_i = (x_i, y_i)$ be a ink point of online data or a pixel of offline data. Let's assume N points form a stroke $P = \{p_0, p_1, \ldots p_{N-1}\}$. Let L_n be the Euclidean distance between two points of p_n and p_{n+1}. The point on n^{th} point of approximated Bezier curve $B(u)$, denoted as u_n, is defined as follows, if the entered point series is dense enough,

$$u_n = \frac{L_n}{\sum_{i=0}^{N-1} L_i} \tag{1}$$

Using the above equation, the second and third Bezier curves can be determined. In the case of the quadratic Bezier curve, the start and end control points r_0 and r_2 are fixed, and only r_1 needs to be calculated. r_1 can be determined by finding the points that minimize the differences between the Bezier curve points and the actual points. The following equation can be used to minimize the resulting values,

$$r_1 = \sum_{i=0}^{N-1} \frac{(1-u_i)u_i p_i - (1-u_i)^3 u_i p_0 + (1-u_i)^3 u_i p_{N-1}}{2(1-u_i)^2 u_i^2} \tag{2}$$

In the case of the cubical Bezier curve, the start and end control points are obtained as the quadratic case, but two off-line control points are need to be calculated. The two unknowns can be calculated using the similar equation of r_1 above.

The differences between the points of the Bezier curve and the actual points, means curve fitting error e are expressed as follows:

$$e = \sum_{i=0}^{N-1} (p_i - B(u_i))^2 \tag{3}$$

2.3 Line Approximation

Some of curve components can be approximated as a 'line' component instead of curve representation within the allowable error range, if the curvature is not large. Since the line approximation from raw digital ink data is a computationally intensive process, the Bezier curve fitting parameters are used directly to examine the possibility of a line approximation. The off-line control point of a Bezier curve always exists outside of fitting curve, i.e. not within the area of fitting curve and straight line between two on-curve points. So, if the off-line control point is located within the error tolerance boundary, we can assume that the fitting curve trajectory exists within the error boundary. In this case we can approximate the Bezier curve into a straight line between the two on-line control points within the allowable fitting error tolerance.

If two conditions are satisfied, i) the Euclidean distances between the on and off control points are smaller than allowable delta tolerance (means maximum allowable value for the first order difference), and ii) the minimum Euclidean distance between the off-line point and the straight line between the two on-line points is smaller than the error tolerance. Then, the off-line control point is assumed to be within the error tolerance. If the test is successful, the Bezier Curve representation is converted into a line component representation by discarding the off-line control point.

3 Experiment

The proposed method has been tested in two different data sets: object drawings, and handwriting characters. The data set collected from various peoples for short messaging system that can be rendered through wireless network.

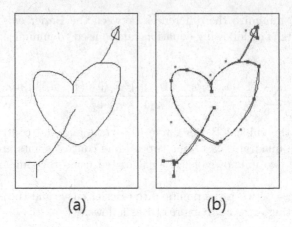

(a)   (b)

Fig. 5. An exmaple of Bezier curve approximation: (a) online input data, (b) approximated results - dots are the control points

Fig. 5 shows one of the examples of Bezier curve approximation on online data. The proposed algorithm generates the essential Bezier curve control points from given input data as shown in Fig 5-(a) and (b), allowing the maximum error of four pixel distance. It also shows the synthesis curves regenerated by the obtained control points. For comparison, the synthesis curves are displayed in blue ink with the original drawings in black ink.

Fig. 6 shows results of stroke segmentation, Bezier curve approximation and the stroke orderings on an offline handwritten character image. The second and third Bezier curves are used for approximation in this experiment. Top to down and left to right ordering based on the centroid of sgemented strokes are used for pseudo time-ordering of the strokes. Directional vectors for the Bezier curve control points were used to estimate the stroke directions. If two or more segmented strokes are generated from a originally connected component and the difference of the stroke directions are less than a threshold value, then the group of strokes are combined as a single stroke as shown right image in Fig. 6.

Fig. 7 shows regenerated character strokes from the control points of approximated Bezier curve and the pseudo ordering information. The ordering of strokes is perfectly associate with actual writing orders. But the generated ordering sequence can be regulated on the characters in several proto types.

4   Summary

In this paper, we present a unified solution for efficient representation of online and offline graphic messages. The goals of the proposed method are to represent hand drawing graphic data for a unified universal symbol recognizer which can work for online and offline environment together. In order to develop the online and offline universal recognition system, common characteristics must be extracted through the generalization process.

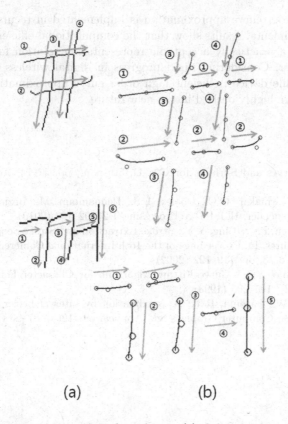

Fig. 6. Stroke segmentation and stroke ordering: (a) skeletonized strokes, (b) approximated result with pseudo stroke ordering

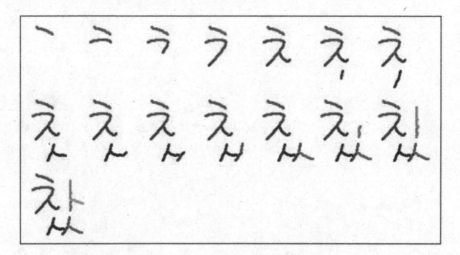

Fig. 7. An example of stroke ordering on a character image

Piecewise Bezier curve approximation is implemented in recursive architecture. The experimental results show that the computational-efficient implementation is to be a practically acceptable representation solution for online and offline recognizer. Considering rapid progress in digital wireless network and developing mobile devices, efficient high order curve approximation and optimization idea are highly desired in the near future.

References

1. Farin, G.: Curves and Surfaces for CAGD, 5th edn., pp. 57–74. Academic Press (2002)
2. Sohel, F.A., Karmakar, G.C., Dooley, L.S., Bennamoun, M.: Bezier curve-based generic shape encoder. IET Image Processing 4(2), 92–102 (2010)
3. Lau, K.K., Yuen, P.C., Tang, Y.Y.: Stroke Extraction and Stroke Sequence Estimation on Signatures. In: Proceedings of the 16th International Conference on Pattern Recognition, vol. 3, pp. 119–122 (2002)
4. Ohno, K., Ohno, Y.: A Curve Fitting Algorithm for Character Fonts. Electronic Publishing 6(3), 195–205 (1993)
5. Sederberg, T.W., Farouki, R.T.: Approximation by interval bezier curves. IEEE Transactions on Computer Graphics and Applications 12(5), 87–95 (1992)

Computing Precision and Recall with Missing or Uncertain Ground Truth

Bart Lamiroy[1] and Tao Sun[2]

[1] Université de Lorraine, LORIA, UMR 7503, Nancy, F-54502, France
Bart.Lamiroy@loria.fr
[2] Lehigh University – Computer Science and Engineering, Bethlehem, PA, USA

Abstract. In this paper we present a way to use precision and recall measures in total absence of ground truth. We develop a probabilistic interpretation of both measures and show that, provided a sufficient number of data sources are available, it offers a viable performance measure to compare methods if no ground truth is available. This paper also shows the limitations of the approach, in case a systematic bias is present in all compared methods, but shows that it maintains a very high level of overall coherence and stability. It opens broader perspectives and can be extended to handling partial or unreliable ground truth, as well as levels of prior confidence in the methods it aims to compare.

1 Introduction

Performance evaluation of information retrieval methods in a broad sense, *i.e.* globally any process associating high level information to a collection of weakly structured data often relies on comparing the output of the methods under evaluation to selected and verified data, for which the expected outcome of the methods is known (*cf.* [20] in graphical document analysis, for instance). These data are usually referred at as *ground truth*.

As long as the retrieval goals can be correctly captured and the scope of the data on which the methods must operate remains controllable, relying on ground-truth is possible [2,7]. However, when the size of the potential data space becomes unmanageable of when it becomes more controversial to fully formalize the required outcome of the methods under investigation, fixing or obtaining ground truth becomes problematic to impossible. In some cases, especially when the data sets grow to a significant size, en when the retrieval process tends to favor *precision* rather than *recall* (*cf.* next section for definitions) performance evaluation approaches may rely on sampling and statistical extrapolation [8], rather than exhaustive validation. This still requires as sufficiently large set of ground-truthed data, however. Other approaches use higher level knowledge to assess coherence patterns in classified data [3].

In this paper we approach the problem differently, by making the assumption that there is either no ground truth available, or that the available ground truth may be unreliable (for instance, coming from crowd-sourced annotation processes, for which no post-processing has been done, or scenarios where human

Y.-B. Kwon and J.-M. Ogier (Eds.): GREC, LNCS 7423, pp. 149–162, 2013.

feedback interferes with pre-established ground truth [19]). We show that by re-formulating classical performance metrics like precision and recall in probabilistic terms we can establish a ranking between competing approaches that is comparable to the one that would be obtained in presence of reliable ground-truth. In that aspect, it shares some very interesting similarities with work related to classifier fusion using majority voting [11,4]. This similarity will be addressed in Section 4.3.

Before that, and after a brief recall of the definitions of Precision and Recall in Section 2, we develop the theoretical framework of our approach in Section 3. Section 4 provides a series of experimental validations of our method and exposes some of its limitations. Further work and extensions are provided in Section 5.

2 Precision and Recall

2.1 General Definitions and Notation

Precision Pr and Recall Rc (and often associated F-measure or ROC curves) are standard metrics expressing the *quality* of Information Retrieval methods [15]. They are usually expressed with respect to a query q (or averaged over a series of queries) over a data set Δ such that:

$$Pr_q^\Delta = \frac{\left|\mathcal{P}_q^\Delta \cap \mathcal{R}_q^\Delta\right|}{\left|\mathcal{R}_q^\Delta\right|} \tag{1}$$

$$Rc_q^\Delta = \frac{\left|\mathcal{P}_q^\Delta \cap \mathcal{R}_q^\Delta\right|}{\left|\mathcal{P}_q^\Delta\right|} \tag{2}$$

where $\mathcal{P}_q^\Delta$ is the set of all documents in Δ, relevant to query q, and where $\mathcal{R}_q^\Delta$ is the set of documents actually retrieved by q. Although we can make a safe assumption by considering $\mathcal{R}_q^\Delta$ known (*i.e.* the query q can actually be executed, and returns a known, manageable set of results), the same assumption does not always hold for $\mathcal{P}_q^\Delta$, as will be shown later. For ease of reading we will refer to respectively Pr, $\mathcal{P}$, Rc, and $\mathcal{R}$, when there is no ambiguity on Δ and q.

Often both are combined in the F_β measure, where

$$F_\beta = \left(1 + \beta^2\right) \frac{Pr\,Rc}{\beta^2 Pr + Rc} \tag{3}$$

and where β expresses the importance of recall with respect to precision. Generally, $\beta = 1$, so that both are considered of equal importance.

2.2 Other Interpretations and Frameworks

Precision, Recall and the F-measure can also be defined with respect to *true positives* τ_p, *false positives* ϕ_p, *true negatives* τ_n and *false negatives* ϕ_n. In that case, the corresponding formulas are:

$$Pr = \frac{\tau_p}{\tau_p + \phi_p} \tag{4}$$

$$Rc = \frac{\tau_p}{\tau_p + \phi_n} \tag{5}$$

$$F_\beta = \frac{\left(1 + \beta^2\right)\tau_p}{\left(1 + \beta^2\right)\tau_p + \beta^2\phi_n + \phi_p} \tag{6}$$

Here again, it is necessary to know the values of τ_p, ϕ_p, τ_n and ϕ_p (as, previously, the sets $\mathcal{P}$ and $\mathcal{R}$) in order to be able to do the computations.

It is also possible to give probabilistic interpretations to Pr and Rc. In that case, Pr would be the probability that a random document retrieved by the query is relevant, and Rc that a random relevant document be retrieved by the query (taking as assumption that documents have uniform distributions). This is the interpretation we are going to use in the next sections.

3   Absence of Ground Truth

Previously enumerated metrics all made the assumption that the returns of queries can, in some way be qualified as "good" or "bad". Most often, there even is the assumption that this can actually be quantified: belonging to set $\mathcal{P}$, τ_p, etc. This implies that there is some absolute knowledge of *ground truth* or an *oracle* function available for the assessment of these quantities. While it is very convenient to rely on established truth to further train or evaluate methods, it is often very costly to obtain in many cases, and even impossible in others. Furthermore, it generally requires some human intervention or validation of some sorts, which makes the ground-truthing process both difficultly scalable and error prone, and therefore costly.

This paper presents a way to estimate precision and recall using a probabilistic model, allowing either to compare algorithms operating on the same data, without the requirement of establishing ground truth, or, to leverage crowd-sourcing to establish ground truth in presence of noise, errors and mistakes. In order to achieve this, we shall first establish the underlying assumptions to our approach, in section 3.1, defining the context in which we have conceived our model. We then develop the mathematical foundations and tools in section 3.2.

3.1   General Assumptions

In what follows we are assuming that the following general conditions and notations apply:

1. We are considering generic system $\mathcal{S}$ that, given a query q, partitions[1] a set of documents $\Delta = \{\delta_i\}_{i=1...d}$ into $\mathcal{S}^{q+}$ and $\mathcal{S}^{q-}$.

---

[1] For the absent-minded reader, *"partitioning"* Δ into $\mathcal{S}^+$ and $\mathcal{S}^-$ entails that $\Delta = \mathcal{S}^+ \cup \mathcal{S}^-$ and $\mathcal{S}^+ \cap \mathcal{S}^- = \emptyset$.

The partitioning function S^q is defined as

$$S^q : \Delta \to \{+, -\}$$
$$\delta_i \mapsto S^q(\delta_i) \tag{7}$$

S^{q+} (resp. S^{q-}) is defined as the inverse image of $\{+\}$ (resp. $\{-\}$).

2. Other systems, similar to S^q exist and their partitioning results are available. It is assumed that these systems operate in the same semantic context, and therefore aim to achieve the same partitioning as S^q. We shall refer to the set of these systems as $\Sigma^q = \{S_i^q\}_{i=1\ldots s}$

In what follows, and where it is obvious, parameter q will be omitted. Table 1 gives an example overview of what three different systems could produce for a given query over a particular document set Δ.

Table 1. Example of query systems S_i operating on document set Δ

Δ	S_1	S_2	S_3	
δ_1	+	+	+	$S_1^+ = \{\delta_1, \delta_2, \delta_4, \delta_5\}$
δ_2	+	+	+	$S_1^- = \{\delta_3, \delta_6, \delta_7\}$
δ_3	-	+	-	
δ_4	+	-	-	$S_2^+ = \{\delta_1, \delta_2, \delta_3\}$
δ_5	+	-	-	$S_2^- = \{\delta_4, \delta_5, \delta_6, \delta_7\}$
δ_6	-	-	+	
δ_7	-	-	-	$S_3^+ = \{\delta_1, \delta_2, \delta_6\}$
				$S_3^- = \{\delta_3, \delta_4, \delta_5, \delta_7\}$

3.2 Performance Evaluation

The question that arises now is how to compare different S_i and decide which one performs best. Traditionally, one would take an evaluation test set $\Delta_\star$ for which the ground truth of a query $q_\star$ is known and available. We shall refer to this ground truth as $\Delta_\star^+$ and $\Delta_\star^-$ (*i.e.* $\Delta_\star^+$ is the partition of $\Delta_\star$ containing the documents corresponding to $q_\star$, $\Delta_\star^-$ its complement). This knowledge then allows to compute precision and recall values, as described in Section 2, for all S_i and establish a performance metric adapted to the context under consideration.

When $\Delta_\star^+$ and $\Delta_\star^-$ are unavailable, it is less obvious to compare the results of the different S_i. One well documented approach is to use statistical estimators by considering each $S_i(\Delta)$ as the outcome of some random variable. What we are going to develop here, is very similar, but particularly focused on the expression of precision and recall.

Simplified Case. First we're making the assumption that all S_i are of equal importance, and that there is no *a priori* knowledge available allowing to presume some of the systems are more reliable than others. This assumption will be alleviated in later work. We also assume all documents have equal frequency and occurrence probability.

For the arguments developed next, we need to introduce two "virtual" query systems, $\mathcal{S}_\top$ and $\mathcal{S}_\perp$. $\mathcal{S}_\top$ always returns all documents for any given query, $\mathcal{S}_\perp$ never returns any. In other terms,

$$\mathcal{S}_\top^+ = \Delta, \mathcal{S}_\top^- = \emptyset \tag{8}$$

$$\mathcal{S}_\perp^+ = \emptyset, \mathcal{S}_\perp^- = \Delta \tag{9}$$

We are also slightly reconsidering the partitioning function defined in equation (7), such that it returns values in $\{1, 0\}$ rather than in $\{+, -\}$.

Under these hypotheses, the probability that a document δ_i belongs to Δ_*^+ is

$$P(\delta_i) = \frac{1}{s+2} \sum_{k=1...s,\perp,\top} S_k(\delta_i) \tag{10}$$

The results of the application of this to the example in Table 1, is represented in Table 2.

Table 2. Example

Δ	$P(\delta_i)$	$\mathcal{S}_\top$	$\mathcal{S}_1$	$\mathcal{S}_2$	$\mathcal{S}_3$	$\mathcal{S}_\perp$
δ_1	0.8	1	1	1	1	0
δ_2	0.8	1	1	1	1	0
δ_3	0.4	1	0	1	0	0
δ_4	0.4	1	1	0	0	0
δ_5	0.4	1	1	0	0	0
δ_6	0.4	1	0	0	1	0
δ_7	0.2	1	0	0	0	0

Given the hypothesis of equidestribution of all documents δ_i in Δ and given the probabilistic definition of precision in Section 2.2, stating that Pr "is the probability that a random document retrieved by a query is relevant", we can now define $Pr(\mathcal{S}_k)$:

$$Pr(\mathcal{S}_k) = \frac{\sum_{i=1...d} P(\delta_i) S_k(\delta_i)}{\sum_{i=1...d} S_k(\delta_i)} \tag{11}$$

Similarly, Rc was defined as "the probability for a random relevant document to be retrieved by the query". In our case, however relevancy has no longer a binary value, but has been replaced by $P(\delta_i)$. By reformulating this conditional probability and using Bayes' theorem (and using the fact that the inverse conditional of Rc is Pr), things smooth out elegantly.

$$Rc\left(S_k\right) = Prob\left(\text{retrievedBy}_{S_k}\left(\delta_i\right) \middle| \text{isRelevant }\left(\delta_i\right)\right)$$

$$= Prob\left(\text{isRelevant}\left(\delta_i\right) \middle| \text{retrievedBy}_{S_k}\left(\delta_i\right)\right) \frac{Prob\left(\text{retrievedBy}_{S_k}\left(\delta_i\right)\right)}{Prob\left(\text{isRelevant}\left(\delta_i\right)\right)}$$

$$= Pr\left(S_k\right) \frac{\frac{1}{d}\sum_{i=1..d} S_k\left(\delta_i\right)}{\frac{1}{d}\sum_{i=1..d} P\left(\delta_i\right)}$$

$$= \frac{\sum_{i=1...d} P\left(\delta_i\right) S_k\left(\delta_i\right)}{\sum_{i=1...d} S_k\left(\delta_i\right)} \frac{\sum_{i=1..d} S_k\left(\delta_i\right)}{\sum_{i=1..d} P\left(\delta_i\right)}$$

$$= \frac{\sum_{i=1...d} P\left(\delta_i\right) S_k\left(\delta_i\right)}{\sum_{i=1..d} P\left(\delta_i\right)} \tag{12}$$

It is interesting to notice the resemblance between equations (1) and (11) as well as between (2) and (12). Table 3 shows the values obtained when applied to the examples of Table 2.

Table 3. Example of precision and recall computations without established ground truth

Δ	$P\left(\delta_i\right)$	$S_\top$	S_1	S_2	S_3	$S_\perp$
δ_1	0.8	1	1	1	1	0
δ_2	0.8	1	1	1	1	0
δ_3	0.4	1	0	1	0	0
δ_4	0.4	1	1	0	0	0
δ_5	0.4	1	1	0	0	0
δ_6	0.4	1	0	0	1	0
δ_7	0.2	1	0	0	0	0
Sum	3.4	7	4	3	3	0
$\sum PS_k$		3.4	2.4	2	2	0
Pr		0.49	0.6	0.67	**0.67**	∞
Rc		1	**0.71**	0.59	0.59	0

4   Experimental Validation

In order to experimentally validate the model developed we have taken two contexts. One consists in taking the results of experiments reported in [10] related to comparing standard symbol recognition techniques. A second is related to evaluation of binarization algorithms on downstream treatment and is very similar to the experiments conducted in [13].

4.1   Symbol Recognition

In this section we use the experimental results reported in [10]. In this paper, the authors compare 5 different symbol recognition methods on a set of electrical wiring diagrams. Since their dataset has no known ground truth, they use a panel of human annotators to select and determine which ground truth corresponds to which query.

Since the authors in [10] report retrieval efficiency, as defined in [9], we have resampled their raw experimental data to extract precision and recall. The results, with respect to the human-defined ground-truth reported by the authors is shown in Figure 1.

Figure 2 reproduces the precision and recall values obtained using our method on the exact same data. It is interesting to note that, with one noteworthy exception, the ordering of the tested methods, with respect to precision or recall (*i.e.* when ordering methods from high precision/recall to low) is respected. Although not reproduced here, this also holds for the F-measure. What is even more compelling, is that the methods 'SC' and 'GFD' maintain their similarity in both cases, with and without consideration of ground truth.

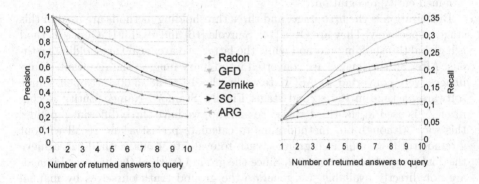

Fig. 1. Precision and Recall as reported in [10]

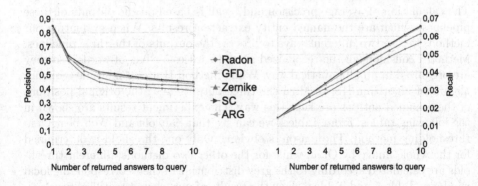

Fig. 2. Precision and Recall as computed without ground truth

The one exception is the 'ARG' method. While considered as a tie with 'SC' and 'GFD' with our method, it significantly outperforms all other approaches according to the ground truth. This is a very interesting result, and is currently under investigation.

4.2   Document Binarization

The data used in this second study are the historical images collected from the Library of Congress on-line data set[1]. A total of 60 TIF format images with a resolution of 300 dpi. Various genres from official documents to private letters are included. The degraded quality of these images, such as uneven illumination, bleeding-through, handwritten marks, *etc*, are be a great challenge for recognition algorithms. In this case, we are going to try and use our approach to evaluating binarization quality to downstream recognition, as in [13]. The document image analysis pipeline consists of three stages: binarization – OCR – named entity recognition.

Binarization is the first stage, and three thresholding methods are used in this stage respectively. They are Otsu [14], Sauvola [16] and Wolf [21]. Otsu's method is a global thresholding method while the latter two are local thresholding methods. After all the images are converted into binary images, the resultant binary images were converted to ASCII texts by the Tesseract-3.00 [17] open source software package in the second stage. Finally, Stanford Named Entity Recognizer [5] is used in the third stage. To sum up, we have three different pipelines this way. Although our method aims to calculate precision and recall without ground truth, we still need ground truth to evaluate if our method can achieve the goal proposed in Section 3.2. Since the ground truth of the historical images are not directly available, we generate the ground truth ourselves by manual typing the text and carefully proofreading.

Since the three different pipelines depend on three different thresholding methods, we use the names of them to stand for the three pipelines, respectively. The calculation of average precision and recall is based on the outputs of these pipelines, which are the named entity extraction results. When evaluating our method, we use two different ways to process the outputs of the three pipelines. Method I considers all the recognized named entities as 'bag-of-words", so they are organized in an alphabetical way. While Method II uses a multiple sequence alignment algorithm [18] to align the three outputs first, the original positions of these named entities are kept this way. The experiment results are shown in the following tables. From Table 4 we can see that Sauvola and Wolf beat Otsu thresholding method. The reason is obvious. Only one threshold is determined for the whole image by Otsu, while for the other two methods, different thresholds are calculated according to the grey distribution of their corresponding local windows. Table 5 and Table 6 show the results of our ground-truthless precision and recall measures using each of the metrics described before (Method I and II). We can see again the performance of Sauvola and Wolf is better than that of

Table 4. Average Recognition Accuracies with Ground Truth

	Otsu	Sauvola	Wolf
Precision	0.6223	0.7715	0.7533
Recall	0.5915	0.7281	0.7230

Table 5. Method I: Average Recognition Accuracies without Ground Truth

	$S^\top$	Otsu	Sauvola	Wolf	$S_\perp$
Precision	0.4000	0.6327	0.6757	0.6722	∞
Recall	1.0000	0.5153	0.5660	0.5662	0

Table 6. Method II: Average Recognition Accuracies without Ground Truth

	$S^\top$	Otsu	Sauvola	Wolf	$S_\perp$
Precision	0.5733	0.6035	0.6450	0.6416	∞
Recall	1.0000	0.6550	0.6988	0.6957	0

Otsu, while recognition accuracies between Sauvola and Wolf are similar. Both of them indicate that even if without ground truth, the precision and recall computed by our method is similar to those computed with ground truth.

4.3   Limitations

It would be an error to consider the approach developed in this paper as a complete and equivalent replacement of ground truth. Since the approach consists in finding an overall consensus between the tested methods, it is sensitive to collective bias. This is illustrated in the following example, taken from the raw data of the ICDAR 2011 contest described in [13].

The contest setup is quite similar than the one used in the previous section where its general aim is concerned. The difference lies in the fact that 24 different 4-stage pipelines are compared to one another. The document analysis pipelines consist in binarization – text segmentation – OCR and named entity detection, using 3 different binarization algorithms, 4 text segmentation methods and 2 OCRs.

As reported in [13], the tested pipeline is very sensitive to the quality of the used OCR engine. The results obtained using the 24 different execution paths, where every other path uses one of the 2 tested OCR engines, show that one of them clearly outperforms the other.

In order to compare these results with the approach developed in this paper we are not going to use raw F-Measure values, since the previous results have shown that there may be a significant difference in range. Instead, we are going to look at the ranking of the different methods with respect to their decreasing F-Measure. Using the Method I of the previous section, we obtain the results represented in Fig. 3.

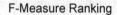
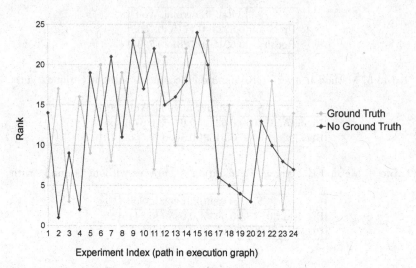

Fig. 3. Comparison of F-Measure ranking between ground truth based and ground truth-less measures

There are two observations to be made regarding these results. The first, quite puzzling one, is that although both curves follow the same global trend, they are in complete opposite phase with respect to the oscillation induced by the OCR quality. Second, a closer look at the figures shows that there is an averaging effect operating. Since both OCR engines are consistent in their errors, they introduce a bias in the consensus values computed by our method, thus pulling the F-Measures toward an average value.

By separating the results in function of the OCR, we observe that we obtain much more coherent, and more encouraging results, in line with what we observed in the previous sections. Fig. 4 shows that the overall ranking pattern is preserved when projecting the F-Measures by OCR. It is clear, on the other hand, that there is no total equivalence between the ranking obtained with ground truth and the one obtained without. However, global ranking (top – middle – bottom tiers) is very consistent.

These results very much recall the experiments reported in [11] in the case of classifier fusion. Although there are some fundamental difference in combining binary classifiers by majority voting and the approach developed here, the underlying formalism is very much the same. The main differences are that one the one hand, we are not applying a full majority vote, in our case. Although the probability of an individual document being relevant depends on the number of systems having classified it as such, and therefore relates to a voting system, this probability is not truncated to either 0 or 1, as it would have been, in the

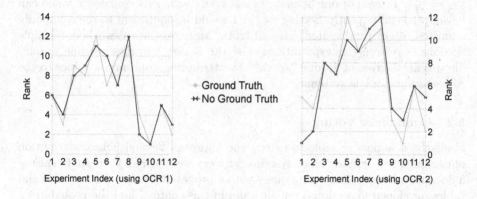

Fig. 4. Comparison of F-Measure ranking between ground truth based and ground truth-less measures in function of the underlying OCR method

case of majority voting. On the other hand, the goal of classifier fusion is to obtain a new classifier, performing better than its individual contributors. This is not the aim in our case, where we just want to express a ranking between the different classifiers. One may argue, however, that the classifier obtained by majority voting may provide a theoretical boundaries to the reliability of the probabilistic Precision and Recall values presented in the previous sections. The math behind this assumption needs to be further developed and assessed.

5   Extensions

The probabilistic model developed in section 3.2 makes the simplifying assumption that both all data and all methods have uniform confidence values: no method is considered more reliable than the others, and all data either belongs or does not belong to the query results.

5.1   Method Weighting

Our model is capable of integrating ground truth, and may even handle uncertain ground truth (*e.g.* coming from reliable, but not fully verified human annotations). To that avail, the ground truth can be integrated as being the result of some "oracle" system $S_{\mathcal{O}}$, and the probability of a document δ_i belonging to $\Delta_\star^+$, as expressed in (10) should be slightly modified.

$$P(\delta_i) = \sum_{k=1\ldots s,\perp,\top,\mathcal{O}} S_k(\delta_i)\,\kappa_{S_k} \tag{13}$$

Where κ_{S_k} is the confidence value associated to system S_k, and $\sum_k \kappa_{S_k} = 1$. In the case we previously developed, all systems had equal confidence, and

$\kappa_{S_k} = \frac{1}{s+2}$. In case of one or more oracle systems S_O, its confidence value can be adapted consequently. Setting $\kappa_{S_O} = 1$ would be equivalent to the commonly admitted use of (undisputed) ground truth. Moreover, in cases where multiple versions of reference interpretations exist [12] it now becomes possible to handle varying degrees of ground "truth"[2] by attributing appropriate values to the corresponding oracle systems.

5.2 Confidence Voting

Similarly, it is now possible to extend the approach beyond binary attribution of documents to queries, since systems can very well express their confidence of a document being relevant to a query with a probability value. All formulae and tables developed in section 3 remain valid in this context, and the probabilistic precision and recall computations are directly transposable to the case where individual documents for a given query have a probability of pertinence rather than a binary valuation. Furthermore, this can be combined with the method weighting expressed in the previous section.

6 Conclusion and Future Work

In this study we have presented how to compute precision and recall without presence of formally identified ground truth. Results indicate that this measure is coherent with real, ground truth based precision and recall measures, although it can obviously not infer ground truth and achieve the exact same performance as if ground truth were actually available.

On the other hand, the mathematical framework supporting the computation of probabilistic precision and recall has the interesting property to handle a continuum of situations ranging from perfectly known and available ground truth, over uncertain ground truth to total absence of it.

The major condition for this method to work, however, is that it has access to a number of competing systems that are providing multiple possible answers to the same queries, each of them supposedly trying to achieve the best possible result. This is particularly well suited for large scale performance evaluation contexts like the one experimented in [13] and formally developed in [12]. Its use in larger scale experiments will also contribute in further establishing the exact differences between full use of ground truth and the approximation presented in this paper.

Further work and development will consist in establishing how to rank or take into account user-contributed "partial" ground truth, especially considering "yes/no/unknown" information. Currently, our framework makes the assumption that all systems operate on the exact same set of queries and documents. There exist models that are capable of integrating overlapping or dissimilar query and document sets [6]. It would be interesting to confront them to our

---

[2] Since there cannot exist varying degrees in truth, we prefer the term of "interpretation".

approach and to study how partial ground truth (for instance, resulting from crowd-sourced contributions) can be integrated and improve overall performance of our approach.

Acknowledgements. The authors would like to acknowledge Dr. Santosh K.C. for having provided the experimental data, used in Section 4.1. They also thank Prof. Dan Lopresti for having pointed them to voting approaches in classifier fusion.

Bart Lamiroy was a visiting scientist at Lehigh University in 2010–2011. This work was conducted at the Computer Science and Engineering Department at Lehigh University and was supported in part by a DARPA IPTO grant administered by Raytheon BBN Technologies.

References

1. Library of congress, http://memory.loc.gov/
2. Antonacopoulos, A., Karatzas, D., Bridson, D.: Ground Truth for Layout Analysis Performance Evaluation. In: Bunke, H., Spitz, A.L. (eds.) DAS 2006. LNCS, vol. 3872, pp. 302–311. Springer, Heidelberg (2006)
3. Baraldi, A., Bruzzone, L., Blonda, P.: Quality assessment of classification and cluster maps without ground truth knowledge. IEEE Transactions on Geoscience and Remote Sensing 43(4), 857–873 (2005)
4. Bauer, E., Kohavi, R.: An empirical comparison of voting classification algorithms: Bagging, boosting, and variants. Machine Learning 36, 105–139 (1999)
5. Finkel, J.R., Grenager, T., Manning, C.D.: Incorporating non-local information into information extraction systems by gibbs sampling. In: ACL. The Association for Computer Linguistics (2005)
6. Goutte, C., Gaussier, E.: A Probabilistic Interpretation of Precision, Recall and F-Score, with Implication for Evaluation. In: Losada, D.E., Fernández-Luna, J.M. (eds.) ECIR 2005. LNCS, vol. 3408, pp. 345–359. Springer, Heidelberg (2005)
7. Grosicki, E., Carree, M., Brodin, J.M., Geoffrois, E.: Results of the rimes evaluation campaign for handwritten mail processing. In: 10th International Conference on Document Analysis and Recognition, ICDAR 2009, pp. 941–945 (July 2009)
8. Hauff, C., Hiemstra, D., de Jong, F., Azzopardi, L.: Relying on topic subsets for system ranking estimation. In: Proceedings of the 18th ACM Conference on Information and Knowledge Management, CIKM 2009, pp. 1859–1862. ACM, New York (2009)
9. Kankanhalli, M.S., Mehtre, B.M., Wu, J.K.: Cluster-based color matching for image retrieval. Pattern Recognition 29, 701–708 (1995)
10. Santosh, K.C., Lamiroy, B., Wendling, L.: Spatio-structural symbol description with statistical feature add-on. In: The Ninth International Workshop on Graphics Recognition (2011)
11. Kuncheva, L., Whitaker, C., Shipp, C., Duin, R.: Limits on the majority vote accuracy in classifier fusion. Pattern Analysis & Applications 6, 22–31 (2003)
12. Lamiroy, B., Lopresti, D., Korth, H., Jeff, H.: How carefully designed open resource sharing can help and expand document analysis research. In: Agam, G., Viard-Gaudin, C. (eds.) Document Recognition and Retrieval XVIII. SPIE Proceedings, vol. 7874. SPIE, San Francisco (2011)

13. Lamiroy, B., Lopresti, D., Sun, T.: Document Analysis Algorithm Contributions in End-to-End Applications. In: 11th International Conference on Document Analysis and Recognition - ICDAR 2011. International Association for Pattern Recognition, Beijing (2011)

14. Otsu, N.: A threshold selection method from gray-level histograms. IEEE Transactions on Systems, Man and Cybernetics 9(1), 62–66 (1979)

15. van Rijsbergen, C.J.: Information Retrieval. Butterworth (1979)

16. Sauvola, J.J., Pietikäinen, M.: Adaptive document image binarization. Pattern Recognition 33(2), 225–236 (2000)

17. Smith, R.: An overview of the tesseract ocr engine. In: ICDAR 2007: Proceedings of the Ninth International Conference on Document Analysis and Recognition, pp. 629–633. IEEE Computer Society (2007),
http://www.google.de/research/pubs/archive/33418.pdf

18. Thompson, J.D., Higgins, D.G., Gibson, T.J.: Clustal w: improving the sensitivity of progressive multiple sequence alignment through sequence weighting, position-specific gap penalties and weight matrix choice. Nucleic Acids Research 22(22), 4673–4680 (1994)

19. Tombre, K., Lamiroy, B.: Pattern Recognition Methods for Querying and Browsing Technical Documentation. In: Ruiz-Shulcloper, J., Kropatsch, W.G. (eds.) CIARP 2008. LNCS, vol. 5197, pp. 504–518. Springer, Heidelberg (2008)

20. Valveny, E., Dosch, P., Winstanley, A., Zhou, Y., Yang, S., Yan, L., Wenyin, L., Elliman, D., Delalandre, M., Trupin, E., Adam, S., Ogier, J.M.: A general framework for the evaluation of symbol recognition methods. International Journal on Document Analysis and Recognition 9, 59–74 (2007)

21. Wolf, C., Doermann, D.S.: Binarization of low quality text using a markov random field model. In: ICPR, vol. (3), pp. 160–163 (2002)

A Semi-automatic Groundtruthing Framework
for Performance Evaluation of Symbol Recognition
and Spotting Systems

Mathieu Delalandre, Jean-Yves Ramel, and Nicolas Sidere

Laboratory of Computer Science, François Rabelais University, Tours city, France
{firstname.lastname}@univ-tours.fr

Abstract. In this paper, we are interested with the groundtruthing problem for performance evaluation of symbol recognition & spotting systems. We propose a complete framework based on user interaction scheme through a tactile device, exploiting image processing components to achieve groundtruthing of real-life documents in an semi-automatic way. It is based on a top-down matching algorithm, to make the recognition process less sensitive to context information. We have developed a specific architecture to achieve the recognition in constraint time, working with a sub-linear complexity and with extra memory cost.

1 Introduction

This paper deals with the the performance evaluation topic. Performance evaluation is a particular cross-disciplinary research field in a variety of domains such as Information Retrieval, Computer Vision, CBIR, etc. Its purpose is to develop full frameworks in order to evaluate, to compare and to select the best-suited methods for a given application. Two main tasks are usually identified: groundtruthing, which provides the reference data to be used in the evaluation, and performance characterization, which determines how to match the results of the system with the groundtruth to give different measures of the performance.

In this work, we are interested with the groundtruthing problem for performance evaluation of symbol recognition & spotting systems. We propose a complete framework based on user interaction scheme through a tactile device, exploiting image processing components to achieve groundtruthing of real-life documents in an semi-automatic way. In the rest of the paper, section 2 will present related work on this topic. Then, in section 3 we will introduce our approach. Section 4 will report our conclusions and perspectives about this work.

2 Related Works

Groundtruthing systems can be considered according three main approaches: automatic (i.e. synthetic), manual and semi-automatic. Concerning performance evaluation of symbol recognition & spotting, most of the proposed systems are automatic [2]. In these systems, the test documents are generated by a generation methods which combines

Y.-B. Kwon and J.-M. Ogier (Eds.): GREC, LNCS 7423, pp. 163–172, 2013.

pre-defined models of document components in a pseudo-random way. Performance evaluation is then defined in terms of generation methods and degradation models to apply. The automatic systems present several interesting properties for performance evaluation (reliability, high semantic content, complete control of content, short delay and low cost, etc.). However, the data generated by these systems still appears quite artificial. Final evaluation of systems should be completed by the use of real data to proof, disprove and complete conclusions obtained from synthetic documents.

Semi-automatic and manual systems deal with the groundtruth extraction from real-life documents. At best of our knowledge only the systems described in [8,3] have been proposed to date for performance evaluation of symbol recognition & spotting, and both of these systems are manual. In [8], the authors employ an annotation tool to groundtruth floorplan images. The groundtruth is defined in terms of RoI[1] and class names. Such an approach remains quite subjective and few reliable due to image ambiguities and errors introduced by human operators. In addition, the obtained groundtruth is defined "a minima" i.e. only rough localization and class names are considered.

The EPEIRES[2] platform [3] is a manual groundtruthing framework working in a collaborative fashion. It is based on on two components: a GUI to edit the groundtruth connected to an information system. The operators obtain from the system the images to annotate and the associated symbol models. The groundtruthing is performed by mapping (moving, rotating and scaling) transparent bounded models on the document using the GUI. The information system allows to collaboratively validate the groundtruth. Experts check the groundtruth generated by the operator by emitting alerts in the case of errors. The major challenge of such a platform is at community level, to federate people in using it. Indeed, the groundtruthing process is time consuming due to the user-interaction with the GUI and the additional validation steps. Due to these constraints, no "significant" datasets have been constituted to date using this platform [2].

A way to solve the limitation of manual systems is semi-automatic groundtruthing [5]. This approach is popular in the field of DIA[3], systems have been proposed for performance evaluation of chart recognition [5], handwriting recognition [4] and layout analysis [6]. Major challenge of these systems is the design of image processing components able to support the groundtruthing process and the user-interaction. Such components are application dependent, and at best of our knowledge none has been proposed to date to support performance evaluation symbol recognition & spotting. This paper presents a contribution on this topic, we present our approach in next section.

3   Our Approach

3.1   Introduction

Our system uses a mixture of auto-processing steps and human inputs. User interaction is done through a tactile device (e.g. smartphone, tablet or tactile screen). Then, for

---

[1] Region of Interest.

[2] http://www.epeires.org/

[3] Document Image Analysis.

every symbol on the document it is asked to the user to outline it in a roughly way. Specific image and recognition processings are then called to recognize & localize the symbol automatically. In the case of miss-recognition, the user can correct the result manually based on results display. Otherwise, implicit validation is obtained when no correction is observed. At last, groundtruth is exported including the class name, the location and the graphics primitives composing the symbols. With this approach, we constraint the user to outline individually each symbol. We didn't consider the automatic spotting methods [8] to gain in robustness. However, due to the support of automatic processings, recognition and positioning of a symbol could be done in a couple of seconds.

Regarding the user-interaction scheme defined above, auto-processing for semi-automatic groundtruthing must deal automatic recognition and positioning of symbols in context. These symbols are obtained following roughly outlines of users. To support the production of groundtruth, the auto-processing must be robust enough and work in constraint time to allow a fluent user-interaction. We propose here a specific system with algorithms that support these constraints. Our recognition & positioning approach is top-down i.e. symbol models will be matched to the RoIs describing symbols for better robustness to context elements. In addition, we define it as partially invariant to scale and rotation change and constraint users on providing rough approximation of scale and rotation parameters (i.e. size and direction of RoI). The full process works with a sub-linear complexity and with an extra memory cost. The Fig. 1 presents the general architecture our system. This one is composed of three main blocks: indexing of models (1), indexing of the drawings (2), and then positioning & matching process (3). We will briefly present each of them in next subsections 3.2, 3.3 and 3.4.

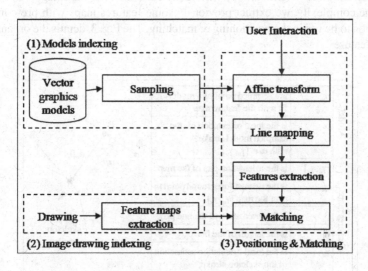

Fig. 1. Architecture of our system

3.2 Indexing of Symbol Models

To support our matching and positioning step, our models are given in a vector graphics form. We complete this representation by applying a sampling process in order to extract a set of representative points of symbol models (Fig. 2). We set this sampling process with sampling frequency f_s. This frequency fixes the number of points n to extract and their inter-distance gap T. The parameter L corresponds to the sum of lengths of vector graphics primitives composing the symbol. Like this, this process will respect an unique inter-distance gap T for all the symbol models. The number of points n will change regarding the number and length of primitives composing the symbol. The frequency parameter has a minimum $\frac{1}{L}$ (i.e. two points at least for a line).

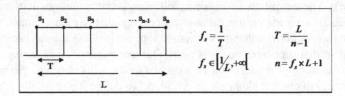

$$f_s = \frac{1}{T} \qquad T = \frac{L}{n-1}$$

$$f_s \in \left[\frac{1}{L}, +\infty \right[\qquad n = f_s \times L + 1$$

Fig. 2. Sampling process

3.3 Indexing of Drawing Images

Our matching and positioning step will exploit on one side the sampled models, and in the other side the neighbourhood information available on the images. In order to reduce the complexity, we extract previously some features maps with pre-computed information to be use in the positioning & matching. The Fig. 3. details the organization of these features.

Model	p_i	is a sampled point of a model to fir with the feature map
	α	is the local orientation of the sampled model stroke with $\alpha \in [\gamma_u, \gamma_v]$
Features map	$[\gamma_u, \gamma_v]$	is the orientation gap of the map
	q_k	is the nearest foreground point to p_i in the map $[\gamma_u, \gamma_v]$
	β_i	is the orientation of the line p_i, q_k
	d_i	is the length of the line p_i, q_k
	γ_k	is the local orientation estimation of the skeleton stroke, with $\gamma_k \in [\gamma_u, \gamma_v]$

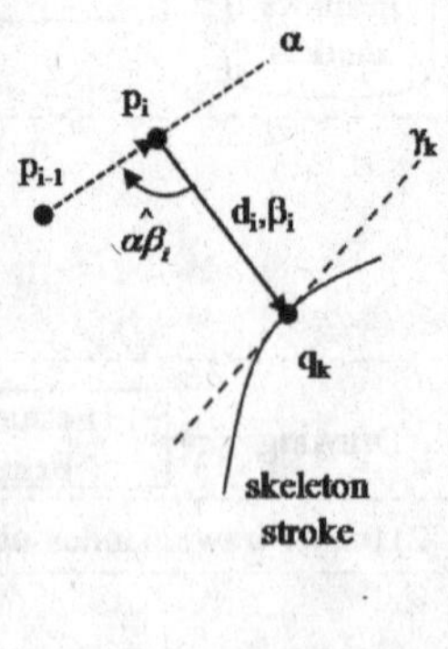

Fig. 3. Extracted features

For a given sampled point p_i of a symbol model, to fit with the features maps, we exploit the α value corresponding to the local orientation of the model stroke that it composes. This value α drives the selection of a features map $[\gamma_u, \gamma_v]$, such as $\alpha \in [\gamma_u, \gamma_v]$. The reading of the pixel p_i will provide directly the features $\{d_i, \beta_i, \gamma_k\}$, corresponding respectively to the distance, the direction and the local orientation estimation of the nearest foreground point q_k in this map.

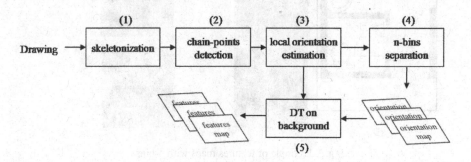

Fig. 4. Computation of features maps

To extract these features maps, we employ the image processing chain presented in Fig. 4. This chain is executed off-line. It is composed of five main steps:

1. The first step is a skeletonization. The key goal is to adapt the drawing image to the sampled representation of our models. We use the algorithm detailed in [1], as it is well adapted for scaling and rotation variations.
2. In this step, we detect the chain-points composing the skeleton's strokes. We chains and separates them from the junction and end points composing the rest of the skeleton. It is achieved using the method described in [7]. Chain-point are stored as Freeman code for further processing in steps 3 and 4.
3. For every chain-point, we compute a local direction estimation. This estimation is done using the chain code of a local neighborhood within a $m \times m$ mask. Local tangent values are computed within the mask from the central pixel to the "up" and "down" chains. The direction estimation is the average of these values.
4. In the step 4, we process the chain points with their direction estimations by a n-bins separation algorithm. This algorithm aims to build-up the orientation maps, that are root versions of our features maps. It stores every point q_k of local orientation estimation γ_k in the map $[\gamma_u, \gamma_v]$, such as $\gamma_k \in [\gamma_u, \gamma_v]$. The parameter n controls the number of maps, and then fixes the extra memory cost of our approach.
5. In a final step, we apply a Distance Transform (DT) on each orientation map. The DT algorithm is applied on the background part, in order to propagate the d_i features (Fig. 3) to every background pixels. We have "tuned" this algorithm to propagate the β_i and γ_k values to each foreground point.

Fig. 5. gives an example of features maps computation. The processed image is given on the left part of the Fig. 5, and the obtained features maps on the right. In the features maps, the dark zones correspond to the lowest distances and the light-gray zones to the highest ones. The filled gray sections in the half circles, right to the maps, indicate the orientations of every maps.

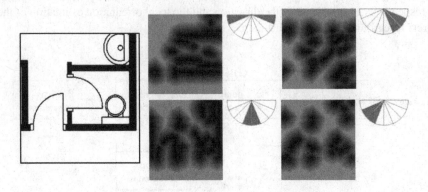

Fig. 5. Example of features maps with 4-bins

3.4   Positioning and Matching

In a final last step, we exploit the indexed model database and the features maps to achieve the positioning & matching of symbols. As presented in Fig. 1. this process relies on four main steps: affine transform, line mapping, features extraction and matching. We will present each of them in next subsections.

Affine Transform. Affine transform is the basic operation to take benefit of localization information provided by the users. When a user defines a RoI, the sampled models are fit within that RoI using some affine transform based operations. These operations exploit standard computational geometry methods resulting in shifting, scaling and then orientation change of symbol models with their sampled points.

Line Mapping. In a next step we achieved a line mapping process Fig. 6. The key goal is to map the strokes composing the model with pixels on the image corresponding to straight lines. This process exploits the features maps computed previously, the local orientations α of the models' strokes are used to drive their selection Fig. 6 (a). In order to be less sensitive to the quantification of features maps, we employ in addition a parameter ϱ such as $[\alpha - \varrho, \alpha + \varrho] \in [\gamma_u, \gamma_v]$. When a multiple selection of maps is observed, the shortest Euclidean distances d_i are considered for selection of q_k Fig. 3.

The sampled points of models are discretized to obtain coordinates and then access the features $\{d_i, \beta_i, \gamma_k\}$ stored in the maps, with an access cost of $o(1)$. Then, we compute for every pair of points p_i the $\triangle d_i$ value Eq. (1). In this equation, i and $i + 1$ are the indexes of two successive sampled points p_i, p_{i+1} of the model stroke, and $\triangle d_i$ the difference between their d_i and d_{i+1} features.

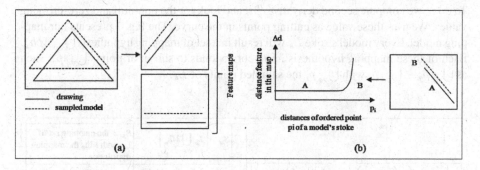

Fig. 6. Line mapping (a) selection of features maps (b) computation of $\triangle d_i$ with line shifting

As shown in Fig. 6 (b), shifting between model and image lines will result in increasing values of $\triangle d_i$. Here, the area B corresponds to increasing distances whereas the area A remains constant. To solve this problem, we tuned the computation of $\triangle d_i$ into $\triangle_\beta d_i$ Eq. (2). This equation combines the distance d_i and the line orientation β_i in such a namer that $\triangle_\beta d_i$ will will not be impacted by shifting. To do it, we compute direct angle value $\widehat{\alpha\beta_i}$ between vector $\overrightarrow{p_{i-1},p_i}$ and $\overrightarrow{p_i,q_k}$ Fig. 4. Direct angle takes into consideration the left and right positions between $\overrightarrow{p_{i-1},p_i}$, $\overrightarrow{p_i,q_k}$ with $\widehat{\alpha\beta_i} \in [0, 2\pi]$. We exploit the $\widehat{\alpha\beta_i}$ value through a φ function Eq. (3) to support the opposite detection cases (i.e. parallel lines at a same distance of the stroke, but on the left and right sides). At the end, the $\triangle_\beta d_i$ curve will present the following properties:

- strict parallel lines,
  $\forall i \, \triangle_\beta d_i \rightarrow 0$
- slightly orientation gap between the lines,
  $\forall i \, \triangle_\beta d_i \rightarrow K$
- local curvature modification on the image line,
  the $\triangle_\beta d_i$ curve will have a non null tangent
- one-to-many mapping,
  the $\triangle_\beta d_i$ curve will present pick values

$$\triangle d_i = d_i - d_{i+1} \tag{1}$$

$$\triangle_\beta d_i = d_i \sin(\varphi(\widehat{\alpha\beta_i})) - d_{i+1} \sin(\varphi(\widehat{\alpha\beta_{i+1}})) \tag{2}$$

$$\widehat{\alpha\beta_i} < pi \qquad \varphi(\widehat{\alpha\beta_i}) = \widehat{\alpha\beta_i} \tag{3}$$
$$\widehat{\alpha\beta_i} > pi \qquad \varphi(\widehat{\alpha\beta_i}) = -(2\pi - \widehat{\alpha\beta_i})$$

Following the computation of $\triangle_\beta d_i$ for a given model stroke, we perform a mathematical analysis on the obtained curve to determinate the mapping hypothesis. The key objective is to detect the tangent variations in the curve, every mapping hypothesis will correspond to a zone of the $\triangle_\beta d_i$ curve where no tangent variations will be observed.

To do it, we compute second derivate $\triangle''_\beta d_i$ and look for the non-null and zero-crossing values. We uses these value as cutting points in the curve. The Fig. 7 presents our mapping model. Every model stroke L_k will result in a set of mapping hypothesis $\bigcup_{\forall p} Mh_p$. Each of these mapping hypothesis Mh_p corresponds to subset of points $\bigcup_{\forall j} p_j$, such as $\bigcup_{\forall j} p_j \in \bigcup_{\forall i} p_i$ with $\bigcup_{\forall i} p_i$ the sampled points of L_k.

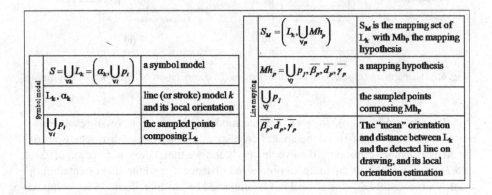

Symbol model	$S = \bigcup_{\forall k} L_k = \left(\alpha_k, \bigcup_{\forall i} p_i \right)$	a symbol model
	L_k, α_k	line (or stroke) model k and its local orientation
	$\bigcup_{\forall i} p_i$	the sampled points composing L_k

Line mapping	$S_M = \left(L_k, \bigcup_{\forall p} Mh_p \right)$	S_M is the mapping set of L_k with Mh_p the mapping hypothesis
	$Mh_p = \bigcup_{\forall j} p_j, \overline{\beta_p}, \overline{d_p}, \overline{\gamma_p}$	a mapping hypothesis
	$\bigcup_{\forall j} p_j$	the sampled points composing Mh_p
	$\overline{\beta_p}, \overline{d_p}, \overline{\gamma_p}$	The "mean" orientation and distance between L_k and the detected line on drawing, and its local orientation estimation

Fig. 7. Mapping model

Features Extraction. Thereafter, we complete our mapping model with $\overline{\beta_p}, \overline{d_p}, \overline{\gamma_p}$ features, corresponding respectively to the orientation and distance between L_k and the detected line on the drawing, and its local orientation estimation. These features are based on the computation of the $\overline{\triangle_\beta d_j p}$ value of the mapping hypothesis Mh_p, as detailed in Eq. (4). Then, this value $\overline{\triangle_\beta d_j p}$ allows to extract the $\overline{\varepsilon_{\alpha_p}}$ corresponding to the direction gap between L_k and the detected line on drawing as shown in Fig. 8. It is computed as detailed in Eq. (4), using the inter-distance gap T parameter of the sampling process (see section 3.1). Then, $\overline{\beta_p}$ and $\overline{\gamma_p}$ are obtained from $\overline{\varepsilon_{\alpha_p}}$ as detailed in Eq. (5). At last, $\overline{d_p}$ is obtained from Eq. (6), with $\hat{D}$ the estimation of mean distance between L_k and the detected line Fig. 8.

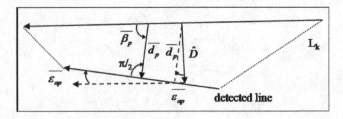

Fig. 8. Computation of mapping features $\overline{\beta_p}, \overline{d_p}, \overline{\gamma_p}$

$$\overline{\triangle_\beta d_j}p = \frac{1}{n}\sum_{j=1}^{n}\triangle_\beta d_j \qquad \overline{\varepsilon_{\alpha_p}} = \arctan\left(\frac{T}{\overline{\triangle_\beta d_i}p}\right) \tag{4}$$

$$\overline{\gamma_p} = \alpha + \overline{\varepsilon_{\alpha_p}} \qquad \overline{\beta_p} = \overline{\gamma_p} + \frac{\pi}{2} \tag{5}$$

$$\overline{d_p} = \widehat{D} \times \cos(\overline{\varepsilon_{\alpha_p}}) \qquad \widehat{D} = \frac{1}{n}\sum_{j=1}^{n}d_j\sin(\widehat{\alpha\beta_j}) \tag{6}$$

Matching. Our final step is matching; it is based on the mapping hypothesis and their associated features $\overline{\beta_p}, \overline{d_p}$. This matching looks for the standard variations of features $\sigma_{\widetilde{\beta}}, \sigma_{\widetilde{d}}$, as a perfected mapping results in null values. Global scores are proposed at symbol level, applying a weighting to take into account the coverage of mapping hypothesis.

For a mapping set S_M Fig. 7, we compute weights w_p for every mapping hypothesis Mh_p as detailed in Eq. (7). We use these weights to compute the weighted mean values $\widetilde{f_{S_M}}$ and the standard deviation $\sigma_{\widetilde{f_{S_M}}}$ as detailed in Eq. (8), where f could be either the feature $\overline{\beta_p}$ or either the feature $\overline{d_p}$. We repeat the computation of weights w_k for every stroke L_k at the symbol model level Eq. (9). Global scores are provided by a features vector $\left(\sigma_{\widetilde{\beta_S}}, \sigma_{\widetilde{d_S}}\right)$ computed as detailed in Eq. (9), where $f = (\overline{\beta_p}, \overline{d_p})$. The best matching is the one resulting in the smallest vector when comparing every models. The implicit validation of symbol is done when the user releases the tactile screen. Otherwise the matching process is repeated for every models and the display results are refreshed.

$$w_p = \frac{j}{i} \qquad Mh_p = \bigcup_{\forall j}p_j \in \bigcup_{\forall i}p_i \tag{7}$$

$$\widetilde{f_{S_M}} = \sum_{\forall p}w_p \times \overline{f_p} \qquad \sigma_{\widetilde{f_{S_M}}} = \sqrt{\sum_{\forall p}w_p \times \left(\overline{f_p} - \widetilde{f_{S_M}}\right)^2} \tag{8}$$

$$w_k = \frac{i_k}{\sum_{\forall k}i_k} \qquad \sigma_{\widetilde{fs}} = \sum_{\forall k}w_k \times \sigma_{\widetilde{f_{S_M}}}^k \tag{9}$$

4 Conclusion and Perspectives

In this paper, we have proposed a complete framework for semi-automatic groundtruthing for performance evaluation of symbol recognition & spotting systems. This one uses a mixture of auto-processing steps and human inputs based on a tactile device. It employs a top-down matching algorithm, to make the recognition process less sensitive to context information. The proposed algorithm is partially invariant to scale and rotation change, constraining users only in rough definition of RoI. The full process works with a sub-linear complexity, allowing like this a fluent user-interaction. This is a work in progress opening different main perspectives. In a near future, our main challenges are the support of arc primitives, final alignement of symbols and complete performance evaluation of our system.

References

1. Baja, G.D.: Well-shaped, stable, and reversible skeletons from the (3,4)-distance transform. Journal of Visual Communication and Image Representation 5(1), 107–115 (1994)
2. Delalandre, M., Valveny, E., Lladós, J.: Performance evaluation of symbol recognition and spotting systems: An overview. In: Workshop on Document Analysis Systems (DAS), pp. 497–505 (2008)
3. Dosch, P., Valveny, E.: Report on the Second Symbol Recognition Contest. In: Liu, W., Lladós, J. (eds.) GREC 2005. LNCS, vol. 3926, pp. 381–397. Springer, Heidelberg (2006)
4. Fischer, A., et al.: Ground truth creation for handwriting recognition in historical documents. In: International Workshop on Document Analysis Systems (DAS), pp. 3–10 (2010)
5. Huang, W., Tan, C.-L., Zhao, J.: Generating Ground Truthed Dataset of Chart Images: Automatic or Semi-automatic? In: Liu, W., Lladós, J., Ogier, J.-M. (eds.) GREC 2007. LNCS, vol. 5046, pp. 266–277. Springer, Heidelberg (2008)
6. Okamoto, M., Imai, H., Takagi, K.: Performance evaluation of a robust method for mathematical expression recognition. In: International Conference on Document Analysis and Recognition (ICDAR), pp. 121–128 (2001)
7. Popel, D.V.: Compact Graph Model of Handwritten Images: Integration into Authentification and Recognition. In: Caelli, T.M., Amin, A., Duin, R.P.W., Kamel, M.S., de Ridder, D. (eds.) SSPR&SPR 2002. LNCS, vol. 2396, pp. 272–280. Springer, Heidelberg (2002)
8. Rusiñol, M., Lladós, J.: A performance evaluation protocol for symbol spotting systems in terms of recognition and location indices. International Journal on Document Analysis and Recognition (IJDAR) 12(2), 83–96 (2009)

The 2012 Music Scores Competitions: Staff Removal and Writer Identification

Alicia Fornés, Anjan Dutta, Albert Gordo, and Josep Lladós

Computer Vision Center - Dept. of Computer Science,
Universitat Autònoma de Barcelona, Edifici O
08193, Bellaterra, Spain
{afornes,adutta,agordo,josep}@cvc.uab.es

Abstract. Since there has been a growing interest in the analysis of handwritten music scores, we have tried to foster this interest by proposing in ICDAR and GREC two different competitions: Staff removal and Writer identification. Both competitions have been tested on the CVC-MUSCIMA database of handwritten music score images. In the corresponding ICDAR publication, we have described the ground-truth, the evaluation metrics, the participants' methods and results. As a result of the discussions with attendees in ICDAR and GREC concerning our music competition, we decided to propose a new experiment for an extended competition. Thus, this paper is focused on this extended competition, describing the new set of images and analyzing the new results.

Keywords: competition, graphics recognition, music scores, writer identification, staff removal.

1 Introduction

In the last years, there has been a growing interest in the analysis of handwritten music scores [1,2,3]. In this context, the focus of interest is two-fold: the recognition of handwritten music scores (Optical Music Recognition), and the identification (or verification) of the authorship of an anonymous music score.

In the Optical Music Recognition systems, staff removal algorithms have attracted many researchers [4,5,6], since a good detection and removal of the staff lines will allow the correct segmentation of the musical symbols, and consequently, will ease the correct recognition and classification of the music symbols.

Concerning writer identification in music scores, some approaches have been proposed in the last decade [7,8,9]. It must be said that musicologists must work very hard to identify the writer of an unknown manuscript. In fact, they do not only perform a musicological analysis of the composition (melody, harmony, rhythm, etc), but also analyze the handwriting style. In this sense, writer identification can be performed by analyzing the shape of the hand-drawn music symbols (e.g. music notes, clefs, accidentals, rests, etc), because it has been shown that the author's handwriting style that characterizes a piece of text is also present in a graphic document.

Y.-B. Kwon and J.-M. Ogier (Eds.): GREC, LNCS 7423, pp. 173–186, 2013.
© Springer-Verlag Berlin Heidelberg 2013

In order to foster the interest in the analysis of handwritten music scores, we have proposed at ICDAR (International Conference on Document Analysis and Recognition) and GREC (International Workshop on Graphics Recognition) two different competitions: Staff removal and Writer Identification. Both competitions have been tested on the CVC-MUSCIMA[1] database [10]. The CVC-MUSCIMA database has been designed for musical scores analysis and recognition. It consists of 1,000 handwritten music score images, written by 50 different musicians. Each writer has transcribed exactly the same 20 music pages, using the same pen and paper.

Details on these two competitions (ground-truth, metrics, participants' methods and results) can be found in the corresponding ICDAR publication [11]. In this paper, however, we would like to focus on the extended competition on staff removal that has been organized after ICDAR and GREC. In fact, during ICDAR and GREC, we received interesting feedback from researchers in music analysis. One of the most common suggestions was to use combinations of distortions for further staff removal competitions. As a result, we decided to generate a new set of images and ask the participants on the staff removal task to participate.

The rest of the paper is organized as follows. Firstly, we will briefly describe the music scores competition proposed in ICDAR and GREC. The writer identification competition is described in Section 2 and 3 describes the staff removal competition. Afterwards, Section 4 is devoted to the extended staff removal competition, describing the new set of images and analyzing the results obtained by the participant's methods. Finally, Section 5 concludes the paper.

2   Writer Identification Competition

For the writer identification competition, the CVC-MUSCIMA dataset [10] is equally divided in two parts, where 500 images (10 images from each writer) were used for training, and 500 images were used for testing. We have provided images without the staff lines, because they are particularly useful here: since most writer identification methods remove the staff lines in the preprocessing stage, this eases the publication of results which are not dependent on the performance of the particular staff removal technique applied. Moreover, these images (see Fig.1) make easy the participation of researchers that do not work on staff removal. The staff lines were initially removed using color cues and manually checked for correcting errors (see more details in [10]).

2.1   Participants

In this subsection, we will describe the methods submitted by the participants.

PRIP02. These methods were submitted by Abdelâali Hassaïne and Somaya Al-Ma'adeed from the Pattern Recognition and Image Processing Research Group of Qatar University; and Ahmed Bouridane from Northumbria University. The authors submitted three methods:

---

[1] http://www.cvc.uab.es/cvcmuscima

Fig. 1. Example of image without staff lines

- PRIP02-edges: The first one uses the edge-based directional probability distribution features (see [13]).
- PRIP02-grapheme: The second one uses grapheme features, described in [14].
- PRIP02-combination: The third method combines both kinds of features, edge-based and grapheme features.

These methods have previously been applied for Arabic writer identification and for signature verification and have shown interesting results. The classification step is performed either using a logistic regression classifier or a k-nearest neighbour algorithm.

TUA03. These methods were submitted by Chawki Djeddi from the Mathematics and Computer Science Department of the Cheikh Larbi Tebessi University, Tebessa, Algeria; and Labiba Souici-Meslati from the LRI Laboratory, Computer Science Department of the Badji Mokhtar University, Annaba, Algeria.

The methods compute run-lengths features, which are determined on the binary image taking into consideration the pixels corresponding to the ink trace. The probability distribution of white run-lengths has been used in the writer identification experiments. There are four scanning methods: horizontal, vertical, left-diagonal and right-diagonal. They calculate the runs-lengths features using the grey level run-length matrices and the histogram of run-lengths is normalized and interpreted as a probability distribution. For further details, see [16].

For the classification step, the authors have used five different approaches:

- TUA03-5NN: A 5 nearest neighbor classifier with cityblock Distance Metric.
- TUA03-SVMOAO: Support Vector Machine (SVM One against one).
- TUA03-SVMOAA: Support Vector Machine (SVM One against all).

- TUA03-MLP: Multilayer perceptron (MLP).
- TUA03-Combination: A combination of the four previous classifiers. The combination rule used is Majority Vote.

2.2   Metrics and Results

A musical score will be considered as correctly classified if the writer decided by the algorithm is the same as the ground-truthed one. The evaluation metric will be the Writer Identification rate *W.I.*, which corresponds to the number of correctly identified documents divided by the total amount of documents:

$$\text{W.I.rate} = 100 \cdot \frac{\text{number of correctly identified documents}}{500} \tag{1}$$

The results of the different methods are shown in Table 1. One can see that most methods obtain a writer identification rate of about 65%. We can see that the best methods are PRIP02-combination and TUA03-SVMOAA, which indeed obtain very similar results (77% and 76.6% respectively). These results are obtained after the combination of different sets of features (PRIP02), or several classifiers (in case of TUA03).

Table 1. Writer Identification results. Number of correctly identified images and the final Writer Identification (W.I.) rate in %.

Method	Correct/Total	W.I.rate (%)
PRIP02-edges	327/500	65.4
PRIP02-grapheme	319/500	63.8
PRIP02-combination	385/500	**77.0**
TUA03-5NN	267/500	53.4
TUA03-MPL	324/500	64.8
TUA03-SVMOAA	383/500	**76.6**
TUA03-SVMOAO	333/500	66.6
TUA03-combination	352/500	70.4
Specific IJDAR	425/500	**85**

It must be said that in the CVCMUSCIMA publication [10], the reference writer identification rate is about 85%. These results are obtained using a specific writer identification method for music scores, which is based on the bag-of-notes approach described in [15]. In addition, the authors of [17] demonstrate that their specific method also obtains better results than some writer identification methods for roman text documents that are adapted for music scores.

Since the competition results reported here are obtained by adapting writer identification methods for arabic documents, we could conclude that specific methods might be the best choice. In summary, all these results demonstrate that the identification of the writer in graphical documents (such as music scores) is still challenging, and more research must be done.

3   Staff Removal Competition

For testing the robustness of the staff removal algorithms, we have applied the following distortion models (see Fig.2) to the original images: degradation with Kanungo noise, rotation, curvature, staffline interruption, typeset emulation, staffline y-variation, staffline thickness ratio, staffline thickness variation and white speckles. Two of these models (staffline y-variation and staffline thickness variation) are applied twice with different parameters. See [10] for details.

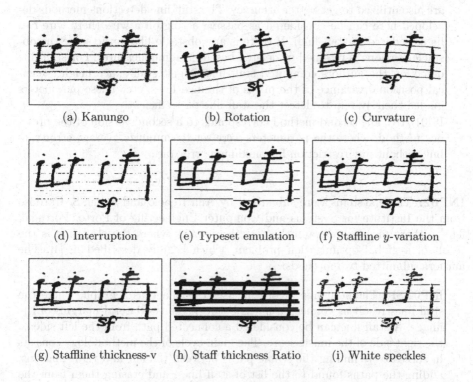

(a) Kanungo   (b) Rotation   (c) Curvature

(d) Interruption   (e) Typeset emulation   (f) Staffline y-variation

(g) Staffline thickness-v   (h) Staff thickness Ratio   (i) White speckles

Fig. 2. Examples of Staff deformations

As a result, we have obtained 11,000 distorted images, with together with the originals yield a total of 12,000 images. For the staff removal competition the entire dataset is equally divided into two parts, of which the first 50% of the images (500 images x 12 variations = 6000 images) will be used as training the algorithms and the other 6000 images will be used for testing them.

3.1 Participants

In this subsection, we will shortly describe the participants' methods.

ISI01. This system was submitted by Jit Ray Chowdhury and Umapada Pal from the Computer Vision and Pattern Recognition Unit of the Indian Statistical Institute, Kolkata, India. The authors submitted two versions of the algorithm:

- ISI01-Rob: First, the images are thinned and, by analyzing the thinned portions, the input images are automatically categorized in two groups: (a) images containing straight staff line and (b) other non-straight or curved staff-lines. Images containing straight staff lines are further divided into horizontal staff lines and non-horizontal straight lines. Next, staff lines are detected based on the characteristics of each group. Some smoothing techniques are also utilized to get better accuracy. The staff line detections methods developed here can be considered as passing a ring on a wire (here wire can be considered as staff-line). If there is any obstacle like music score the obstacle portions is retained or deleted based on some measures. For staff-line detection the authors computed staff line height, staff space height, vertical positional variance of the pixels of thinned lines, etc. These parameters guided their system to detect the staff line part efficiently.
- ISI01-HA: The second method corresponds to a second version of the previous method, where the parameters were set to minimize average error rate but without any restriction for maximum error rate.

INP02. These systems were submitted by Ana Rebelo and Jaime S. Cardoso from the Institute for Systems and Computer Engineering of Porto, Portugal. The authors propose a graph-theoretic framework where the staff line is the result of a global optimization problem, which is fully described in [4]. The authors submitted two methods:

- INP02-SP: The staff line algorithm uses the image as a graph, where the staff lines result as connected paths between the two lateral margins of the image. A staff line can be considered a connected path from the left side to the right side of the music score. The main cycle of the methodology consists in successively finding the stable paths between the left and right margins, adding the paths found to the list of staff lines, and erasing them from the image. To stop the iterative staff line search, a sequence of rules is used to validate the stable paths found; if none of them passes the checking, the iterative search is stopped. A path is discarded if it does not have a percentage of black pixels above a fixed threshold. Likewise, a path is discarded if its shape differs too much from the shape of the line with median blackness. After the main search step, valid staff lines are post-processed. The algorithm eliminates spurious lines and cluster them in staves. Finally, lines are smoothed and can be trimmed.

– INP02-SPTrim: In this version, the aim is to eliminate the initial white pixels of the paths. Hence, for each staff, a sequence of median colours is computed as follows: for each column, the median of the colours (black and white values) of the lines is added to the sequence. Next, the trimming points are found on this sequence: starting on the centre, we traverse the sequence to the left and right until a run of $whiterun = 2 \cdot staffspaceheight$ white pixels is found. The pixels between the left and right runs are kept in the staff lines. The weight function was designed to favour the black pixels of the staff lines. Hence, the function assigns high costs for white pixels and black pixels of the music symbols.

NUS03. This method was submitted by Bolan Su from the School of Computing of the National University of Singapore; Shijian Lu from the Institute for Infocomm Research, Singapure; Umapada Pal from the Computer Vision and Pattern Recognition Unit of the Indian Statistical Institute, India; and Chew-Lim Tan from the School of Computing of the National University of Singapore.

The method consists in the following: First the staff height and staff space are estimated using the histogram of vertical run length. Those staff lines are assumed parallel, then the estimated staff height and space are used to predict the lines' direction and fit an approximate staff line curve for each image. The fitted staff line curve can be used to identify the actual location of staff lines on the image. Then those pixels who belong to staff lines are removed.

NUG04. These systems were submitted by Christoph Dalitz and Andreas Kitzig from the Niederrhein University of Applied Sciences, Institute for Pattern Recognition (iPattern), Krefeld, Germany. They submitted three different systems:

– NUG04-Fuji: The method identifies long horizontal runs as staffline candidates. To allow for possible curvature, the image is in a preprocessing step deskewed by alignment of vertical strips based on their projection correlation. This however only works for a very limited range of curvature or rotation. For more details on the Fujinaga's approach, see [12]. The source code is available in the website: *http://music-staves.sourceforge.net/* (class $MusicStaves\_rl\_fujinaga$).

– NUG04-LTr: The method simply removes all vertical runs shorter than $2 *$ $staffline - height$ around a found staff line. The $staffline - height$ is measured as the most frequent black vertical runlength. The staff finding is done by vertically thinning long horizontal runs with an average blackness above a certain threshold, vertically linking these filaments based upon their vertical distance and then identifying staff systems as connected subgraphs. The first step of identifying long horizontal dark windows makes this method inappropriate for strongly curved stafflines. For more details, see [5] (Section 3.1, method "Linetrack Height" with the staff finder described at the end of section 2). The source code is available in the website: *http://music-staves.sourceforge.net/* (class $MusicStaves\_linetracking$).

– NUG04-Skel: The method directly discriminates staff segments from musical symbols. It is based on splitting the skeleton image at branching and corner points and building a graph with vertical and horizontal links from those segments fulfilling heuristic rules that make them likely to be staffline segments. As the horizontal linking is based on extrapolation, this method fails for heavily curved stafflines. For more details, see [5] (Section 3.4). The source code is available in the website: *http://music-staves.sourceforge.net/* (class *MusicStaves_skeleton*).

3.2 Metrics and Results

The performance of the algorithms was measured based on pixel based metric. Here the staff removal is considered as a two-class classification problem at the pixel level. The error rate of classification for each of the images ranges from 0 to 100, and was computed as:

$$\text{E.R.} = 100 \cdot \frac{\#\text{misclassified } sp + \#\text{misclassified non } sp}{\#\text{all } sp + \#\text{all non } sp} \tag{2}$$

where $\#$ means "number of" and sp means "staff pixels". So lower being the error rate, better the performance.

Since it may occur that one system obtains very good results but rejects many images, the participants' methods have been evaluated in two ways:

– Error rate without rejection: The average error rate is computed as the mean of the error rate of the images that the system could evaluate. Thus, the rejected images are not included here.
– Error rate with rejection: The average error rate is computed taking into account all the set of images (the 500 images of each kind of distortion). Thus, the rejected images are considered to have an E.R.=100%.

The results of the different methods are shown in Table 2. Most methods have an error rate without rejection between 1.9 and 2.8, being ISI01-HA the one which obtains better results in most cases, and also without rejecting any image. Not surprisingly, most methods obtain very similar results when dealing with the original ideal images (1.5%) and Kanungo noise (2.85%). However, differences are significant when dealing with Curvature, Interruption or Thickness Ratio.

It is interesting to notice that there is no agreement in the kind of distortion that all staff removal methods solve in the best way. This means that some methods are more suitable to a specific kind of distortion, whereas others solve in a better way another kind of distortions.

Concerning the rejected images, one can see how the NUS03 method has lower Error Rate than the INP02 methods, but discards all the *Thick* distorted images. In this sense, it must be said that some severe distortions (such as Interruption or Thickness) make the staff detection very difficult, and consequently, most images are rejected by the systems (in many cases, all the images are discarded).

Table 2. Staff Removal results. Error Rate (E.R.) in % for each one of the 12 distortions. For each one of the participant's methods, we show the Error Rate with rejection (With R.) and without rejection (No R.). In case of the Error rate without rejection, we also show the number # of rejected images. The last row corresponds to the overall Error Rate.

Distortion	Error Rate	ISI01-Rob	ISI01-HA	INP02-SP	INP02-SPTrim	NUS03	NUG04-Fuji	NUG04-LTr	NUG04-Skel
01-	No R.	1.50	1.50	1.5	1.51	1.54	1.53	2.08	2.11
-	#	0	0	0	0	0	0	0	1
Ideal	With R.	1.50	1.50	1.5	1.5	1.54	1.53	2.08	2.31
02-	No R.	1.66	1.66	1.8	1.80	2.83	38.45	–	13.38
-	#	0	0	0	0	0	3	**500**	148
Curvature	With R.	1.66	1.66	1.8	1.8	2.83	38.82	**100**	39.02
03-	No R.	0.92	0.91	5.16	5.19	1.04	18.79	–	–
-	#	0	0	5	5	0	**499**	**500**	**500**
Interruption	With R.	0.92	0.91	6.10	6.14	1.04	**99.84**	**100**	**100**
04-	No R.	2.84	2.84	2.86	2.87	2.91	2.84	4.33	7.93
-	#	0	0	0	0	0	0	0	0
Kanungo	With R.	2.84	2.84	2.86	2.87	2.91	2.84	4.33	7.93
05-	No R.	1.76	1.76	2.03	2.03	3.06	40.40	–	4.60
-	#	0	0	0	0	0	8	**500**	48
Rotation	With R.	1.76	1.76	2.03	2.03	3.06	41.35	**100**	13.76
06-	No R.	2.44	2.17	2.70	2.71	3.38	2.53	3.74	4.14
staffline	#	0	0	0	0	0	0	0	0
thickness v1	With R.	2.44	2.17	2.70	2.71	3.38	2.53	3.74	4.14
07-	No R.	2.18	2.15	3.01	3.02	3.41	2.20	3.74	3.72
staffline	#	0	0	0	0	0	0	0	0
thickness v2	With R.	2.18	2.15	3.01	3.02	3.41	2.20	3.74	3.72
08-	No R.	2.00	1.89	2.43	2.45	3.01	3.21	5.56	6.34
staffline	#	0	0	0	0	0	0	2	0
y-variation v1	With R.	2.00	1.89	2.43	2.45	3.01	3.21	5.94	6.34
09-	No R.	1.92	1.83	2.27	2.28	3.02	3.28	3.34	4.98
staffline	#	0	0	0	0	0	0	2	0
y-variation v2	With R.	1.92	1.83	2.27	2.28	3.02	3.28	3.72	4.98
10	No R.	2.86	2.86	6.89	6.89	–	–	10.78	15.96
Thickness	#	0	0	0	0	**500**	**500**	0	0
Ratio	With R.	2.86	2.86	6.89	6.89	**100**	**100**	10.78	15.96
11-	No R.	1.61	1.60	1.60	1.61	1.70	7.95	3.29	18.41
TypeSet	#	0	0	0	0	0	0	8	**477**
emulation	With R.	1.61	1.60	1.60	1.61	1.70	7.95	4.83	**96.25**
12-	No R.	1.48	1.48	1.73	1.74	2.04	1.92	1.76	6.69
White	#	0	0	0	0	0	0	0	0
Speckles	With R.	1.48	1.48	1.73	1.74	2.04	1.92	1.76	6.69
Overall	No R.	**1.93**	**1.89**	**2.83**	**2.84**	**2.54**	**10.37**	**4.29**	**6.87**
Error	#	0	0	5	5	500	1010	1512	1174
Rate	With R.	1.93	1.89	2.91	2.92	10.66	25.46	28.41	25.09

4   Staff Removal Extended Competition

During the GREC 2011 workshop and the ICDAR 2011 conference, we had the opportunity to discuss about our music competition with some attendees and researchers working on music analysis. As a result of this feedback, we decided to contact the staff removal participants again in order to propose them to run their algorithms with a new set of distorted images.

The goal of this new experiment is to test the robustness of the participants' algorithms in a more realistic case: a combination of different distortions. The idea behind is that in a real scenario, a document may contain several kinds of distortions.

Next, we will describe the new set of images and the obtained results.

4.1   Images Description

In this new experiment, for each one of the original image, we have generated one distorted image. Thus, the new set of distorted images is composed of 1000 images, 500 images for training and 500 images for testing. These images have been generated by the combination of four different distortion methods: staffline y-variation, curvature, white speckles and kanungo. However, and contrary to the GREC and ICDAR competition, we have generated three different levels of distortions, namely low, medium and severe. Table 3 shows the number of images for each level of distortion and the parameters used for each distortion. The staff distortion code that has been used for generating these images is available in the CVC-MUSCIMA website.

Table 3. Staff Removal - Extended Competition. Number of images and parameters used.

Distortion Level	Number of Images	staffline y-variation (maxdiff,c)	curvature (amplitude, period)	white speckles (p, n, k)	kanungo (eta, a0, a, b0, b, k)
Low	200	(1, 0.5)	(0.05, 1)	(0.03, 6, 2)	(0, 1, 1, 1, 1, 2)
Medium	200	(3, 0.7)	(0.05, 5)	(0.04, 8, 2)	(0 , 1 , 1, 1, 1, 2)
Severe	100	(5, 0.9)	(0.05, 8)	(0.05, 10, 2)	(0 , 1 , 1, 1, 1, 2)

As an illustrative example, Figure 3 shows the same music score with a low, medium and severe distortion. Notice that, although the original document is the same, the resulting images look quite different, especially in terms of curvature and noise (see Fig.(d-e)).

4.2   Results

The performance of the algorithms in this new set of images has been measured using the same metrics as the ones used for the previous staff removal competition: Error Rate (E.R.) with and without rejection. Table 4 shows the results of

(a) Low distortion

(b) Medium distortion

(c) Severe distortion

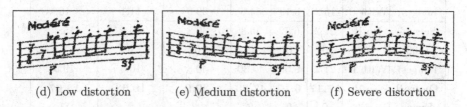

(d) Low distortion   (e) Medium distortion   (f) Severe distortion

Fig. 3. Combination of distortion methods applied to the same music score and with different distortion levels. (a) Low, (b) Medium and (c) Severe distorted images. Captions of these images: (d) Caption of the image (a), (e) Caption of the image (b), and (f) Caption of the image (c).

the extended staff removal competition. In most cases, the Error Rate increases when increasing the level of distortion (e.g. ISI01, NUG04-Fuji, etc.). However, some of the methods are quite stable, with a variation of less than one percent, such as INP02 (5.86-6.52%) or NUG04-LTr (11.2-10.6%).

Comparing with the results from the previous staff removal competition, there are two main aspects to remark. Firstly, and as expected, these error rates are higher than the ones shown in Table 2. The main reason is that these methods could be individually trained to cope with each isolated distortion, in other words, the parameters could be different depending on the distortion to be treated. However, when images are generated through a combination of distortions, it is hardly impossible to find one set of parameters that is suitable for all the distortions. Secondly, the amount of rejected images is lower than the rejected images in Table 2). This can be explained because, although the resulting image is more complex, the staff lines look more realistic and consequently, the staff detection method has a better performance.

One interesting aspect is that, in this extended competition, the best results are obtained by INP02, followed by NUG04-LTr (with an overall Error Rate of 6.19% and 10.63%. respectively). Consequently, these methods are a priori more suitable for dealing with realistic images (complex images with several kinds of distortions) than the best methods (ISI01 and NUS03) described in the previous staff removal competition, which seem to be very sensitive to parameter configuration.

Table 4. Staff Removal results of the Extended Competition. For each submitted method and distortion level, we show the Error Rate (E.R.) in % with rejection (With R.) and without rejection (No R.), and the number # of rejected images. The last row corresponds to the overall (average) Error Rate.

Distortion	Error	ISI01	INP02	NUS03	NUG04-Fuji	NUG04-LTr	NUG04-Skel
Low-	No R.	14.1	5.86	39.6	21.3	11.2	11.7
(200	#	0	0	2	5	0	3
Images)	With R.	14.1	5.86	40.6	23.8	11.2	13.2
Medium-	No R.	16.2	6.19	54.6	30.6	10.1	14
(200	#	0	0	0	18	2	4
Images)	With R.	16.2	6.19	54.6	39.6	11.1	16
Severe-	No R.	21.2	6.52	49.3	40.8	10.6	15.3
(100	#	0	0	0	0	0	4
Images)	With R.	21.2	6.52	49.30	40.8	10.6	19.3
Overall	No R.	**17.17**	**6.19**	**47.83**	**30.9**	**10.63**	**13.67**
Error	#	0	0	2	23	2	11
Rate	With R.	17.17	6.19	48.17	34.73	10.97	16.17

5   Conclusion

The first music scores competition held in ICDAR2011 and GREC2011 has shown to wake up the interest of researchers, with 8 participant methods in the staff removal competition, and another 8 participant methods in the writer identification competition.

In the writer identification task, the participants' results have shown that more research is required for dealing with the identification of graphical documents. In this context, and since the adaptation of writer identification methods from other kind of documents have obtained modest results, one may conclude that specific approaches for music scores are the best choice.

The staff removal methods submitted by the participants have obtained very good performance in front of severe distorted images, although it has also been shown that there is still room for improvement, especially concerning the detection of the staff lines. In addition, we have extended this competition by adding a new set of images which have been generated from a combination of different kinds of distortions. The new results of the participants have demonstrated that most methods significantly decrease their performance when dealing with a combination of distortions, which is precisely a more realistic scenario than the previous one. In future competitions, it would be also interesting to see how the systems could cope with real distortions, especially the ones that appear in historical documents.

Finally, we hope that the competition results on the CVC-MUSCIMA database will foster the research on handwritten music scores in the near future.

Acknowledgments. We would like to thank Joan Casals and all the musicians who contributed to the CVC-MUSCIMA dataset; and Dr. Christoph Dalitz for providing the code which generates the staff distortions. We thank all the participants, because without their interest the competition would not have been possible. We thank the writer identification participants: Abdelâali Hassaïne, Somaya Al-Ma'adeed, Chawki Djeddi, Labiba Souici-Meslati. Especially, we would like to thank the researchers that kindly agreed to participate in the extended staff removal competition: Jit Ray Chowdhury, Dr. Umapada Pal, Ana Rebelo, Dr. Jaime S. Cardoso, Bolan Su, Dr. Shijian Lu, Dr. Chew-Lim Tan, Dr. Christoph Dalitz and Andreas Kitzig.

This work has been partially supported by the Spanish projects TIN2011-24631, TIN2009-14633-C03-03, CONSOLIDER-INGENIO 2010 (CSD2007-00018) and 2011 FIB 01022.

References

1. Miyao, H., Maruyama, M.: An online handwritten music symbol recognition system. International Journal on Document Analysis and Recognition 9(1), 49–58 (2007)
2. Fornés, A., Lladós, J., Sánchez, G., Otazu, X., Bunke, H.: A combination of features for symbol-independent writer identification in old music scores. International Journal on Document Analysis and Recognition 13(4), 243–259 (2010)

3. Rebelo, A., Capela, G., Cardoso, J.: Optical recognition of music symbols. International Journal on Document Analysis and Recognition 13(1), 19–31 (2010)

4. Cardoso, J.S., Capela, A., Rebelo, A., Guedes, C., da Costa, J.P.: Staff detection with stable paths. IEEE Trans. on Pattern Analysis and Machine Intelligence 31(6), 1134–1139 (2009)

5. Dalitz, C., Droettboom, M., Pranzas, B., Fujinaga, I.: A Comparative Study of Staff Removal Algorithms. IEEE Trans. on Pattern Analysis and Machine Intelligence 30(5), 753–766 (2008)

6. Cui, J., He, H., Wang, Y.: An adaptive staff line removal in music score images. In: IEEE 10th International Conference on Signal Processing (ICSP), pp. 964–967 (2010)

7. Luth, N.: Automatic identification of music notations. In: Proceedings of the Second International Conference on WEB Delivering of Music (WEDELMUSIC), pp. 203–210 (2002)

8. Bruder, I., Temenushka, I., Milewski, L.: Integrating knowledge components for writer identification in a digital archive of historical music scores. In: Proceedings of the 4th ACM/IEEE-CS Joint Conference on Digital Libraries (JCDL), p. 397 (2004)

9. Marinai, S., Miotti, B., Soda, G.: Bag of Characters and SOM Clustering for Script Recognition and Writer Identification. In: International Conference on Pattern Recognition, pp. 2182–2185 (2010)

10. Fornés, A., Dutta, A., Gordo, A., Lladós, J.: CVC-MUSCIMA: A Ground-Truth of Handwritten Music Score Images for Writer Identification and Staff Removal. International Journal on Document Analysis and Recognition 15(3), 243–251 (2012)

11. Fornés, A., Dutta, A., Gordo, A., Lladós, J.: The ICDAR 2011 Music Scores Competition: Staff Removal and Writer Identification. In: International Conference on Document Analysis and Recognition, pp. 1511–1515 (2011)

12. Fujinaga, I.: Staff Detection and Removal. In: George, S. (ed.) Visual Perception of Music Notation, pp. 1–39. Idea Group (2004)

13. Al-Ma'adeed, S., Mohammed, E., Al Kassis, D.: Writer identification using edge-based directional probability distribution features for Arabic words. In: International Conference on Computer Systems and Applications (AICCSA), pp. 582–590 (2008)

14. Al-Ma'adeed, S., Al-Kurbi, A.-A., Al-Muslih, A., Al-Qahtani, R., Al Kubisi, H.: Writer identification of Arabic handwriting documents using grapheme features. In: Int'l Conf. on Computer Systems and Applications (AICCSA), pp. 923–924 (2008)

15. Gordo, A., Fornés, A., Valveny, E., Lladós, J.: A bag of notes approach to writer identification in old handwritten musical scores. In: International Workshop on Document Analysis Systems, pp. 247–254 (2010)

16. Djeddi, C., Souici-Meslati, L.: A texture based approach for Arabic Writer Identification and Verification. In: Int'l Conf. on Machine and Web Intelligence (ICMWI), pp. 115–120 (2010)

17. Fornés, A., Lladós, J.: A Symbol-Dependent Writer Identification Approach in Old Handwritten Music Scores. In: International Conference on Frontiers in Handwriting Recognition, pp. 634–639 (2010)

Final Report of GREC'11 Arc Segmentation Contest: Performance Evaluation on Multi-resolution Scanned Documents

Hasan S.M. Al-Khaffaf[1,2], Abdullah Zawawi Talib[2], and Mohd Azam Osman[2]

[1] Image Understanding and Pattern Recognition Research Group (IUPR),
Technische Universität Kaiserslautern, Kaiserslautern, Germany
[2] School of Computer Sciences, Universiti Sains Malaysia,
11800 USM Penang, Malaysia
hasansm@rhrk.uni-kl.de, {azht,azam}@cs.usm.my

Abstract. This paper presents the final report of the outcome of the sixth edition of the Arc Segmentation Contest. The theme of this edition is segmentation of images with different scanning resolutions. The contest was held offline before the workshop. Nine document images were scanned with three resolutions each and the ground truth images were created manually. Four participants have provided the output of their research prototypes. Two prototypes are more established while the other two are still in development. In general, vectorization methods produces better results with low resolution scanned images. Participants' comments on the behavior of their methods are also included in this report. A website devoted for this edition of the contest to hold the newly created dataset and other materials related to the contest is also available.

Keywords: Empirical Performance Evaluation, Graphics Recognition, Raster to Vector Conversion, Line Drawings, Statistical Analysis.

1 Introduction

This edition of the Arc Segmentation Contest 2011 was held in conjunction with the Ninth IAPR International Workshop on Graphics RECognition (GREC) held in Chung-Ang University, Seoul, Korea, in September 2011. This contest was organized by the School of Computer Sciences, Universiti Sains Malaysia, Malaysia. The theme of this contest is multi scanning resolutions and its effect on line detection. The test images were selected from a text book. Three scanning resolutions were employed: 200, 300, and 400 DPI. Ground truth data were created manually using a vector editor and they were stored in the VEC file format. The output of research prototypes as well as commercial software were accepted. Two methods of participation were available. The first option involves using the DAE platform [1,2] while the second option was participation through email. In both cases the output of participating methods should be in the VEC or DXF file formats.

Y.-B. Kwon and J.-M. Ogier (Eds.): GREC, LNCS 7423, pp. 187–197, 2013.
© Springer-Verlag Berlin Heidelberg 2013

2   Test Images, Ground Truthing, and Expected Vectors

A set of mechanical engineering drawings were selected from an old textbook [3]. The selected images were then scanned by AstraSlim scanner with three different resolutions: 200, 300, and 400 DPI. In the scanning process, trial and error were employed to ensure that the graphical elements in the paper drawing were captured with minimum rotation angle. The scanned color images were then cropped and binarized with 50% threshold. We have nine images for each scan resolution and a total of 27 test images. The images are shown in Fig. 1.

For the generation of the ground truth data, we started with images with high resolution (400 DPI). Vectors were created for each corresponding raster entity (arc or circle) in the image using a vector editor. Contextual knowledge was put into effect during the creation of the vector data such as arcs/circles that are co-centered and an arc/circle passing through the center of another arc/circle. After creating the vectors for all necessary primitives, the vectors were combined into one block and copied to the image with lower resolutions (300 and 200 DPI). The block of vector entities were then fitted manually on the raster image by continuous resizing/moving till it fitted well on the corresponding raster image. We opted to retain the text strings in the scanned image. The reason for not whiting out the text strings is to make the vectorization scenario as close as possible to real situations. Additionally, all text strings in the original raster images were not vectorized. This dataset does not support line width information, hence the width for all ground truth arcs/circles is set to the value of 1.

As in the previous editions of the arc segmentation contest, the focus is on circle and arc detections only. For this reason, straight lines were ignored. The text strings were also ignored and not saved to the vector file. Dashed circle/arc entities are not supported. However, circular segments that are parts of dashed circles/arcs and large enough to be recognized can be saved as separate arcs. Each of these arcs will has center, radius, start angle, and end angle. The detected circles were stored as circle entities identified by a center and a radius in the output vector file. The pixel is the unit of measure and the top-left corner of the image/screen is at point (0,0).

A website[1] is available for the contest. The test images generated in this contest were hosted in the website as well as within the DAE platform (Section 3).

3   Methods of Participation

As with previous edition of the contest [4], research prototypes as well as commercial software were accepted in this edition of the contest. However, all the four participants (as shown in Table 1) have provided the output of their own research prototypes. Nevertheless, commercial software were also tested on the newly created dataset [5]. Two options of participation were available:

---

[1] http://www.cs.usm.my/arcseg2011/

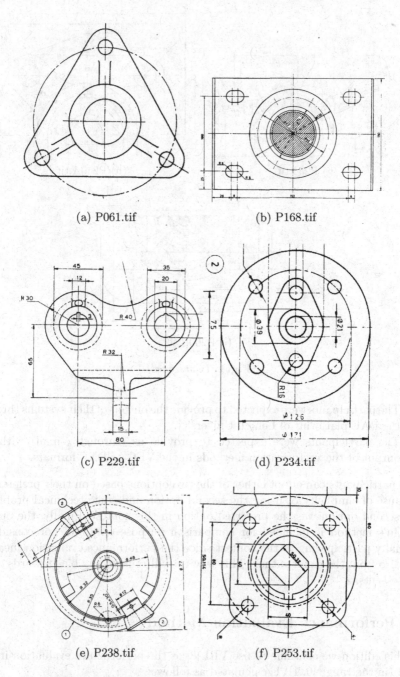

(a) P061.tif   (b) P168.tif

(c) P229.tif   (d) P234.tif

(e) P238.tif   (f) P253.tif

Fig. 1. Test images (Scanned from Sidheswar et al. [3])

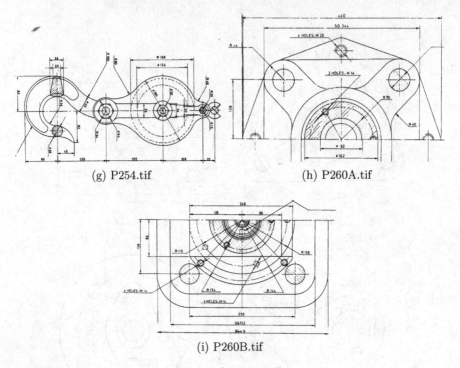

(g) P254.tif   (h) P260A.tif

(i) P260B.tif

Fig. 1. (*Continued*)

1. The participants were expected to provide the output of their systems through the DAE platform[2] of Lehigh University.
2. The participants were expected to provide us (through e-mail) with the output of the vectorization methods in the VEC or DXF formats.

The participants can adopt either of the two options based on their preferences. Because of simplicity of using the second option and some technical problems, the second option was the preferred option in this contest. Finally, the output of Liu's method is included for comparison purpose only and not considered officially participating in the contest since the performance evaluation measure are also from the same author. This way we will remove any bias towards other contestants.

4   Performance Evaluation Method

In this edition we continue to use VRI [8] as the performance evaluation index. VRI (in the range [0..1]) is calculated as follows:

$$VRI = \sqrt{D_v * (1 - F_v)} \qquad (1)$$

---

[2] DAE platform [1,2]: http://dae.cse.lehigh.edu/dae/

Table 1. Participated Methods

Vectorizer	Author(s)	Affiliation
Liu's method [6]	Liu Wenyin	Department of Computer Science, City University of Hong Kong, Hong Kong, China
ArcFind[†] 3.1	Dave Elliman	School of Computer Science, University of Nottingham, UK
Effective Arc Segmentation[†] (EAS) 1.0	Zili Zhang, Xuan Wang, Yanjun Ma	Shenzhen Graduate School, Harbin Institute of Technology, ShenZhen, China
Qgar-Lamiroy [7]	Bart Lamiroy	Université de Lorraine, LORIA, Nancy, France

[†]Unpublished work

where D_v is the detection rate and F_v is the false alarm rate. A high VRI score indicates better recognition rate. Under this measure, the detected vector quality is the geometric mean of five factors: endpoints quality, overlap distance quality, line width quality, line style quality, and line shape quality. In this contest the dataset does not include width information hence the line width quality factor is eliminated (neutralized) when calculating the VRI index.

5 Results and Discussion

For each of the participated methods, we obtained 27 VRI scores (nine images * three resolutions) and a total of 108 scores for the four participated methods. Table 2 shows performance scores of the four participated methods. In terms of stability, the two best performers, Liu and Qgar-Lamiroy are stable with one exception for the latter where it fails (VRI=0) at image P229-400dpi. These two methods are more mature than the other two and have participated in past editions of this contest. For the other two methods ArcFind and EAS, the former is more stable (fails on one image P229-400dpi) while the latter fails on five images. These two methods are currently under development[3] which could be one of the reasons for getting this sort of performance. As mentioned in §3, Liu's method is included for comparison purposes only. Objectively and in terms of VRI scores, the Qgar-Lamiroy method is the highest performer, and hence it is the winner of this contest.

In order not to limit ourselves to finding a winner for the contest, we opted to perform a more rigorous analysis on the effect of scanning resolution on the performance of the participated methods. In this edition of the contest, we have studied the resolution factor as well as the vectorization factor. Instead of performing a superficial test on the data and relying on the mathematical mean, we opted to go a step further and used a robust statistical analysis. The use of statistical test will also provide answers to research questions that were not

---

[3] The argument is based on email communication with the authors.

Table 2. Performance scores $[D_v, F_v, VRI]$ for the participated methods

Image	Liu's	ArcFind	EAS	Qgar-Lamiroy
P061[†]	[.770, .174, **.798**[‡]] [.690, .331, **.679**] [.616, .292, **.660**]	[.144, .845, .149] [.288, .924, .148] [.436, .909, .200]	[.240, .599, .310] [.226, .525, .328] [0, 1, 0]	[.286, .160, .490] [.243, .315, .408] [.347, .186, .532]
P168	[.705, .227, **.738**] [.470, .541, **.464**] [.285, .695, .295]	[.429, .869, .237] [.222, .936, .119] [.126, .973, .058]	[.034, .807, .081] [.050, .894, .073] [.016, .880, .044]	[.072, .775, .127] [.320, .547, .381] [.306, .623, **.340**]
P229	[.553, .422, **.565**] [.429, .547, .441] [.327, .681, **.323**]	[.494, .800, .314] [.352, .895, .192] [0, 1, 0]	[.196, .693, .245] [.238, .650, .288] [.015, .979, .018]	[.354, .225, .524] [.384, .239, **.540**] [0, 1, 0]
P234	[.290, .486, **.386**] [.658, .257, .699] [.469, .496, .486]	[.145, .950, .085] [.176, .937, .105] [.236, .912, .144]	[.178, .339, .343] [.201, .716, .239] [.150, .314, .321]	[.121, .545, .235] [.695, .100, **.791**] [.687, .133, **.772**]
P238	[.204, .718, .240] [.397, .646, **.375**] [.284, .745, **.269**]	[.221, .950, .105] [.093, .974, .049] [.194, .970, .077]	[.057, .750, .119] [0, 1, 0] [0, 1, 0]	[.139, .308, **.311**] [.146, .610, .239] [.139, .708, .201]
P253	[.909, .214, **.846**] [.645, .399, **.623**] [.488, .569, .459]	[.122, .966, .065] [.136, .937, .093] [.517, .855, .274]	[.130, .811, .157] [.129, .587, .231] [.060, .876, .086]	[.507, .355, .572] [.507, .275, .606] [.435, .419, **.503**]
P254	[.422, .406, **.501**] [.368, .550, **.407**] [.525, .469, **.528**]	[.327, .908, .174] [.099, .970, .054] [.109, .978, .049]	[.042 .643, .123] [0, 1, 0] [.034, .685, .103]	[.106 .365, .260] [.178, .572, .276] [.198, .594, .283]
P260A	[.467, .449, **.507**] [.528, .471, **.528**] [.525, .559, **.481**]	[.149, .959, .078] [.396, .934, .162] [.058, .989, .025]	[.037, .814, .083] [.025, .903, .049] [.087, .775, .140]	[.054, .213, .207] [.205, .227, .398] [.125, .576, .230]
P260B	[.379, .525, **.424**] [.318, .647, **.335**] [.218, .769, **.224**]	[.061, .976, .038] [.114, .971, .057] [.024, .996, .009]	[.097, .597, .198] [0, 1, 0] [.048, .618, .135]	[.074, .498, .193] [.176, .700, .230] [.084, .866, .106]
Avg	0.492	.113	.138	.361

[†]1st, 2nd, and 3rd rows of each image, corresponds to 200, 300, and 400 DPI
[‡]Highest VRI score in each resolution is shown in bold

possible to be answered using the mean or at least could not be answered with confidence. A precision of 95% is used for all the statistical tests of this paper.

In our experiment, we have two independent variables (*Method* and *Resolution*) and one dependent variable (*VRI*). Each paper image (subject) was used many times, and thus producing many VRI scores for any single paper drawing. Repeated measure ANOVA is the statistical test which is suitable to handle experiments with similar nature [9,10]. However, before starting with ANOVA, we need to check it's three requirements: (i) order effect should be avoided, (ii) the data should be normally distributed, and (iii) the Sphericity condition should not be violated.

The order effect is avoided since the original paper drawings were used in scanning and the raster images were not changed during the run of any software.

Shapiro-Wilk test [11] is used to check the normality condition. The null (H_0) and the alternative (H_1) hypotheses are as follows:

$$H_0 : \text{There is no difference between the distribution} \tag{2}$$
$$\text{of the data and the normal.}$$

$$H_1 : \text{There is a difference between the distribution} \tag{3}$$
$$\text{of the data and the normal.}$$

The ρ of the Shapiro-Wilk for all the cells (values are not shown in this paper) are not significant ($Sig. > .05$), indicating a failure to reject the null hypothesis, and hence the data are considered normally distributed.

In order to test the validity of the Sphericity condition, Mauchly's Test [12] needs to be performed. In Table 3, $\rho > .05$ for the two factors *Method* and *Resolution*; and the interaction between them, *Method * Resolution*. Hence the Sphericity condition is not violated.

Table 3. Mauchly's Test of Sphericity‡

Within Subjects Effect	df	Sig. (ρ)
Method	5	.408
Resolution	2	.280
Method * Resolution	20	.657

‡Tests the null hypothesis that the error covariance matrix of the orthonormalized transformed dependent variables is proportional to an identity matrix.

After validating the three conditions for using repeated measure ANOVA, it will be possible to proceed with the statistical method by analyzing the Test of Within-Subjects Effects (Table 4). The *Method* variable is significant while the *Resolution* variable as well as the interaction between the two variables are not significant ($\rho \geq .05$). The significance of the *Method* variable means that we fail to reject the null hypothesis (H_0). On the other hand, the insignificance of the *Resolution* variable indicates that we reject the null hypothesis and accept the alternative one. The hypotheses for each of the variables are as follows:

$$H_0 : \mu_{\text{Liu}} = \mu_{\text{ArcFind}} = \mu_{\text{EAS}} = \mu_{\text{Qgar-Lamiroy}} \tag{4}$$

$$H_1 : \text{Not all the means are equal} \tag{5}$$

$$H_0 : \mu_{\text{200DPI}} = \mu_{\text{300DPI}} = \mu_{\text{400DPI}} \tag{6}$$

$$H_1 : \text{Not all the means are equal} \tag{7}$$

In other words, there are significant differences between the vectorization methods in terms of VRI scores. However, there are little differences between the scanning resolutions in terms of VRI scores. It is shown in Table 5 that the mean differences between Liu method and the other three methods, Qgar-Lamiroy, EAS and ArcFind are significant ($\rho < .05$). Qgar-Lamiroy method is also significantly better than the other two methods EAS and ArcFind. However, Qgar-Lamiroy has a special case of high VRI scores with moderate resolution (300 DPI) while all the other methods get the best results with the lowest resolution (200 DPI). The performance of methods within the three resolutions is shown in Fig. 2.

With regard to scanning resolution, it is shown in Fig. 3 that the mean VRI scores drops with the increase in scanning resolution. However, the drop is not statistically significant.

Table 4. Tests of Within-Subjects Effects

Source	df	F	Sig. (ρ)
Method	3	54.33	.000
Error (Method)	24		
Resolution	2	2.39	.124
Error (Resolution)	16		
Method * Resolution	6	1.55	.183
Error (Method*Resolution)	48		
Sphericity Assumed			

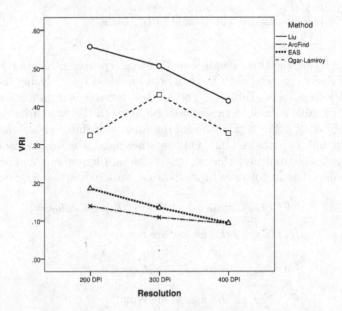

Fig. 2. Performance of vectorization methods with different scanning resolutions

Table 5. Pairwise Comparisons

(I) Method	(J) Method	Mean Difference (I-J)	Std. Error	Sig.[a]
Liu	ArcFind	.379	.035	.000
	EAS	.354	.038	.000
	Qgar-Lamiroy	.131	.035	.034
ArcFind	EAS	.024	.025	1.000
	Qgar-Lamiroy	-.248	.042	.002
EAS	Qgar-Lamiroy	-.224	.031	.001

Based on estimated marginal means

[a]. Adjustment for multiple comparisons: Bonferroni.

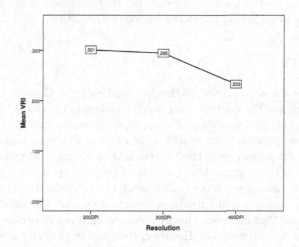

Fig. 3. VRI score means for the three resolutions

6 Post Contest Discussion

After the GREC event, we invited the authors to comment on the performance of their methods. In this section we highlight the outcome of the discussion. One paragraph is devoted to each author and their revised comments are presented next.

Qgar-Lamiroy method is based on matching an algebraic circle formula on a set of discrete points retrieved from the skeleton and measuring the overall fitting error. The higher the resolution, the more robust the skeleton is and the more precise the fitting error is measured. On the other hand, when the resolution gets higher, the algorithm starts detecting any small distortion in the shape of the circle (e.g. slightly oval in shape due to perturbations in the image processing chain whereby the human eye will not notice but the algorithm will). Although most parameters are scale/resolution invariant, there is one -tolerance on radius error- which is set in pixels, and therefore influencing the result when resolution becomes too high. Further work will eliminate these parameters (or at least try and make them scale invariant).

The ArcFind method is developed to detect circular arcs in scanned document images. It works well when arc shapes are close to full circle, but its performance drops when arcs are small and when short arcs are connected to straight lines causing small arcs to be detected as polyline. The contest images have a variety of arcs and circles that distract the ArcFind method and cause a drop in detection and hence causing it to get low VRI scores.

The EAS method has difficulty in obtaining accurate values for the center and radius of a circle. The method is better in detecting circles than in detecting arcs. The method also has difficulty in detecting arcs/circles that are tangents to other graphical elements.

Liu Wenyin commented on the experiment and gave feedbacks to improve its robustness. The feedbacks were incorporated in this report. However, no comments were provided on the performance of his method.

7   Summary

The outcome of the sixth edition of the Arc Segmentation Contest has been presented in this paper. The contest was held off-line before the GREC'11 workshop. Empirical performance evaluation of multi scan resolution was the theme of this contest. Four participants have provided the output of their own research prototypes. The highest performer in this contest is Qgar-Lamiroy method, and hence, it is the winner of this contest. One outcome of this contest is the creation of new multi-resolution ground truth data. This work is also the first study on research prototypes that involves multi resolution scanned images. The other outcome is in the new finding that increasing image resolution has negative effect on the performance of the tested methods. However, the drop in performance with higher scanning resolutions is not statistically significant. Actually, we have invited the authors to explain to us the reason behind any unusual performance of their methods. Lamiroy provides justification (See §6) on why his method gives good results with mid-resolution images. For two other authors, their methods are still under development and the details of their method are not published yet.

Acknowledgment. The authors appreciate the efforts of Abdul Halim Ghazali in preparing the ground truth images and Wong Poh Lee for creating and maintaining the contest website. We would also like to thank all participants for their contribution to the success of this contest. During the organization of the contest, the first author was a Post-Doctoral Fellow in the School of Computer Sciences, USM, Malaysia.

References

1. Lamiroy, B., Lopresti, D.: A Platform for Storing, Visualizing, and Interpreting Collections of Noisy Documents. In: Fourth Workshop on Analytics for Noisy Unstructured Text Data - AND 2010. ACM International Conference Proceeding Series. IAPR, ACM, Toronto, Canada (2010)

2. Lamiroy, B., Lopresti, D.: An Open Architecture for End-to-End Document Analysis Benchmarking. In: 11th International Conference on Document Analysis and Recognition - ICDAR 2011. International Association for Pattern Recognition, Beijing (2011)

3. Sidheswar, N., Kannaiah, P., Sastry, V.V.S.: Machine Drawing. Tata McGraw-Hill, New Delhi (1992)

4. Al-Khaffaf, H.S.M., Talib, A.Z., Osman, M.A., Wong, P.L.: GREC'09 Arc Segmentation Contest: Performance Evaluation on Old Documents. In: Ogier, J.-M., Liu, W., Lladós, J. (eds.) GREC 2009. LNCS, vol. 6020, pp. 251–259. Springer, Heidelberg (2010)

5. Al-Douri, B.A.T., Al-Khaffaf, H.S.M., Talib, A.Z.: Empirical Performance Evaluation of Raster to Vector Conversion with Different Scanning Resolutions. In: Badioze Zaman, H., Robinson, P., Petrou, M., Olivier, P., Shih, T.K., Velastin, S., Nyström, I. (eds.) IVIC 2011, Part I. LNCS, vol. 7066, pp. 176–182. Springer, Heidelberg (2011)

6. Liu, W.Y., Dori, D.: Incremental arc segmentation algorithm and its evaluation. IEEE Transactions on Pattern Analysis and Machine Intelligence 20(4), 424–431 (1998)

7. Lamiroy, B., Guebbas, Y.: Robust and Precise Circular Arc Detection. In: Ogier, J.-M., Liu, W., Lladós, J. (eds.) GREC 2009. LNCS, vol. 6020, pp. 49–60. Springer, Heidelberg (2010)

8. Liu, W.Y., Dori, D.: A protocol for performance evaluation of line detection algorithms. Machine Vision and Applications 9(5-6), 240–250 (1997)

9. Roberts, M.J., Russo, R.: A Student's Guide to Analysis of Variance. Routledge (1999)

10. Al-Khaffaf, H.S.M., Talib, A.Z., Salam, R.A.: Empirical performance evaluation of raster-to-vector conversion methods: A study on multi-level interactions between different factors. IEICE Transactions on Information and Systems E94.D(6), 1278–1288 (2011)

11. Shapiro, S.S., Wilk, M.B.: An analysis of variance test for normality (complete samples). Biometrika 52(3/4), 591–611 (1965)

12. Mauchly, J.W.: Significance test for sphericity of a normal n-variate distribution. The Annals of Mathematical Statistics 11(2), 204–209 (1940)

Report on the Symbol Recognition and Spotting Contest

Ernest Valveny[1], Mathieu Delalandre[2], Romain Raveaux[3], and Bart Lamiroy[4]

[1] Computer Vision Center, Univ. Autònoma de Barcelona
Edifici O, Campus UAB, 08193 Bellaterra, Spain
ernest@cvc.uab.es
[2] Laboratoire d'Informatique
Université de Tours, France
mathieu.delalandre@univ-tours.fr
[3] L3i laboratory
Université de La Rochelle, France
romain.raveaux01@univ-lr.fr
[4] LORIA / INPL - École des Mines de Nancy
Bart.Lamiroy@loria.fr

Abstract. In this paper we summarize the framework and the results of the fourth edition of the International Symbol Recognition Contest, organized in the context of GREC'11. The contest follows the series started at the GREC'03 workshop and it is the first time that, in addition to recognition of isolated symbols, the contest includes the evaluation of symbol spotting. In this report we describe the evaluation framework – including datasets and evaluation measures – and we summarize the results obtained by the only participant method.

Keywords: Performance evaluation, symbol recognition, symbol spotting.

1 Introduction

Symbol recognition has been a topic of active research within the graphics recognition community with many different approaches described in the literature [2,7,11]. Thus, there is a real need for a generic and standard framework that permits a fair comparison of all existing methods. Such a framework was discussed in [12] in terms of datasets, ground-truth, evaluation metrics and protocol of evaluation. Following these ideas, several competitions have been organized. The first work on evaluation of symbol recognition was undertaken at ICPR'00 [1]. The dataset consisted of 25 electrical symbols that were scaled and degraded with a small amount of binary noise to generate images of non-connected symbols. The series of contests on symbol recognition linked to the GREC workshop started in 2003. In the first edition [13], the dataset was composed of 50 architectural and electrical symbols that were rotated, scaled, degraded with binary noise and deformed through vectorial distortion in order to

Y.-B. Kwon and J.-M. Ogier (Eds.): GREC, LNCS 7423, pp. 198–207, 2013.

generate up to 72 different tests with increasing levels of difficulty and number of symbols. In the second edition of the contest [4] the set of symbols was increased up to 150 different symbols, allowing the definition of more pertinent tests for the evaluation of the scalability. Degradation models included some very extremely hard models in order to test the robustness of the methods under very extreme conditions. In the third edition [5] a dataset of logos was included in the framework in order to test the genericity of the participant methods. With the same goal different types of randomly selected degradations were included in the same test in order to generate blind tests.

In this paper we summarize the framework and the results of the new edition of the contest following the series of previous GREC contests. Three are the main novelties of this edition of the contest. Firstly, a new set of images for isolated symbol recognition is generated. This new set is composed of a set of blind tests – mixing different kinds of degradations in the same test – and intends to be representative enough of the kind of degradations encountered in graphics recognition applications. It has been carefully designed to permit the evaluation of the scalability of the methods. Secondly, a new type of test has been created including images of symbols that have been directly cropped from real drawings. The goal is to evaluate the performance of isolated symbol recognition when it is not possible to achieve a perfect segmentation of the symbol. Thirdly, a set of complete architectural and electrical drawings has been defined allowing to include, for the first time, the evaluation of symbol spotting. This was one of the missing issues in the past editions of the contest. Recently, there have been interesting contributions regarding both the creation of datasets [3] and the definition of metrics [10] for performance evaluation of spotting systems in graphics recognition. We have taken advantage of these works to include symbol spotting in this edition of the contest.

In the rest of the paper, in section 2 we describe the datasets generated for the contest. Then, in section 3 we explain the evaluation metrics used both for recognition and spotting. In section 4 we analyze the results obtained by the only participant method. Finally, in section 5 we state the main conclusions and discuss open issues for next editions of the contest.

2   Dataset

For the generation of the dataset we have used the same set of 150 symbols of the previous GREC contests. We have created different datasets for symbol recognition and symbol spotting that are described in the next sections. Tables 1 and 2 summarize the contents of these datasets for training and test respectively.

2.1   Symbol Recognition

Datasets for isolated symbol recognition have already been generated for the past editions of the contest. However, we decided to create new datasets in order to provide a set of tests that could complement some of the drawbacks of previous ones and could become a kind of generic datasets to be used from now on as a reference for any evaluation of symbol recognition methods. Thus, we designed the new datasets with the following goals: first, to provide a set of tests that could evaluate scalability of methods; second, to be able to test the performance of methods under some realistic increasing degradations; third, to be able to test the genericity of the methods. It is worth to mention that this option prevents from comparing the results with those of previous contests.

Table 1. Training datasets. (S/M is the instance of (S)ymbols per (M)odel)

id	Type	Domain	Models	S/M	Symbols	Noise
#1	recognition	Technical	150	10	1500	Rotation
#2	recognition	Technical	150	10	1500	Scaling
#3	recognition	Technical	150	10	1500	Rotation/Scaling
#4	recognition	Technical	150	25	3750	Kanungo-Level α
#5	recognition	Technical	150	25	3750	Kanungo-Level β
#6	recognition	Technical	150	25	3750	Kanungo-Level η
#7	recognition	Technical	36	25	900	Context
					16650	

id	Type	Domain	Models	Images	Symbols	Noise
#8	localization	Architectural	16	5	142	Ideal
#9	localization	Architectural	16	5	133	Kanungo-Level 1
#10	localization	Architectural	16	5	144	Kanungo-Level 2
#11	localization	Architectural	16	5	128	Kanungo-Level 3
#12	localization	Electrical	21	5	54	Ideal
#13	localization	Electrical	21	5	81	Kanungo-Level 1
#14	localization	Electrical	21	5	91	Kanungo-Level 2
#15	localization	Electrical	21	5	62	Kanungo-Level 3
				40	**835**	

As a result we generated three different sets of images each with an increasing number of symbols (50, 100 and 150). For each of these tests, we synthetically generated 50 images of every symbol with different degradations. To generate degradations, as in previous contests, we used the method of binary degradation proposed by Kanungo et al.[6]. This is a well founded and established method for generating document distortions. We started by generating basic images of each symbol by applying a very slight binary degradations to the ideal image of the symbol – figure 1(a)–. Using these basic images we generated a set of images with rotation, scaling and combined rotation and scaling (training sets #1 to #3 in table 1). Then, we generated more degraded images according to different settings of Kanungo's method parameters. We just modified each of the parameters independently in order to get a set of increasing different types of distortions. Changing parameter α we were able to generate images where lines are thinned with respect to the original ones – figure 1(b)-(c) and set #4 in table 1–. Parameter β allows to simulate thicker lines – figure 1(d)-(e) and set #5 in table 1–. Finally, parameter η influences the level of global noise – figure 1(f)-(g) and set #5 in table 1–. In order to test the genericity of methods we mixed randomly all degradations in the final tests so that participants couldn't have any a priori information about the kind of noise of images – see table 2–.

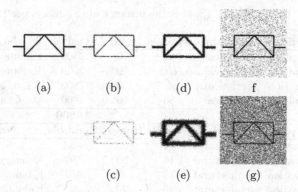

Fig. 1. Examples of images generated for the symbol recognition tests. (a) Basic image. (b)-(c) Degradation according to parameter α. (d)-(e) Degradation according to parameter β. (f)-(g) Degradation according to parameter η.

Fig. 2. Examples of images cropped from complete drawings

In addition to these three sets of images of isolated symbols, we generated an additional fourth set consisting of images directly cropped from complete drawings. Thus, images were instances of symbols not perfectly segmented. The goal of this fourth test set was to evaluate recognition performance under more realistic conditions where a perfect segmentation can not be usually achieved. It can only be seen as a way of involving user interaction in the tests. These tests propose query symbols (i.e. cropped images of symbols) that can be affected by the way the user makes the selection. They try to imitate this effect by randomly growing the bounding box of the symbol. In that sense, they constitute a tradeoff between the recognition and localization problems. This work has been motivated by the interest of the community on such a problem, as highlighted in some recent contributions [8]. Only 36 different symbols were used to generate this set. Some examples of these images can be seen in figure 2 – tests #7 and #4 in tables 1 and 2 respectively –.

2.2 Symbol Spotting

This is the first time that images of complete drawings are provided for evaluation of symbol spotting in the series of GREC contests. The main difficulty up to now was the unavailability of public datasests for symbol spotting. In this edition we have taken advantage of a recent work describing the synthetic generation of complete architectural floorplans and electronic diagrams [3]. The approach is based on the definition of a set of constraints that directs the placement of a

Table 2. Final datasets. (S/M is the instance of (S)ymbols per (M)odel)

id	Type	Domain	Models	S/M	Symbols	Noise
#1	recognition	Technical	50	50	2500	Kanungo-Mixed
#2	recognition	Technical	100	50	5000	Kanungo-Mixed
#3	recognition	Technical	150	50	7500	Kanungo-Mixed
#4	recognition	Technical	36	50	1800	Context
					16800	

id	Type	Domain	Models	Images	Symbols	Noise
#5	localization	Architectural	16	20	633	Ideal
#6	localization	Architectural	16	20	597	Kanungo-Level 1
#7	localization	Architectural	16	20	561	Kanungo-Level 2
#8	localization	Architectural	16	20	593	Kanungo-Level 3
#9	localization	Electrical	21	20	246	Ideal
#10	localization	Electrical	21	20	274	Kanungo-Level 1
#11	localization	Electrical	21	20	237	Kanungo-Level 2
#12	localization	Electrical	21	20	322	Kanungo-Level 3
			160		**3463**	

given set of symbols on a pre-defined background according to the properties of a particular domain (architecture, electronics, engineering, etc.). In this way, we can obtain a large amount of images resembling real documents by simply defining the set of constraints and providing a few pre-defined backgrounds. As documents are synthetically generated, the groundtruth (the location and the label of every symbol) becomes automatically available. All the documents generated in the context of this work have been published in a dataset called SESYD[1] made publicly available[2] for performance evaluation purpose.

To generate the localization tests for this GREC contest, we have used samples of the SESYD dataset. The whole SESYD dataset is composed of 20 collections, 10 collections from the architectural domain plus 10 from the electrical one. The architectural floorplans are composed of 16 symbol models whereas the electrical diagrams are composed of 21. We have selected 14 collections from the initial dataset, those that permit to guarantee the homogeneity of line thickness across different images. Images have been randomly selected in order to get a mix of different backgrounds in tests . Tables 1, 2 give the details about these tests. We have generated 8 different tests both for training (#8 to #15) and test (#5 to #12) datasets, four corresponding to architectural floorplans and four corresponding to electronic diagrams. For each domain, one test contains ideal instances of the symbols while the other three contain increasingly degraded versions of the symbols using the Kanungo's method [6] as in the tests for symbol recognition. We have employed different parameters of the method to provide four levels of degradation: ideal (i.e. without noise), levels 1, 2 and 3. The training tests are composed of 5 drawings each, whereas the final tests are composed of 20. Some examples of these images are shown in Fig. 3.

---

[1] Systems Evaluation SYnthetic Documents.
[2] http://mathieu.delalandre.free.fr/projects/sesyd/

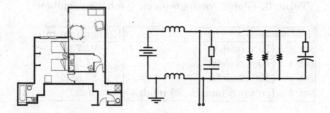

Fig. 3. Examples of images of complete drawings for symbol spotting

3   Evaluation Metrics

For symbol recognition we just used the recognition rate as in previous editions
of the contest. For symbol spotting we have adopted the measures proposed in
a recent work that redefined classical retrieval performance measures for the
case of spotting in graphics recognition [10]. For completeness we recall in the
following the definition of these measures as described in the original paper.
They are based on the overlapping of the set of polygons describing the ground-
truth and the set of polygons returned as a result of spotting. In our case we
have constrained the polygons to rectangular bounding boxes of symbols both
in the ground-truth and in the results.

Then, being $A(P)$ the area of a set of polygons, being $\oplus$ the operator that
denotes the intersection of two sets of polygons, P_{rel} the set of polygons in the
ground-truth and P_{ret} the set of polygons retrieved by the spotting system,
precision P, recall R and F-score F are defined as follows:

$$P = \frac{A(P_{ret} \oplus P_{rel})}{A(P_{ret})} \tag{1}$$

$$R = \frac{A(P_{ret} \oplus P_{rel})}{A(P_{rel})} \tag{2}$$

$$F = \frac{P \cdot R}{P + R} \tag{3}$$

In addition to these measures two additional measures are defined to evaluate
the recognition at symbol level, that is, the percentage of symbols that are found
at some degree by the spotting system. This degree of confidence that controls
if a symbol has been found is defined in terms of overlapping between the area
of the symbol in the ground-truth and the result of the retrieval. Thus, if the
overlapping area is above a certain threshold (that is fixed to 75%) of the area
of the symbol in the ground-truth the symbol is considered as correctly identified. Then, recognition rate, as the percentage of symbols in the ground-truth
correctly identified, and average false positives $AveFP$ as the average number
of returned symbols that do not correspond to any ground-truth symbols, are
also defined as complementary evaluation metrics.

Table 3. Global results tests on symbol recognition

Test name	Recognition rate
set #1 (50 models)	94,76%
set #2 (100 models)	91,98%
set #3 (150 models)	85,88%
set #4 (cropped images, 36 models)	96,22%

4   Results

There was only one participant in the contest, in both entries, symbol recognition and symbol spotting. The method, based on geometric matching, was developed by Nayef et. al. [9], IUPR research group of the university of Kaiserslautern. The method is based on geometric matching. In the next subsections we will report detailed results for symbol recognition and symbol spotting.

Table 4. Detail of results for set #3 for each kind of deformation

Degradation	Recognition rate
Basic	85,33%
Rotation & scaling	84,84%
Degradation α	88,07%
Degradation β	85,73%
Degradation η	85,67%

4.1   Symbol Recognition

As it has been described in section 2 we generated 4 different tests for symbol recognition. Three of them were created after applying several deformations to an increasing number of symbol models: 50, 100 and 150. The fourth test consisted of images of symbols directly segmented from the drawings including lines of their neighboring elements . The global results for each test are shown in table 3. As expected we can observe that accuracy decreases as the number of symbol models increase. However, the method seems to be robust to segmentation noise. Accuracy for set #4 is higher than in the other tests. These better results could be justified by the lower number of symbol models (only 36) in this test, and also by the fact that the symbols in this test are clean images with no noise at all. The background lines connected to the symbols did not affect the performance since the method works for recognizing symbols in context.

Table 5. Results for set #3 for images with rotation and scaling

Level of degradation	Recognition rate
Rotation	81,07%
Scaling	89,20%
Rotation-Scaling	84,27%

In tables 4–8 we show detailed results for each kind of transformation applied to the images. Table 4 shows the details for each kind of deformation according to the different parameters of Kanungo's degradation model or to the affine transforms (rotation and scaling) applied to the images. We have only included results for set #3 as it is the set with the larger number of symbol models and thus, where differences could be a priori more significant. However, we do no appreciate significant differences in the accuracy for the different kinds of deformations. It is surprising that results for degradation according to parameter α – which generates images with thin lines, as shown in figure 1 – are better than those for the basic set of images with a very slight noise – figure 1 –. A possible explanation could be that the method includes an adaptive preprocessing and noise removal module to deal with different kinds of heavy binary noise.

Table 6. Results for set #3 for different levels of degradation based on parameter α

Level of degradation	Recognition rate
Level 1	88,40%
Level 2	87,73%

Analyzing in more detail the results for each kind of distortion we can observe that the method seems to be more robust to scaling than to rotation – table 5 –. For degradations generated with the Kanungo's model, the performance decreases slightly as the amount of noise increases, although not in a significant way – tables 6–8–.

Table 7. Results for set #3 for different levels of degradation based on parameter β

Level of degradation	Recognition rate
Level 1	85,87%
Level 2	85,60%

4.2   Symbol Spotting

In the spotting tests, participants were asked to spot all instances of all symbol models included in the test. In table 9 we show the results for the tests including images of architectural floorplans with increasing levels of noise. Although there is not a completely linear relation, we can observe a degradation of all the performance indices as the amount of noise increases. This relation is not so clear for images of electrical diagrams 10. At this point, it is probably worth noting

Table 8. Results for set #3 for different levels of degradation based on parameter η

Level of degradation	Recognition rate
Level 1	86,00%
Level 2	85,33%

that the performance of a symbol spotting system can depend on many factors, being the level of noise only one of them. There are other parameters such as the number and location of the symbols that can also have a great influence in the final results. Since all these parameters have been determined at least partially in a random way, we do not have a complete control on the difficulty of every test. In addition, analyzing the results on symbol recognition in the previous section, we can see that the method seems to be quite robust to binary noise.

Table 9. Spotting results for images of architectural floorplans

Test name	Precision	Recall	F-Score	Recognition rate	Average false positives
Set #5 (ideal)	0.62	0.99	0.76	99,31	18,75
Set #6 (level 1)	0.64	0.98	0.77	97,00%	13,68
Set #7 (level 2)	0.62	0.93	0.74	98,80%	13,62
Set #8 (level 3)	0.57	0.98	0.72	97,74%	17,37

Table 10. Spotting results for images of electrical diagrams

Test name	Precision	Recall	F-Score	Recognition rate	Average false positives
Set #9 (ideal)	0.37	0.56	0.45	94,02%	2.66
Set #10 (level 1)	0.44	0.63	0.52	86,27%	3.19
Set #11 (level 2)	0.40	0.61	0.48	85,25%	2.66
Set #12 (level 3)	0.43	0.64	0.51	88,40%	3.76

5   Conclusions

In this paper we have described the framework for the fourth edition of the Symbol Recognition Contest and we have reported the results achieved by the only participant method. This is the first time that the contest includes an entry on symbol spotting.

Concerning symbol recognition, after several editions of the contest we have evolved the dataset including a systematic way of generating several kinds of distortions from a basic set of images of the symbols. We think that this dataset can serve without further significant modifications for future editions of the contest and can become a stable platform for continuous evaluation and comparison of symbol recognition methods, maybe with the only additional inclusion of hand-drawn symbols.

With respect to symbol spotting, this is the first important attempt to provide a complete framework for evaluations, including a significantly large dataset along with a set of performance measures. We feel that the final result is encouraging, although probably some improvement should be done in the creation of the dataset, particularly regarding the generation of noise, to be able to characterize the difficulty of each test. And, obviously, we need to foster participation in the contest to validate the framework.

Acknowledgments. This work has been partially supported by the Spanish projects TIN2009-14633- C03-03, TSI-020400-2011-50 and a CONSOLIDER-INGENIO 2010(CSD2007-00018).

References

1. Aksoy, S., Ye, M., Schauf, M., Song, M., Wang, Y., Haralick, R., Parker, J., Pivovarov, J., Royko, D., Sun, C., Farneback, G.: Algorithm performance contest. In: Proceedings of the 15th International Conference on Pattern Recognition, vol. 4, pp. 870–876 (2000)
2. Chhabra, A.K.: Graphic Symbol Recognition: An Overview. In: Chhabra, A.K., Tombre, K. (eds.) GREC 1997. LNCS, vol. 1389, pp. 68–79. Springer, Heidelberg (1998)
3. Delalandre, M., Valveny, E., Pridmore, T., Karatzas, D.: Generation of synthetic documents for performance evaluation of symbol recognition & spotting systems. Int. J. Doc. Anal. Recognit. 13, 187–207 (2010)
4. Dosch, P., Valveny, E.: Report on the Second Symbol Recognition Contest. In: Liu, W., Lladós, J. (eds.) GREC 2005. LNCS, vol. 3926, pp. 381–397. Springer, Heidelberg (2006)
5. Valveny, E., Dosch, P., Fornes, A., Escalera, S.: Report on the Third Contest on Symbol Recognition. In: Liu, W., Lladós, J., Ogier, J.-M. (eds.) GREC 2007. LNCS, vol. 5046, pp. 321–328. Springer, Heidelberg (2008)
6. Kanungo, T., Haralick, R.M., Stuezle, W., Baird, H.S., Madigan, D.: A statistical, nonparametric methodology for document degradation model validation. IEEE Trans. Pattern Anal. Mach. Intell. 22, 1209–1223 (2000)
7. Lladós, J., Valveny, E., Sánchez, G., Martí, E.: Symbol Recognition: Current Advances and Perspectives. In: Blostein, D., Kwon, Y.-B. (eds.) GREC 2002. LNCS, vol. 2390, pp. 104–128. Springer, Heidelberg (2002)
8. Luqman, M.M., Delalandre, M., Brouard, T., Ramel, J.-Y., Lladós, J.: Fuzzy Intervals for Designing Structural Signature: An Application to Graphic Symbol Recognition. In: Ogier, J.-M., Liu, W., Lladós, J. (eds.) GREC 2009. LNCS, vol. 6020, pp. 12–24. Springer, Heidelberg (2010)
9. Nayef, N., Breuel, T.M.: On the use of geometric matching for both: Isolated symbol recognition and symbol spotting. In: Proceedings of the 9th International Conference on Graphics Recognition, GREC 2011 (2011)
10. Rusiñol, M., Lladós, J.: A performance evaluation protocol for symbol spotting systems in terms of recognition and location indices. International Journal on Document Analysis and Recognition 12, 83–96 (2009)
11. Tombre, K., Tabbone, S., Dosch, P.: Musings on Symbol Recognition. In: Liu, W., Lladós, J. (eds.) GREC 2005. LNCS, vol. 3926, pp. 23–34. Springer, Heidelberg (2006)
12. Valveny, E., Dosch, P., Winstanley, A., Zhou, Y., Yang, S., Yan, L., Wenyin, L., Elliman, D., Delalandre, M., Trupin, E., Adam, S., Ogier, J.M.: A general framework for the evaluation of symbol recognition methods. Int. J. Doc. Anal. Recognit. 9, 59–74 (2007)
13. Valveny, E., Dosch, P.: Symbol Recognition Contest: A Synthesis. In: Lladós, J., Kwon, Y.-B. (eds.) GREC 2003. LNCS, vol. 3088, pp. 368–385. Springer, Heidelberg (2004)

Bag-of-GraphPaths Descriptors for Symbol Recognition and Spotting in Line Drawings

Anjan Dutta[1], Josep Lladós[1], and Umapada Pal[2]

[1] Computer Vision Center, Universitat Autònoma de Barcelona, Bellaterra,
Barcelona, Spain
{adutta,josep}@cvc.uab.es
[2] CVPR Unit, Indian Statistical Institute, 203 B.T. Road, Kolkata-700108, India
umapada@isical.ac.in

Abstract. Graphical symbol recognition and spotting recently have become an important research activity. In this work we present a descriptor for symbols, especially for line drawings. The descriptor is based on the graph representation of graphical objects. We construct graphs from the vectorized information of the binarized images, where the critical points detected by the vectorization algorithm are considered as nodes and the lines joining them are considered as edges. Graph paths between two nodes in a graph are the finite sequences of nodes following the order from the starting to the final node. The occurrences of different graph paths in a given graph is an important feature, as they capture the geometrical and structural attributes of a graph. So the graph representing a symbol can efficiently be represent by the occurrences of its different paths. Their occurrences in a symbol can be obtained in terms of a histogram counting the number of some fixed prototype paths, we call the histogram as the Bag-of-GraphPaths (BOGP). These BOGP histograms are used as a descriptor to measure the distance among the symbols in vector space. We use the descriptor for three applications, they are: (1) classification of the graphical symbols, (2) spotting of the architectural symbols on floorplans, (3) classification of the historical handwritten words.

Keywords: Graphic recognition, Symbol recognition, Symbol spotting, Focused Retrieval, Bag-of-GraphPaths.

1 Introduction

Nowadays graphical symbol recognition and spotting has become an important research activity. There is a good demand of effective tools for searching of symbolic objects. The goal is to develop an efficient search engine to find similar graphical objects from a large collection. Shape is an important visual feature and it is one of the basic features used to describe image content. However, shape representation and description is a difficult task, since the real symbol often become corrupted with noise, defects, arbitrary distortion, occlusion etc. Shape representation generally looks for effective and perceptually important features

Y.-B. Kwon and J.-M. Ogier (Eds.): GREC, LNCS 7423, pp. 208–217, 2013.

based on either shape boundary information or boundary with interior content. Various features have been designed, including shape signature, signature histogram, shape invariants, moments, curvature, shape context, shape matrix, spectral features etc. These various shape features are often evaluated how accurately they allow one to retrieve similar shapes from a designated database. However, it is not sufficient to evaluate a representation technique only by the effectiveness of the features employed. This is because the evaluation ignores other important characteristics of a shape representation technique.

There is a long list of shape descriptors available in the literature and majority of them are developed for some specific applications. The major shape descriptors include some simple geometrical, topological properties viz. area, circularity, eccentricity, convexity, ratio of principle axis, circular variance, major axis orientation, bending energy and some combination of them, interested readers are referred to [16] for detailed review. Some of the shape descriptors are based on the points features [1,3], where the points lie on the boundary of the shape. They use some of the distance measures to get the point to point correspondence between two shapes. Boundary moment of a shape is also used as a shape descriptors. Time series models and especially auto-regressive modeling is also used for calculating shape descriptors [2,4,15]. Shape signatures which represent a shape as an one dimensional function derived from the shape boundary points [17] are also used for this purpose. Shapes can be efficiently represented with attributed graphs and for that graph matching, embedding are used to get the similarity measure among graphs representing shapes. The recent major methods work with the graph representation of shapes are mentioned in [9–11, 14]. Usually graph matching or embedding costs lot computational efforts. Moreover, to cope with real world image distortion, these algorithms include some kind of noise model within it which further increases the cost. So this kind of algorithm works aiming to minimize the computational costs while maintaining the matching efficiency even in the presence of distortion.

In this work we try to explore the power of graphs as a tool for structural representation and for that we propose a graph based shape descriptor for shape recognition. The descriptor is based on the graph representation of the objects where the graph is constructed from the vectorized information of binarized images. Our graph representation considers the critical points detected by the vectorization method as the nodes and the lines joining them as the edges. Our description of a symbol depends on the occurrences of the graph paths. A graph path (Hamiltonian path) between two nodes is the sequence of ordered nodes from the starting node to the ending node. Graph paths capture structural attributes as the topological features. Moreover, graph paths give the serialized representation of graphs, which is efficient in terms of computation. Graph paths also give one type factorized representation which allows tolerance to structural error to a certain level. The occurrences of different graph paths in a symbol contain an important and discriminative structural information which is similar for similar symbols and different for different symbols. The distribution of different paths are obtained in terms of a histogram resulted in counting the number of occurrences of each of the paths in a set of prototype paths.

The rest of the paper is outlined as follows: In Section 2 we describe the propose descriptor. We present our experimental results in Section 3, followed by a general discussions in 4. Finally, in Section 5 we conclude the paper and future research works are defined.

2   Proposed Descriptor

In this paper we present a descriptor for graphical symbol recognition. The descriptor is based on the graph representation of the objects where the graph is constructed from the vectorized information of the binarized images. Our graph representation considers the critical points detected by the vectorization method as the nodes and the lines joining them as the edges. Our description of a symbol depends on the occurrences of the graph paths. A graph path (Hamiltonian path) between two nodes is the ordered sequence of nodes from the starting node to the ending node. Graph paths capture structural attributes as the topological features. As mentioned earlier the occurrences of different graph paths in a symbol contain an important and discriminative structural information which is similar for similar symbols and different for different symbols. To capture the path information in each of the symbols, we calculate all the acyclic paths between each of the connected nodes and assign each of them a label of the nearest prototype paths. So at the end we calculate the frequencies of the prototype paths in a symbol. These frequencies create the histogram representation of counting number of prototype paths in a symbol. These histograms capture the distribution of paths in each of the symbols which is discriminative.

2.1   Graph Based Representation of Symbols

To represent an object with a graph we use the binarized images, which again vectorized to get the light weight representation of images. The vectorization process detects the critical points in the binarized images by checking the bending curvature of the point compared to the neighboring points. We consider the critical points detected by the vectorization process as the nodes of graphs and the lines joining them as the edges (see fig. 1).

2.2   Bag-of-GraphPaths (BOGP)

An acyclic path between any two connected nodes in a graph is the ordered sequence of nodes from the source node to the destination following the order of the terminal nodes [6, 7]. For describing a symbol with the BOGP descriptors, we represent it as a graph and then compute all possible acyclic graph paths between each pair of connected nodes of the graph (see fig. 2). Then all the paths are then described with some shape descriptors. In our case we use the Zernike moments descriptors of order 7 for that purpose, this order is experimentally

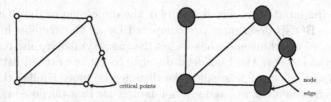

Fig. 1. The critical points detected by the vectorization method are considered as the nodes and the lines joining them are considered as the edges

chosen to give the best performance. Let us call the set of descriptors of all the graph paths as $P_m = \{p_1, ..., p_m\}$, and also call a set of prototype paths that are selected by a random prototype selection technique from P_m as $P_n = \{p_1, ..., p_n\}$ and $P_n \subseteq P_m$, $m \geq n$. Random selection technique is followed since the usual methodologies to create vocabularies such as clustering are computationally expensive to apply here because of the large number of graph paths. Then each of the paths in a symbol is assigned as one of the prototype paths using Euclidean distance measure. So at the end it is possible to count the frequency of each of the prototype paths in a graph representing the symbol. This finally represent each of the graphs with a histogram by counting the number of nearest prototype paths occurred in the symbol. Here since the symbol is represented by the count of graph paths and the graph paths are rotation invariant the resulting descriptors of the symbols are also rotation invariant.

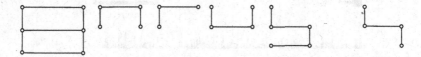

Fig. 2. Different acyclic paths between each pair of connected nodes

A descriptor for a symbol S_1 with the set of paths $P_{S_1} = \{p_l, ..., p_m\}$ is the histogram of counting the number of paths similar to each of the prototype paths:

$$BOGP(S_1) = [\#p_1 \in P_{S_1}, ..., \#p_n \in P_{S_1}] \tag{1}$$

These descriptors contain similar distribution for similar symbols and different distribution for different symbols (see fig. 3).

3 Experimental Results

3.1 Symbol Matching

In order to evaluate the proposed methodology, we present a symbol matching experiment. The set of prototype paths is created by randomly selecting 1000 paths from the input data, which results in the dimension of the BOGP vector as 1000. The BOGP descriptors are computed for all the symbols in which we perform symbol matching and when we get the query symbol we also compute the descriptor and measure the Euclidean distance to get the ranked list of symbol for a particular query. The smaller the distance is, more similar the symbols are. We use two different isolated symbol dataset for that purpose and they are: (i) SESYD Queries (floorplans) [5] and (ii) GREC-POLY [12] (see fig. 4). Both of these two datasets are created with some kind of noise and distortion model to simulate the noise introduced by the real world situation. We compute the precision (P), recall (R) and average precision ($AveP$) of the retrieval list to get the quantitative measure of the results. The readers are referred to [13] for further details about those measures in information retrieval.

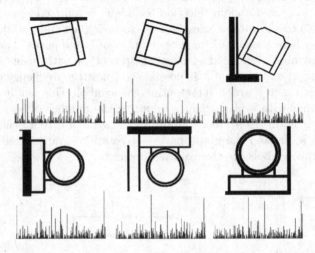

Fig. 3. Histogram to compute the number of paths is shown for similarity measure. BOGP descriptors give similar distribution for similar symbols and different distribution for different symbols.

SESYD Queries (Floorplans). This dataset contains synthetically generated corpus of symbols cropped from complete documents. These experiments are focused on evaluating the robustness of the proposed algorithm against the context noise i.e. the structural noise introduced in symbols when they are cropped from the documents. We believe that being successful on this kind of noise is very important when the algorithm is intended to apply for symbol spotting on a whole document. This dataset contains 3 levels of difficulties of structural noise each level containing 1000 images results in 3000 floorplan symbols in total and 16 ideal symbols used as the model symbols.

We got 60.79% precision (P), 80.58% recall (R) and 85.26% average precision ($AveP$) on this dataset, which indicates the success of the proposed algorithm. But in case of symbols having similar substructures the algorithm confuses, this explains the small amount of errors in the results. But we got good average precision which shows the true positives occur at the beginning of the ranked list.

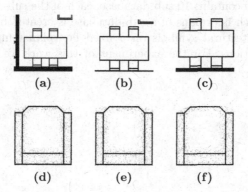

Fig. 4. (a)-(c) Example of symbols from the SESYD Queries database, (d)-(f) Example of symbols from the GREC-POLY database

GREC-POLY. This dataset is mainly adapted from the symbol recognition contest of GREC '2005. The bitmap images are degraded with the noise model proposed by Kanungo et al [8], which simulates the datasets with the noise introduced by the scanning process. The authors have applied three separate sets of parameters to generate three different degradation levels, where each of the total 150 model symbols are degraded to generate 300 degraded images, which results in total 45000 isolated symbols. The dataset is available in vectorized form which is proceeded by a simple morphological operation and a connected component analysis to label the closed regions and the internal and external contours composing a symbol. This dataset also contains arbitrary rotation and scaling.

For this dataset, we got 78.76% precision (**P**), 88.67% recall (**R**) and 93.83% average precision (**AveP**). The method is more successful in this dataset, because it creates the descriptors based on the factorized substructures of graph representation of the symbol which can efficiently tolerate the deformation that this dataset contains.

As we mentioned the vocabulary or the set of prototype paths is created by randomly selecting the graph paths from the available data. To show that the results are independent of the vocabulary selection technique, we repeat this experiment with another randomly selected vocabulary on the SESYD Queries (floorplans) dataset. The experiments results in 61.17% precision (**P**), 88.12% recall (**R**) and 94.29% average precision (**AveP**), which is the same result obtained from the previous settings. This proves that the random selection of the vocabulary does not effect much on the results.

3.2   Symbol Spotting

This experiment is done to show the effectiveness of the proposed descriptors for spotting symbols on documents. We use the SESYD floorplan database [5] for the experiment purpose. This is a collection of synthetically generated images. The database contains 10 sub-database, each of the sub-database contains 100 floorplans. Each floorplans of a sub-database is created by randomly placing different architectural symbols on a fixed floorplan template in different scales and orientations. For the experiment of this work we use one of those sub-databases.

Query:

Results:

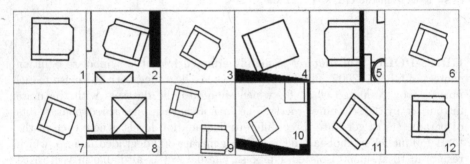

Fig. 5. Qualitative results for the SESYD dataset by our method for the armchair symbol

For spotting or detection we need some localization technique, for that we run sliding window of size 30×30 pixels with 60% overlapping and capture the path information in the window. Then a BOGP histogram is computed for each window. The set of prototype paths is created by taking the 1000 randomly selected paths from the given documents. So in this case each of the sliding windows result in a BOGP histogram vector of size 1000. Since spotting intended to work with large dataset, searching of the query should be more efficient. For that we organize the descriptors of each of the window in hash tables with locality sensitive hashing (LSH) technique. So when the query is invoked, it is described by a BOGP descriptors and then looking into the hash tables results in set of retrievals. The retrievals are then ranked in ascending order based on the distance measure. The retrievals at beginning of the list are supposed to be more relevant to the queried one.

The algorithm results in 35.61% precision (**P**), 65.24% recall (**R**) and 45.76% average precision (**AveP**). The lower recall value implies that the system misses many true instance on the documents. Also the system detects many false positives which further lowers the precision value. The average precision is also bad which implies that the retrieved true symbols do not appear at the beginning of the lists. The lower results for symbol spotting noted the difficulties of sliding window based detection technique which is used in this case. In this case we only use single resolution sliding window but it could be interesting to work with multiple sized sliding windows, but this will further increase the computation time.

3.3   Handwritten Word Recognition

It is obvious that any graphical object can be given symbolic representation. This experiment is done to check whether our BOGP descriptor is also eligible to capture the information of handwritten words. For that we choose to apply the descriptor to a word recognition scenario. We use a corpus that contains 27 pages from a collection of marriage registers from the Barcelona Cathedral, where all the pages are well segmented upto the word level. To apply our descriptor we consider each of the segmented words as a symbol and use the same experimental settings as of sub-section 3.1. In this case also the set of prototype paths is created from 1000 randomly selected paths from the given data. The method needs a preprocessing step including binarization which is done by the Otsu algorithm.

The precision (**P**), recall (**R**) and average precision (**AveP**) attend by the system are respectively 0.65%, 93.77% and 9.73%. Although the quantitative results seem to be quite bad, the results contain visual similarity with the queried word. In fig.6 we present a qualitative result for a given query word "Farrer" for the Barcelona Cathedral collection. We can see that the method present some false positives in the first ten responses. In general handwritten words are very cursive in nature. So in a small region where the curvature of the writing is high,

Query:

Results:

Fig. 6. Qualitative results for the Barcelona Cathedral collection by our method for the word "Farrer"

it creates lot of spurious points. So small variation of in the writing styles creates lot of difference after they are represented by the graphs. This can explain the bad results in case of the hand writing recognition.

4   Discussions

In previous papers [6, 7] we presented two techniques for symbol spotting on graphical documents. The methods were also graph paths based, but we used serialized matching and some hashing scheme for comparing different path structure. The results in those cases were better than this one, this is definitely due to the sliding window technique which compromise some of the accuracy.

5   Conclusions and Future Works

In this paper we have presented a symbol description technique based on the graph representation of objects. The descriptor is based on the distribution of the graph paths of a graph representing the symbols. Graph paths contain structural attributes as features and the distribution of those paths in a similar symbol is similar but different for different symbols. We tested the methods on the recognition of isolated symbols and for symbol spotting, the results are encouraging.

We also investigated whether we could apply our descriptor for representing handwritten words but in that case our results are not as expected. This is due to the cursive nature of the handwritten words, where little variance creates lot of difference in the our graph representation. So the future work will concentrate on introducing more efficient noise model to the existing system.

Acknowledgement. This work has been partially supported by the Spanish projects TIN2009-14633-C03-03, TIN2008-04998, CSD2007-00018 and the PhD scholarship 2011FI_B 01022 by the AGAUR.

References

1. Belongie, S., Malik, J., Puzicha, J.: Shape matching and object recognition using shape contexts. IEEE Transactions on Pattern Analysis and Machine Intelligence 24(4), 509–522 (2002)
2. Chellappa, R., Bagdazian, R.: Fourier coding of image boundaries. IEEE Transactions on Pattern Analysis and Machine Intelligence PAMI-6(1), 102–105 (1984)
3. Chetverikov, D., Khenokh, Y.: Matching for Shape Defect Detection. In: Solina, F., Leonardis, A. (eds.) CAIP 1999. LNCS, vol. 1689, pp. 367–374. Springer, Heidelberg (1999)
4. Das, M., Paulik, M.J., Loh, N.K.: A bivariate autoregressive technique for analysis and classification of planar shapes. IEEE Transactions on Pattern Analysis and Machine Intelligence 12(1), 97–103 (1990)
5. Delalandre, M., Pridmore, T., Valveny, E., Locteau, H., Trupin, E.: Building synthetic graphical documents for performance evaluation, pp. 288–298. Springer, Heidelberg (2008)

6. Dutta, A., Lladós, J., Pal, U.: Symbol spotting in line drawings through graph paths hashing. In: Proceedings of 11th International Conference of Document Analysis and Recognition (ICDAR 2011), pp. 982–986 (2011)
7. Dutta, A., Lladós, J., Pal, U.: A Bag-of-Paths Based Serialized Subgraph Matching for Symbol Spotting in Line Drawings. In: Vitrià, J., Sanches, J.M., Hernández, M. (eds.) IbPRIA 2011. LNCS, vol. 6669, pp. 620–627. Springer, Heidelberg (2011)
8. Kanungo, T., Haralick, R.M., Phillips, I.: Global and local document degradation models. In: Proceedings of the Second International Conference on Document Analysis and Recognition, October 20-22, pp. 730–734 (1993)
9. Luqman, M.M., Brouard, T., Ramel, J.-Y., Lladós, J.: A content spotting system for line drawing graphic document images. In: 2010 20th International Conference on Pattern Recognition (ICPR), pp. 3420–3423 (2010)
10. Nayef, N., Breuel, T.M.: A branch and bound algorithm for graphical symbol recognition in document images. In: Proceedings of Ninth IAPR International Workshop on Document Analysis System (DAS 2010), pp. 543–546 (2010)
11. Qureshi, R.J., Ramel, J.-Y., Barret, D., Cardot, H.: Spotting Symbols in Line Drawing Images Using Graph Representations. In: Liu, W., Lladós, J., Ogier, J.-M. (eds.) GREC 2007. LNCS, vol. 5046, pp. 91–103. Springer, Heidelberg (2008)
12. Rusiñol, M., Borràs, A., Lladós, J.: Relational indexing of vectorial primitives for symbol spotting in line-drawing images. Pattern Recognition Letters 31(3), 188–201 (2010)
13. Rusiñol, M., Lladós, J.: A performance evaluation protocol for symbol spotting systems in terms of recognition and location indices. International Journal on Document Analysis and Recognition 12(2), 83–96 (2009)
14. Rusiñol, M., Lladós, J., Sánchez, G.: Symbol spotting in vectorized technical drawings through a lookup table of region strings. Pattern Analysis and Applications 13, 1–11 (2009)
15. Sekita, I., Kurita, T., Otsu, N.: Complex autoregressive model for shape recognition. IEEE Transactions on Pattern Analysis and Machine Intelligence 14(4), 489–496 (1992)
16. Young, I.T., Walker, J.E., Bowie, J.E.: An analysis technique for biological shape. i. Information and Control 25(4), 357–370 (1974)
17. Zhang, D., Lu, G.: A comparative study of fourier descriptors for shape representation and retrieval. In: Proc. of 5th Asian Conference on Computer Vision (ACCV), pp. 646–651. Springer (2002)

A Scoring Model for Clothes Matching Using Color Harmony and Texture Analysis

Donghyun Kim, Young-Bin Kwon, and Jaehwa Park

Dept. of Computer Science and Engineering,
Chung-Ang University, Seoul, Korea
{dhkim,ybkwon,jaehwa}@cau.ac.kr

Abstract. A contents based scoring model for clothes matching is represented. The major color sets for upper and lower clothes are extracted using color grouping and clustering after discarding background. The all possible combinations between two color sets are considered to measure the overall color harmony. The regions in which printed patterns on the clothes are detected and the pattern types are classified. The pattern matching score is also calculated using statistical characteristics of dispersity and directional uniformity of edge lines. The final score of clothes matching are obtained via linear weighted sum of the scores of color harmony and pattern matching. In the experimental, the scores generated by the proposed model are compared with the scores offered by human observers for real clothes images collected from internet shopping malls.

Keywords: Clothes Matching Score, Color Harmony, Clothes Pattern Extraction.

1 Introduction

Recently, commercial online access to product information is popular. Due to the bounds of electronic media, the information and features about goods and services available to the consumers are very limited. The weak physical reality of online information lowers the convenience of online shopping than in-person shopping. Functionality of merchandise recommendation is one of the key features for pursuing customer in online shopping mall. A computational scoring method is essential for automated recommend operations.

Clothes matching means selecting a set of two or more clothes items intended to be used or worn together in stylish manner [1]. The best approach for clothes matching is to take items and try them on physically, which is impossible in online shopping. A number of approaches has been tried to bridge the gap between online shopping and real shopping where clothing items are in hand to try on [2].

Since the clothes matching is highly depends on ones preference an objective measuring method for the matching score is hardly found. For the reason, the most developed methods adopt attribute based filtering assisted by database or ontology. The attribute informations are usually generated from the collaborative links or additional information about the clothes items, not from the actual

Y.-B. Kwon and J.-M. Ogier (Eds.): GREC, LNCS 7423, pp. 218–227, 2013.
© Springer-Verlag Berlin Heidelberg 2013

characteristics of the clothes such as style, pattern, texture or colors. Contents based computational scoring models for clothes matching have been not studied much.

In this paper, a contents based computation scoring model for clothes matching is represented. The statistical preference to a pair of upper and lower garments is measured in general sense of color harmony and pattern matching. A dominant color palette with weight coefficients for a cloth is extracted using K-means clustering after discarding background image for color features. Also the regions on a pair of upper and lower clothes which have printed patterns such as symbols, letterings or marks are detected. And their pattern types are estimated using statistical characteristics of dispersity and directional uniformity of edge lines extracted from pattern features.

A color harmony in pair of clothes is defined as a weighted average of the color harmony for two color combinations defined in [3]. The all possible combinations between two color sets of the pair are considered for the color harmony. From the pattern features, the degree of matching preference is transformed into a value based on the pre-determined prototypes obtained by human assistance. The final score of clothes matching is obtained via linear combination of the scores of color harmony and pattern matching with proper weights.

In the experimental, the scores generated by the proposed model are compared with the scores offered by human observers for real clothes images collected from internet shopping malls.

2   Clothes Matching

The preference of clothes matching is very subjective and highly depends on one's personality. There are many studies on clothes matching methods. But they are simply based on the counting of recommendations in the community without considering the contents of clothes. These approaches reflects the peoples preferences well on the products but has some problems too. For example, a recommendation system seldom offers new items, since no additional informations about the items are found in the database.

The harmony of a pair of clothes, top and bottom is difficult to evaluate objectively in a unitary numeric value. For this reason, computational models for measuring the harmony on clothes matching are hardly found. A contents driven approach might be essential for the cases. Also the approach should include a computational metric that works in a uniform procedure.

Table 1 shows the statistical characteristics on pairs of clothes. Total 3208 images of clothes pairs are collected from the popular Internet shopping malls. The clothes pairs on the collected mages are assumed to be 'good matching', if the images have top and bottom together as a pair. The 'good matching' may be not always true but most of cases it is acceptable. In Table 1, the tops and bottoms are categorized by symbols and texture patterns. As shown in the table, 97% of bottoms has no symbols or texture features and only 3% of them has some stripes and check patterns. In some cases of tops, the distributions of

Table 1. Statistics on Clothes Matching (No=No pattern or symbol, HS = Horizontal Stripped, VS = Vertical Stripped, CK = Check pattern, SC = Symbol on Center of top, SL = Symbol on Left side of top, SY = Symbols on Bottom)

Cothes Matching		Tops						Sum	%
		No	HS	VS	CK	SC	SL		
Bottoms	No	864	520	1	315	1167	243	3113	97.0
	HS							0	0.0
	VS	23				16		39	1.2
	CK	15						15	0.5
	SY					17	24	41	1.3
Sum		902	520	1	315	1200	270	3208	
%		28.0	16.0	0.0	10.0	37.0	8.0		100

patterns are somewhat spreaded. Since the shopping malls usually sell casual wears such as T-shirts, the tops with symbols (or figures with text characters) have larger portions.

In the table, 864 pairs, which has no texture patterns or symbols in both of top and bottom, is assumed to be well matched. It means that at least 1/4 of clothes matching is only based on color combination. When it is considered that the most of the bottoms has no patterns, the color information is the most important key feature for scoring the clothes matching. Other features of patterns or symbols also work as the key features for the scoring in other cases. Based on the information of Table 1, the color information, texture patterns and symbols are selected as feature set to evaluate the degree of clothes matching. In this paper, a contents based computation scoring model for clothes matching

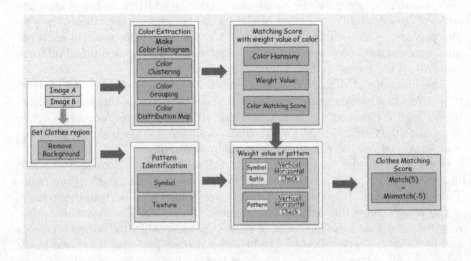

Fig. 1. System Overview

is developed. Fig. 1 shows overall system structure. For the features to measure the matching preference, primitive characteristics of clothes, such as colors, texture patterns, and existence of symbols or text characters, are considered based on the information of Table 1. We only consider the case of matching tops and bottoms on casual wears without considering styles, functionality of clothes etc.

2.1 Preprocessing

To the given top and bottom images, a preprocessing step is applied. The major purpose of the preprocessing is to extract clothes region. The mean shift algorithm [4] is used to region segementation. After region segmentation, the color value of 4 corners as shown in Fig. 2 are selected and the average values of RGB from the extracted color are assumed to be those of background color. And concatenated regions from the corner points, in which the Euclidian distances of RGB values to the background color is less than a threshold, are classified as background regions. The right image of Fig. 2 shows an example of processing results. The background region is marked in pink color.

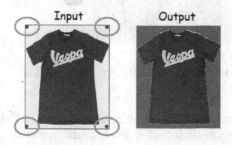

Fig. 2. Clothes region extraction

2.2 Color Feature Extraction

After removing background, two different types of features, color and texture, are extracted. Human can only distinguish just several hundred colors [5]. If pixels, which have similar colors, are neighbored, we can't detect the color difference and perceive them as a color. A process of color grouping and clustering are necessary to extract meaningful information on colors. For the color feature, the major color palette and their weight distributions are extracted. Fig. 3 shows the processing steps to extract major color set.

The mean shift image segmentation algorithm is applied for color grouping. The color given by averaged values of RGB in the segmented region is defined as the representative color of the region. The ratio of the number of pixels of the region to the extracted cloth region is the weight value of the color. After grouping, major color sets are extracted by tje K-means clustering algorithm.

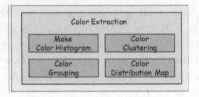

Fig. 3. Major Color Extraction

Since the case in which a clothes item has more than six major colors is seldom found, maximum six colors are extracted for the color set based on the weight values of clusters.

Fig. 4. An Example of Color Detection

Fig. 4 shows an example of processing results on color grouping and clustering. The left image shows the input after background removal, and colors on the bars of right image shows the extracted major color set. The length of bar mean the normalized weight value. The center image shows the result of color transformation using the extracted major color set. In the center image, the each pixel color is exchanged into the closest color in the major color set.

2.3 Symbol and Texture Extraction

For texture pattern and symbol features, the regions that have printed graphic patterns or symbols are detected and the pattern types are estimated in statistical informations of edge line distributions.

By the observation of collected data set, the texture patterns of clothes are categorized into three types of horizontal stripped, vertical stripped and check patterns, though there are lots of varieties on combination of colors, width of strips, etc. Also symbols such as text characters, marks or figures usually exist on top clothes and seldom exist on bottoms. It seems that location and the portion of the symbols in clothe region play more significant roles on clothes matching than actual contents of symbols, such as meaning of text characters. Thus the location and ratio of symboled regions are considered as features.

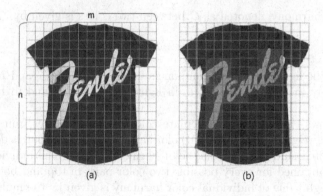

Fig. 5. Symbol and Texture Extraction

To extract texture patterns and symbol features, the bounding box of extracted clothe region is equally divided into $m \times n$ grids as shown in Fig. 5-(a). Then edge detection method is applied to the clothe regions and the number of edge points is obtained on each grid. If the ratio of edge points to the grid size is larger than a threshold, the grid is assumed to have symbols or patterns in it as shown in Fig. 5-(b). The threshold is determined by the ratio of entire edge points to the size of entire clothe regions.

If the number of grids which have edges are lager than 50% then the existence of texture pattern detection procedure is applied. If edge ratio of entire region is larger than a predetermined threshold, and if both of the difference between the edge ratio of entire region and the average of grid edge ratios are smaller than the variance of grid edge ratios, then the clothe is assumed to have texture patterns.

If a clothes item has texture patterns, the pattern type classification is applied also. The Sobel operator is applied for all the edge points and the gradient is obtained at the edge points. The orthogonal direction of the gradient becomes edge direction. Only 8 directions are considered for gradient direction. If the normalized ratio of one directional feature is dominant, the texture pattern is assumed to be stripped with that direction. If the ratio of two orthogonal directions are larger than other sets, the texture pattern is assumed to be checked.

2.4   Clothes Matching Score

The score of clothes matching is calculate by a weighted sum of the scores of color and pattern matching. A color harmony defined in [3] is adopted. The weighted average of color harmony measurement on all possible combinations of two color sets of the top and bottom is assumed to be measurement of color matching. From the pattern matching, the normalized value of matching preference shown in Table 1 is obtained based on the detected pattern types.

The color harmony, denoted as C between two colors is given by

$$C = 0.33L_\Sigma + H_{\Delta C} + H_{\Delta L} + 1.1H_H - 2.2 \qquad (1)$$

L_Σ denotes the lightness sum of component colors. $H_{\Delta C}$, $H_{\Delta L}$ and H_H denote color harmony in chroma difference, in lightness difference and in hue effects respectively.

Fig. 6 shows the process to calculate color matching scores from the color harmony and weight values. The final color harmony in clothes pair is determined by the weighted sum of individual color harmony values. The individual color harmony is obtained for every possible two color pairs of top and bottom color sets. The weigh value of individual color harmony is given by the multiplication of weights of two colors.

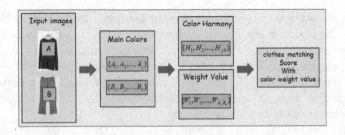

Fig. 6. Color Matching Scoring

The normalized ratio of Table 1 is used as the matching score for texture pattern and symbol matching. A case is assumed to be bad matching, if the same matching case is not detected in Table 1. If combination count is not zero, the normalized ratio value is to be the matching score of the combination.

Finally the cloth matching score, denoted as H, is defined by linear combination of

$$H = \alpha C + (1 - \alpha)P \qquad (2)$$

where P denotes the matching score of pattern and symbols. α is a control parameter, $0 < \alpha < 1$.

3   Experiment

A simple clothes matching recommendation system is implemented. The presented method is adopted to obtain the matching scoring for given clothes pair of top and bottom. For the experiments, total more than 3,000 clothes images are collected from web pages of fashions, magazines, and shopping malls. The images are filtered manually 1000 each for top and bottom. The library functions of CxImage [6] have been used.

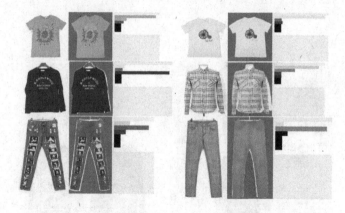

Fig. 7. Experiment Data Set

Fig. 7 shows preprocessing results and extracted major color sets of given input images. The images in the left are original image and the image in the middle are result of preprocessing. The pink colored regions of the center images are the removed regions as backgrounds. The most of cases, the cloth regions are correctly extracted. But sometimes, if the colors of cloth and background are similar, errors are generated. Color bars of the right images show the extracted major color sets and the distributions. The color of first row shows the color of background. Maximum six colors are extracted based on the weight of histogram excluding the background color. The length of bars mean their normalized weights. The short black bar means empty color, when the number of major colors is less than 6.

Fig.8 shows the results of symbol region extraction. The image regions are equally divided into horizontal 9 divisions and vertical 8 divisions. Total 72 rectangular grids are used for the symbol region extraction. In each grid box, the edges are extracted and if the ratio of edges are larger than a predetermined threshold, the whole grid is treated as a region with symbols.

If the ratio of symboled regions is larger than a threshold then the clothes image is classified to have texture pattern. To detect texture pattern type, 8 directions in all edge points are extracted and translated into 4 directional features of Vertical, Horizontal, Diagonal-right, Diagonal-left. Fig.9 shows the examples in which texture patterns are detected.

The performance of matching scoring is compared with that of humans. 10 tops and 10 bottoms shown in Fig. 10 are selected from the collected data. For the entire 100 combinations, the matching score of each pair is recorded manually. The degree of matching is scored as [-5 ~ 5], -5 :the worst matching ~ 5: the best matching. 50 persons aged between [22 ~ 32] are participated in the experiment. The top ranked 100 pairs are selected based on the average score of 50 participants.

The same combinations are given to the implemented matching scoring system and the ranked list of 100 pairs are obtained. To evaluate the performance of

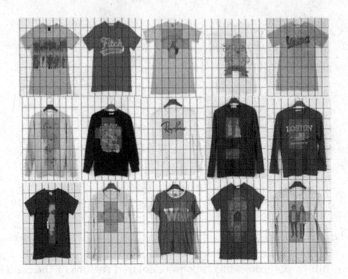

Fig. 8. Extracted symbol regions

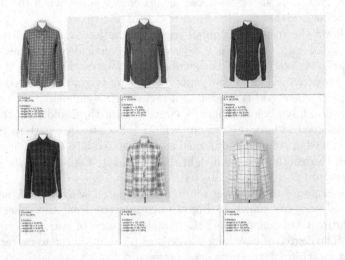

Fig. 9. Clothes images which has texture patterns

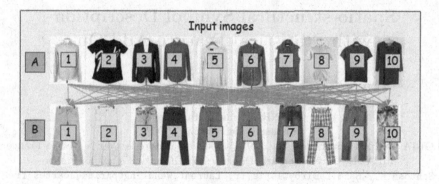

Fig. 10. Experiment Data Set

proposed method, the sets of 10 best matching pairs (rank 1 ∼ 10) and the sets of 10 worst matching pairs (rank 91 ∼ 100) are considered obtained from human scoring ranked list and machine scoring ranked list respectively. The 5 common pairs are found in both best 10 matching pairs. and 4 common pairs are found in both worst 10 matching pairs.

4 Summary

A computational model to measure the degree of clothes matching is presented. The color, texture and symbols are used as the key features to score the matching degree of a pair of top and bottom. Since the clothes matching is very subjective, an objective measurement is hard to define. However, the proposed method provides a primary computational tool to simulate the emotional factors of selecting clothes pairs. Since many factors are involved to select clothes and to find a matched pair, research on methods to quantize the characteristics for clothes are essential to build a practically acceptable system.

References

1. Eun, C., Song, C.: Personalized Apparel Coordinate System using Multiple Hybrid-Filtering on Semantic Web. Journal of Korean Institute of Information Scientists and Engineers 33(2(B)) (2006)
2. Zhang, W.: Real-time clothes comparison based on multi-view vision (2008)
3. Ou, L.-C., Luo, M.R.: A Study of Colour Harmony for Two-colour Combinations. Color Reserch & Application 31(3), 191–204 (2006)
4. Cheng, Y.: Mean shift, mode seeking, and clustering. IEEE Transactions on Pattern Analysis and Machine Intelligence 17(8), 790–799 (1995)
5. Orchard, M., Bouman, C.: Color Quantization of Images. IEEE Transactions on Signal Processing 39(12), 2677–2690 (1991)
6. CxImage Library, http://www.xdp.it/cximage.htm/

Spatio-structural Symbol Description with Statistical Feature Add-On

K.C. Santosh[1], Bart Lamiroy[2], and Laurent Wendling[3]

[1] INRIA Nancy Grand Est
[2] Université de Lorraine – INPL
LORIA Campus Scientifique, BP 239 - 54506 Vandoeuvre-lès-Nancy Cedex, France
[3] LIPADE, Université Paris Descartes, 75270 Paris Cedex 06, France
Santosh.KC, Bart.Lamiroy@loria.fr, Laurent.Wendling@parisdescartes.fr

Abstract. In this paper, we present a method for symbol description based on both spatio-structural and statistical features computed on elementary visual parts, called 'vocabulary'. This extracted vocabulary is grouped by type (e.g., *circle*, *corner*) and serves as a basis for an attributed relational graph where spatial relational descriptors formalise the links between the vertices, formed by these types, labelled with global shape descriptors. The obtained attributed relational graph description has interesting properties that allows it to be used efficiently for recognising structure and by comparing its attribute signatures. The method is experimentally validated in the context of electrical symbol recognition from wiring diagrams.

1 Introduction

Graphics recognition has an extremely rich state-of-the-art literature in symbol recognition and localisation. However, most methods are particularly suited for isolated line symbols, not for composed symbols connected to a complex environment [1,2]. Considering the problem of symbol localisation in real documents, composed of individual parts and constrained by spatial relations for instance, one needs to be able to extract visual parts, characterise their shape description and formalise the possible links that exist between them. This integration of spatial relations and shape description of the extracted visual parts is going to be the core of this paper. The method is very much inspired by a real world industrial problem [3,4,5]. Fig. 1 shows a few samples of the data related to it.

Global signal based descriptors [6] present a number of inconvenients in our context. They difficultly accommodate with connected or composite symbols and they are generally not well adapted for capturing small detail changes. In statistical approaches, signatures are simple with low computational cost. They are, unfortunately, primarily designed for applications where line symbols are isolated [7]. Furthermore, discriminative power and robustness in general applications usually require optimal selection of features [8] or the fusion of different classifiers [9]. Besides global signal based descriptors, another idea is to decompose the symbols into either vector based primitives like *points*, *lines* and *arcs* or

Y.-B. Kwon and J.-M. Ogier (Eds.): GREC, LNCS 7423, pp. 228–237, 2013.

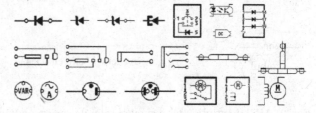

Fig. 1. A few symbols in FRESH dataset containing both linear as well as composite symbols

into meaningful parts like *circles*, *triangles* and *rectangles*. These primitives are then used in structural descriptors like attributed relational graphs (ARG) [10], region adjacency graphs (RAG) [11], as well as deformable templates [12]. In addition to the common drawback related to stability issues coming from segmentation and, error-prone raster-to-vector conversion, variability of the size of the underlying graph structures leads to computational complexity in matching. Structural approaches however, provide a powerful relational representation, conveying how parts are connected to each other, and are usually considered to be preserving generality and extensibility.

In this paper, we aim to combine the best of both structural and statistical approaches, and try to avoid the shortcomings of each of them. To do so, we decompose symbols by expressing their various parts in a fixed visual vocabulary, using spatial relations, graphs and signal based descriptors to describe the whole shape. Our symbol description is explained in Section 2. Symbols can be compared by computing matching scores based on vertex and edge alignment (*cf.* Section 3). In Section 4, we validate our method and compare it with the state-of-the-art. The paper concludes in Section 5. This paper is the extension of the previously published work [13], where we have validated the use of spatial relations for symbol recognition, but which did not include the vertex signatures developed here.

2 Symbol Description

Expanding on previously published work [3,13], we use a set of well controlled elementary part detectors to define a visual *vocabulary*. In our case, they consist of: *circles*, *corners*, *loose ends* and *thick* (filled) components. More formally, we denote the type set as, $\sum_{\mathbb{T}} = \{\mathbb{T}_{thick}, \mathbb{T}_{circle}, \mathbb{T}_{corner}, \mathbb{T}_{extremity}\}$. Such visual elementary parts are extracted with the help of image treatment analysis operations [14]. While, in the general case, this vocabulary can be of any kind from any type of bag-of-features, related to what is visually pertinent in the application context under consideration, our current vocabulary is related to electrical symbols. It can be easily extended to adapt to other domains.

Rather than using the detected elements as a basis for expressing and computing spatial relations, we group them together according to their types, as shown in Fig. 2. Now, we represent whole symbol by a complete ARG as a 4-tuple $G = (V, E, F_A, F_E)$ where V is the set of vertices, $E \subseteq V \times V$ is the set of graph edges, $F_A : V \rightarrow A_V$ is a function assigning attributes to the vertices and

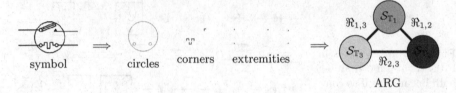

Fig. 2. ARG description for a symbol from its corresponding visual parts – an example

A_V representing a set of vocabulary type set $\sum_{\mathbb{T}}$ as well as their global shape signatures $\mathcal{S}$, and $F_E : E \to \Re_E$ is a function assigning labels to the edges where $\Re$ represents spatial relations of the edge E. Following the symbol in Fig. 2, the resulting graph whose attribute type set is $\{\mathbb{T}_1, \mathbb{T}_2, \mathbb{T}_3\}$, can be expressed as $G = \{$

$$V = \{\mathbb{T}_1, \mathbb{T}_2, \mathbb{T}_3\},$$
$$E = \{(\mathbb{T}_1, \mathbb{T}_2), (\mathbb{T}_1, \mathbb{T}_3), (\mathbb{T}_2, \mathbb{T}_3)\},$$
$$F_A = \{((\mathbb{T}_1, \mathbb{T}_{circle}), \mathcal{S}_{\mathbb{T}_1}), ((\mathbb{T}_2, \mathbb{T}_{corner}), \mathcal{S}_{\mathbb{T}_2}), ((\mathbb{T}_3, \mathbb{T}_{extremity}), \mathcal{S}_{\mathbb{T}_3})\},$$
$$F_E = \{((\mathbb{T}_1, \mathbb{T}_2), \Re_{1,2}), ((\mathbb{T}_1, \mathbb{T}_3), \Re_{1,3}), ((\mathbb{T}_2, \mathbb{T}_3), \Re_{2,3})\}\}.$$

Since this forms a complete graph, it is obvious that there exist $r = \frac{t(t-1)}{2}$ edges for t attribute types. However, because of the use of fixed and completely labelled attributes, we can avoid the NP-hardness of the matching problem (*cf.* Section 3).

In what follows, we explain how edges are labelled with spatial relations, computed between the vertices, and how vertices are labelled with shape features. This results in symbols being represented by ARGs like the one depicted in Fig. 2.

Edge Signatures Using Spatial Relations. The choice of spatial relation models depends on configuration of the studied objects. If the objects are far enough from each other, their relations can be approximated by their centres and their discretised angle [15]. Otherwise, if they are neither too far nor too close, relations can be approximated by their minimum bounding rectangle (MBR) [16] as long as the objects are regular in shape (and their respective MBR are non-overlapping). Approaches like angle histograms [17], tend to be more capable of dealing with overlapping. However, since they consider all pixels, their computational cost increases dramatically. Our work is inspired by the concept of fuzzy relations that take degrees of truth which is more natural than using standard, all-or-none relations [18].

Our model can be explained as follows. Given two shapes $\mathbb{A}$ and $\mathbb{B}$ for which we want to compute the relative position, and given a reference point $\mathbb{R}_p$, we cover the surrounding space at regular radial intervals of $\Theta = 2\pi/m$ by using a radial line. We compute this unique reference point $\mathbb{R}_p = \frac{\mathbb{C}_\mathbb{A} + \mathbb{C}_\mathbb{B}}{2}$ from the centroids $\mathbb{C}_\mathbb{A}$ and $\mathbb{C}_\mathbb{B}$ of the shapes under consideration. The uniqueness of $\mathbb{R}_p$ thus avoids possible errors related to the choice of either of them as a reference.

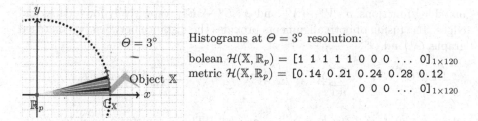

Histograms at $\Theta = 3°$ resolution:

bolean $\mathcal{H}(\mathbb{X}, \mathbb{R}_p) = $ [1 1 1 1 1 0 0 0 ... 0]$_{1 \times 120}$

metric $\mathcal{H}(\mathbb{X}, \mathbb{R}_p) = $ [0.14 0.21 0.24 0.28 0.12

0 0 0 ... 0]$_{1 \times 120}$

Fig. 3. Computing spatial relations using radial line rotation $\circlearrowright$

As depicted in Fig. 3, the line rotates over a cycle, and intersecting with object $\mathbb{X}$ ($\mathbb{A}$ or $\mathbb{B}$), generates a boolean histogram $\mathcal{H}$,

$$\mathcal{H}(\mathbb{X}, \mathbb{R}_p) = [I(\mathbb{R}_p, j\Theta)]_{j=0,\ldots,m-1}, \text{ where } I(\mathbb{R}_p, \theta_i) = \begin{cases} 1 \text{ if } line(\mathbb{R}_p, \theta_i) \cap \mathbb{X} \neq \emptyset \\ 0 \text{ otherwise.} \end{cases}$$

This is extended *wlog* to the sector defined by two successive angle values (θ_i and θ_{i+1}) and is normalised with respect to the total area of the studied object such that $\sum \mathcal{H}(.) = 1$. This histogram provides both spatial and structural information. Fig. 3 provides an illustration for an arbitrary object $\mathbb{X}$.

The histogram can be made rotationally invariant by projecting the smallest angle made by $\mathbb{R}_p$ and $\mathbb{C}_{\mathbb{X}}$ on the horizontal axis. Also, translation does not affect at all, since it uses $\mathbb{C}_{\mathbb{X}}$. Scaling does not produce any difference in $\mathcal{H}$ as it is normalised.

Vertex Signature via Shape Features. Each vertex has a distinct vocabulary type containing different shape and size information. Since spatial relations only encode relative positioning and point distributions, and do not completely exploit global shape information in the way shape descriptors do, we study the pertinence of $\mathcal{R}$−signature [19], region based Zernike moments (ZM) [20], generic fourier descriptors (GFD) [21] and shape context (SC) [22].

3   Symbol Recognition

Based on our symbol description, matching of two symbols is done by matching their corresponding ARGs. Consider two ARGs, query $G^q = (V^q, E^q, F_A^q, F_E^q)$ and database $G^d = (V^d, E^d, F_A^d, F_E^d)$, where the set of vertices $V = \{\mathbb{T}_1, \ldots, \mathbb{T}_t\}$, and the set of edges $E = \{E_1, \ldots, E_r\}$.

Our matching is straightforward i.e., matching has been made between the candidates only having the exact same set of vertices as well as exact labels. To generalise this, we define a binary indicator function $\tau_A^V : \Sigma_\mathbb{T} \to \{0, 1\}$ to check the presence of vertices in the ARG, where the value of $\tau_A^V(\mathbb{T})$ is 1 if $\mathbb{T}$ is present in V and 0, otherwise. For example, for the symbol shown in Fig. 2, the indicator $\tau_A^V = [0, 1, 1, 1]$ refers to the absence of *thick* components and the presence of *circle*, *corner* and *extremity*. Now, we can then set up bijective matching functions: $\sigma : V^q \to V^d$ and $\varphi : E^q \to E^d$, respectively for vertices and edges. The fusion of both alignments provides the distance between two matched graphs G^q and G^d,

$$\text{Dist.}(G^q, G^d) = \alpha \sum_{t \in V} \delta(F_A^q(t), F_A^d(\sigma(t))) + (1 - \alpha) \sum_{r \in E} \delta(F_E^q(r), F_E^d(\varphi(r))),$$

where $\alpha \in [0, 1]$ and $\delta(a, b) = \sum_{l=1}^{L} ||a_l - b_l||_2$. The parameter α provides weight while matching.

- $\alpha = 0$: only vertex signature;
- $\alpha = 1$: only edge signature; and
- $\alpha = 0.5$: equal weights to both vertex and edge signature.

In our experiments, we provide equal weights for both relations and shape distribution of the whenever they are integrated together.

4   Experiments

4.1   Dataset, Ground-Truth and Evaluation Metric

Fig. 1 gives an overview of the dataset we are using for our experiments. The global dataset is composed of roughly 500 different known symbols, some of which come from [5]. It shows that symbols may either be very similar in shape – and only differ by slight details – or either be completely different from a visual point of view. Symbols may also be composed of other known and significant symbols and need not necessary be connected.

Since there is no absolute ground-truth associated to our dataset, we have asked 6 volunteers to manually select what they consider as "similar" symbols, and we have merged their inputs to reduce possible subjective bias. They have chosen the candidates which have similar visual overall appearance or contain significantly similar parts with respect to the chosen query. In our testing protocol, we consider that a result returned from an algorithm is correct if at least one evaluator has selected the same result among similar items. In more formal terms, for each query the "ground-truth" is considered to be the set of symbols formed by the union of all human selected sets.

For every query, we rank the symbols at the output based on distance measure as described in Section 3. Since the number of similar symbols, according to the ground-truths, may vary a lot from one query to another, we use retrieval efficiency [23] as a measure for retrieval quality. For a chosen query and for a fixed number of K returned symbols, it can be expressed as,

$$\eta_K = \begin{cases} n/N \text{ if } N \le K \\ n/K \text{ otherwise,} \end{cases}$$

where n is the number of returned relevant symbols and N the total number of relevant symbols.

4.2   Results and Discussions

We perform a series of tests, focussing on three major issues one after another.

1. Choice of optimal resolution for radial line model (as edge signature) and comparison with other relation models;
2. Choice of the best shape descriptors on vocabulary (as vertex signature) and comparison with global symbol shape descriptors;
3. Integration of both vertex and edge signatures.

In what follows, we compute the average retrieval efficiency for 30 queries, and vary K from 1 to 10.

Test 1. We consider the influence of different resolutions Θ in our edge signature. Its value represents the trade-off between the optimal choice of resolution – and thus precision of spatio-structural information capture – and time/space requirements. Without surprise, the lower Θ, the better the results. Following results in Fig. 4 (a), and given the relatively low gain of efficiency between 3° and 1°, we adopt 3° for the rest of our experiments. We then compare our approach with state-of-the-art spatial relation models: cone-shaped [15], angle histogram [17] and MBR [16] as shown in Fig. 4 (b). Compared to the best performing model (MBR), our radial-line approach increases performance with a substantial difference. These resuls were already reported in [13].

Test 2. In section 2 we already listed the set of global schape-descriptors we consider state-of-the-art: $\mathcal{R}$−signature [19], ZM [20], GFD [21] and SC [22]. For those descriptors, it is important to fit the best parameters. For GFD, we have tuned the radial and angular frequency parameters to achieve the best performance. For SC, we attempt to follow the indications given in [22] but they are restricted by the number of sample points of some symbols (i.e., we have images ranging from a few tens of pixels to thousands of pixels). In the case of ZM, we have used 36 *Zernike* functions of order less than or equal to 7. For Radon, projecting range is $[0, \pi[$.

We first employ them as vertex signatures only and then confront them with the same shape descriptors, applied to the overall shape. This comparison is illustrated in Fig. 5 (a) and (b), respectively. In this test, SC, $\mathcal{R}$−signature and ZM are lagging behind GFD. Therefore, we consider GFD to be the best performing descriptor and will use it as a benchmark for further experiments.

Test 3. We integrate both edge and vertex signatures in the ARG described in Section 2. However, integrating signatures on all vertices is not necessary since our spatial relation signature already carries sufficient information for those vocabulary types less influenced by shape variations (*corner* and *extremity*, for instance). Therefore, we have examined the use of signature from some specific types only, and on some combinations like, *thick*, *thick* and *circle*, *thick*, *circle* and *corner*, and so on. It is important to notice that we have never left out *thick* components from all tested combinations because those vocabulary elements

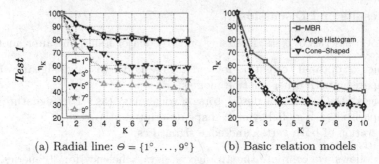

(a) Radial line: $\Theta = \{1°, \ldots, 9°\}$ (b) Basic relation models

Fig. 4. Average retrieval efficiency using spatial relations

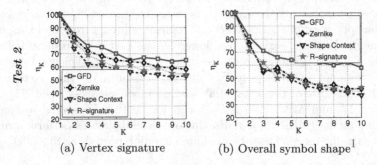

(a) Vertex signature   (b) Overall symbol shape[1]

Fig. 5. Average retrieval efficiency using global signal based shape descriptors

provide the largest amplitude in shape and size variations. To handle this, we use all aforementioned global signal based descriptors as vertex signatures in order to see how well they improve retrieval efficiency. In our tests, substantial advancement is achieved from the combination of vertices, labelled with *thick* and *circle* vocabulary types. Fig. 6 shows results from using different shape signatures combined with the edge signature using a radial line model at 3° resolution. GFD provides the best results. Surprisingly, not all vertex shape descriptors improve upon the plain edge signatures, but some even decrease in performance. $\mathcal{R}$–signature provides an example.

Comparison. In Fig. 7, a comparison is made among the best of all experiments: MBR from the basic spatial relation model and GFD from shape descriptors. Our method outperforms all with a difference of more than 16%. For a few queries, an illustration is shown in Fig. 8.

Another important issue accounting for retrieval performance is execution time. In Table 1, we provide it based on comparison of the methods in Fig. 7.

---

[1] Compared to our previous work [13] where the $1D$ (vanilla) version of the $\mathcal{R}$–signature has been employed, the complete version reported here provides better performance, without altering the global validity of our findings, however.

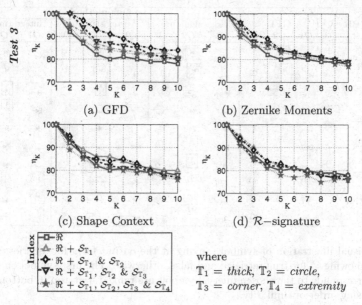

(a) GFD

(b) Zernike Moments

(c) Shape Context

(d) $\mathcal{R}$−signature

where
$\mathbb{T}_1 = thick$, $\mathbb{T}_2 = circle$,
$\mathbb{T}_3 = corner$, $\mathbb{T}_4 = extremity$

Fig. 6. Average retrieval efficiency while integrating vertex signature in our ARG framework

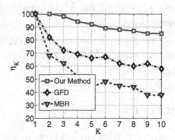

Fig. 7. Comparison among the best of all categories

This proves that the increase in recogition efficiency comes at a cost in execution time. This cost remains in a reasonable limit, however.

| | Test 1 | | Test 2 | Test 3 |
	MBR	Edge sign.	GFD	Edge sign. + GFD vertex sign.
Time	02	04	09	14

Table 1. Average running time (sec.) for matching for a single pair

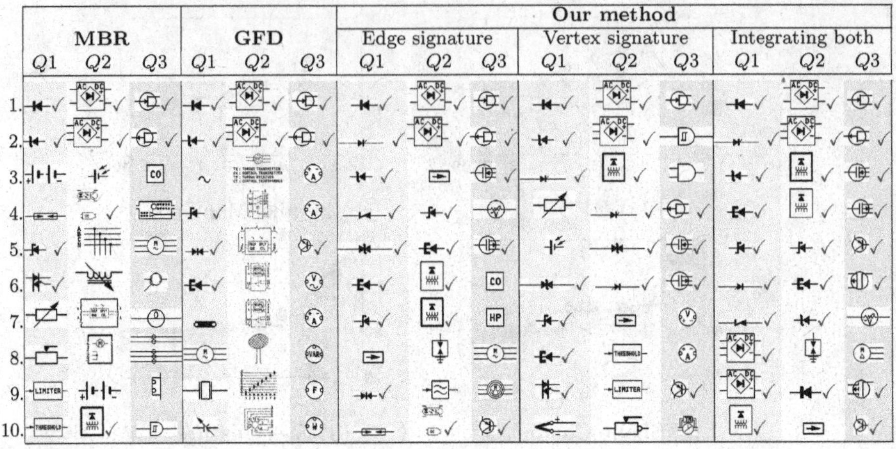

Fig. 8. Visual illustration of symbol ranking at the output for a few queries: $Q1$, $Q2$ and $Q3$, showing ✓ for true retrieval and false, otherwise. The first symbol on the top always corresponds to the chosen query. Symbols are ranked from top to bottom based on decreasing order of similarity.

5   Conclusions

We have presented an ARG based symbol description method, where relational signatures formalise all possible connections between the vocabulary types which are labelled with global shape signatures. Our method has proven to significantly outperform state-of-the-art basic spatial relation models as well as global signal based descriptors.

References

1. Cordella, L.P., Vento, M.: Symbol recognition in documents: a collection of techniques? IJDAR 3(2), 73–88 (2000)
2. Lladós, J., Valveny, E., Sánchez, G., Martí, E.: Symbol Recognition: Current Advances and Perspectives. In: Blostein, D., Kwon, Y.-B. (eds.) GREC 2001. LNCS, vol. 2390, pp. 104–127. Springer, Heidelberg (2002)
3. Tombre, K., Lamiroy, B.: Pattern Recognition Methods for Querying and Browsing Technical Documentation. In: Ruiz-Shulcloper, J., Kropatsch, W.G. (eds.) CIARP 2008. LNCS, vol. 5197, pp. 504–518. Springer, Heidelberg (2008)
4. Santosh, K.C., Lamiroy, B., Ropers, J.P.: Inductive logic programming for symbol recognition. In: ICDAR, pp. 1330–1334 (2009)
5. Tooley, M., Wyatt, D.: Aircraft electrical and electronic systems: principles, operation and maintenance. In: Aircraft Engineering Principles and Practice. Butterworth-Heinemann (2008)
6. Zhang, D., Lu, G.: Review of shape representation and description techniques. PR 37(1), 1–19 (2004)
7. Tombre, K., Ah-Soon, C., Dosch, P., Habed, A., Masini, G.: Stable, robust and off-the-shelf methods for graphics recognition 1, 406 (1998)

8. Barrat, S., Tabbone, S.: A bayesian network for combining descriptors: application to symbol recognition. IJDAR 13(1), 65–75 (2010)
9. Terrades, O.R., Valveny, E., Tabbone, S.: Optimal classifier fusion in a non-bayesian probabilistic framework. IEEE PAMI 31(9), 1630–1644 (2009)
10. Conte, D., Foggia, P., Sansone, C., Vento, M.: Thirty years of graph matching in pattern recognition. IJPRAI 18(3), 265–298 (2004)
11. Lladós, J., Martí, E., Villanueva, J.J.: Symbol recognition by error-tolerant subgraph matching between region adjacency graphs. IEEE PAMI 23(10), 1137–1143 (2001)
12. Valveny, E., Martí, E.: A model for image generation and symbol recognition through the deformation of lineal shapes. PRL 24(15), 2857–2867 (2003)
13. Santosh, K.C., Lamiroy, B., Wendling, L.: Symbol recognition using spatial relations. PRL 33(3), 331–341 (2011)
14. Rendek, J., Masini, G., Dosch, P., Tombre, K.: The Search for Genericity in Graphics Recognition Applications: Design Issues of the Qgar Software System. In: Marinai, S., Dengel, A.R. (eds.) DAS 2004. LNCS, vol. 3163, pp. 366–377. Springer, Heidelberg (2004)
15. Miyajima, K., Ralescu, A.: Spatial Organization in 2D Segmented Images: Representation and Recognition of Primitive Spatial Relations. Fuzzy Sets and Syst. 2(65), 225–236 (1994)
16. Papadias, D., Theodoridis, Y.: Spatial relations, minimum bounding rectangles, and spatial data structures. Int. J. Geographical Inform. Sci. 11(2), 111–138 (1997)
17. Wang, X., Keller, J.M.: Human-Based Spatial Relationship Generalization Through Neural/Fuzzy Approaches. Fuzzy Sets and Syst. 101, 5–20 (1999)
18. Freeman, J.: The modelling of spatial relations. CGIP 4, 156–171 (1975)
19. Tabbone, S., Wendling, L., Salmon, J.P.: A new shape descriptor defined on the radon transform. CVIU 102(1), 42–51 (2006)
20. Kim, W.-Y., Kim, Y.-S.: A region-based shape descriptor using zernike moments. Signal Process.: Image Commun. 16(1-2), 95–102 (2000)
21. Zhang, D., Lu, G.: Shape-based image retrieval using generic fourier descriptor. Signal Process.: Image Commun. 17, 825–848 (2002)
22. Belongie, S., Malik, J., Puzicha, J.: Shape matching and object recognition using shape contexts. IEEE PAMI 24(4), 509–522 (2002)
23. Kankanhalli, M.S., Mehtre, B.M., Wu, J.K.: Cluster-based color matching for image retrieval. PR 29, 701–708 (1995)

De-blurring Textual Document Images

Daniel M. Oliveira[1], Rafael Dueire Lins[1], Gabriel P. Silva[1],
Jian Fan[2], and Marcelo Thielo[3]

[1] Universidade Federal de Pernambuco
Recife - Brazil
{daniel.moliveira,rdl,gabriel.psilva}@ufpe.br
[2] Hewlett-Parckard Labs.
Palo Alto - USA
[3] Hewlett-Parckard Labs.
Porto Alegre - Brazil
{jian.fan,marcelo.resende.thielo}@hp.com

Abstract. Document images may exhibit some blurred areas due to a wide number of reasons ranging from digitalization, filtering or even storage problems. Most de-blurring algorithms are hard to implement, slow, and often try to be general, attempting to remove the blur in any kind of image. In the case of text document images, the transition between characters and the paper background has a high contrast. With that in mind, a new algorithm is proposed for de-blurring of textual documents; there is no need to estimate the PSF and the filter proposed can be directed applied to the image. The presented algorithm reached an improvement rate of 17.08% in the SSIM metric.

Keywords: De-blurring, blur, camera documents, scanner documents.

1   Introduction

Noise is any phenomenon that degrades information. A taxonomy for noises in document images is proposed in reference [9] which besides providing an explanation of how different noises appeared in the final image, it gives pointers to the literature that show ways of avoiding or removing them. In the classification proposed [9], there are four kinds of noise:

1. *The physical noises – whatever "damages" the physical integrity and readability of the original information of a document. It may be further split into the two subcategories proposed in as internal and external.*
2. *The digitization noises – introduced by the digitization process. Several problems may be clustered in this group such as: inadequate digitization resolution, unsuitable palette, framing noises, skew and orientation, lens distortion, geometrical warping, out-of-focus digitized images, motion noises.*
3. *The filtering noise – unsuitable manipulation of the digital file may degrade the information that exists in the digital version of the document (instead of increasing it).*
4. *The storage/transmission noise – the noise that appears either from storage algorithms with losses or from network transmission. JPEG artifact is a typical example of this kind of undesirable interference.*

Y.-B. Kwon and J.-M. Ogier (Eds.): GREC, LNCS 7423, pp. 238–250, 2013.

The blur noise has the effect of unsharpening images. Depending on how it arises it may be included in any of the four categories above. The physical blur may be the result of document "washing", for instance, in which a document, printed with water soluble ink, gets wet. Blur may also be the result of unsuitable digitization, due to several reasons: non-flat objects, digitization errors, out of focus, motion etc. The presence of blur may be an indicator of low quality digitization, but can also be associated with other problems such as the scanning of hard-bound volumes. Blur may be the result of unsuitable filtering, such as a Gaussian or low-pass filter. And finally, blur may appear as the result of storing images in a file format with losses that perceptually degrades the image.

The technical literature points at several approaches proposed for de-blurring images in general. To list a few of them: Demoment [2] uses statistics, Neelamani, Choi, and Baraniuk [3] use Fourier and wavelet transforms, references [4] and [5] apply variational analysis, and Roth and Black [6] use total variation and Field of experts. Most of times, the computational complexity of those algorithms is prohibitively high and can yield undesirable artifacts such as ringing [7] as presented in Figure 1.

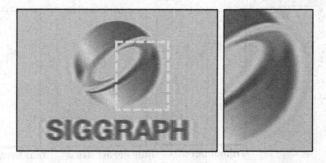

Fig. 1. Ringing artifact [7]

The most successful approaches to blur removal focus at one specific kind of blur. For instance, the literature presents several algorithms [11, 12, 13, 14, 15, 16, 17] that address the problem of motion blur, an specific kind of digitization noise.

In this paper, to increase the chances of better de-blurring, the application domain is restricted to monochromatic scanned documents with book binding warping [10]. The resulting image has uneven blur and illumination. The document images treated here are basically constituted by text and plain paper background. The transition between them in the original physical document is sharp. Using this fact a new algorithm is proposed by using nearby pixels to increase the difference between them. No Point Spread Function (PSF) [18] estimation is done and blur is minimized into a direct application of the image.

2   The New Method

The study performed here focus on the compensation of the blur noise which appears in scanning hardbound documents. Patterns were arranged in an elevated plane model

[1] as shown in Figure 2 to simulate the hardbound warp. Two HP scanners (PhotoSmart C4280 and a HP ScanJet 5300c) were used to digitize a pattern of lines in a grid. Two examples of blurred cross sections can be seen on Figures 3 and 4, corresponding to the two different scanning devices, respectively with two elevation and skew angles.

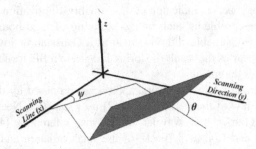

Fig. 2. Elevated plane [1]

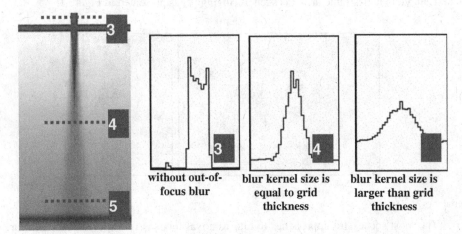

Fig. 3. Line grid scanned with HP PhotoSmart C4280 with $\psi = 0°$ and $\theta = 30°$

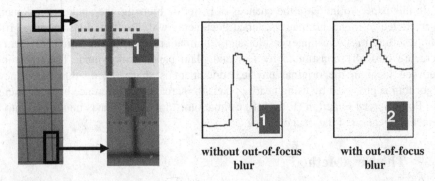

Fig. 4. Line grid scanned with HP ScanJet 5300c with $\psi = 0°$ and $\theta = 45°$

In Figures 3 and 4, as the paper is further away from the scanner flatbed, the blur increases and illumination is fades out; as the scanning device is calibrated to digitize documents at a pre-defined distance, which is exactly the flatbed surface.

These figures also present several cross sections at different parts of the calibration grid images. They show regions without blur (cross sections "1" and "3") and regions with blur kernel size larger than the grid thickness. The line labeled with number "4" is the limit when is not possible to remove the blur totally.

In the case of characters, corners of the strokes are vulnerable regions to the blur. The kernel area in this region is dominated by the information not related to the given point. Figure 5 shows two kinds of corners in the letter "M" that can be irrecoverable.

Fig. 5. Corners of upper case "M" which are vulnerable to the blur noise

2.1   Reconstruction Function

Thoulin and Chang [21] identify document background and foreground locally for the resolution expansion of document images. Proposed method obtains these colors by searching the maximum and minimum on the pixel neighborhood and uses it into the reconstruction function.

Most pixels that belong to the paper background have their intensities values closer to the background intensity. Similarly, for blurred stokes values are closer to the foreground intensity. In this way an S-function can be built, with input and output varying from 0 to 1, whereas the output is below the line of the identity function between 0 and 0.5, and above it between 0.5 and 1.0.

In this work the function $S(t)$ is defined by equation 1 with the fixed parameter p that varies between 0 and 1.0, which controls how strong the correction will be. For p values closer to 0, the function shape looks similar to a step function with higher transitions; for values closer to 1.0, the shape gets closer to a sin function scaled by π. Figure 6 shows two plots for $p = 0.06$ and $p = 1.00$.

$$S(t) = 0.5 - 0.5 \times sign(\cos t\pi) \times |\cos t\pi|^p \qquad (1)$$

To apply the *S-shape* function, two reference values must be determined for the paper background and character stroke. This is done by looking out in a window for the pixel with largest and lowest intensity. The un-blurred value is obtained by eq. (2), where I_b is the blurred intensity value (i.e. original image); min and max are the lowest and the highest intensity values in the given window, respectively.

$$I_u = \left[S\left(\frac{(I_b - min)}{(max - min)} \right) \times (max - min) \right] + min \qquad (2)$$

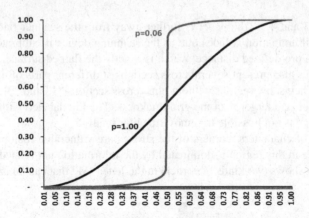

Fig. 6. S-function plots for *p* equal to 1.00 and 0.06

One may notice that using large windows and low values for *p* is more intrusive than the other way round. The choice of this parameter will depend on the blur level.

3   Results and Analysis

The evaluation of the proposed algorithm is done in three parts. The first part uses computer generated images to obtain blurred and un-blurred images; the latter is used as the ground-truth. At the second part, a study is done in scanned images using the elevated plane model [1]. At last, processing results of real documents are presented.

Unfortunately, comparing the method proposed here with other algorithms described in the literature was not possible as they do not offer enough details for granting their implementation, their executable code is not available, and the evaluation datasets used by them do not include document images.

3.1   Computer Generated Images

In order to provide objective quality measures of the proposed algorithm processing, letters and chess shape were generated. Several levels of blur were applied in these images using the GaussianBlur filter available in ImageJ [20]; two examples are presented in Figure 7. The Gaussian radius represents the region with 61% of the whole Gaussian, thus the kernel size is not restricted to this radius [20].

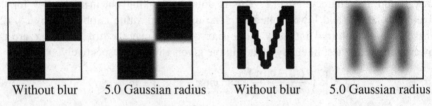

Without blur   5.0 Gaussian radius   Without blur   5.0 Gaussian radius

Fig. 7. Blur applied to chess pattern image and upper case "M"

The de-blurring method proposed herein was applied to the blurred images. Images corrected and without blur were compared using SSIM [19] index. It measures how images are perceptually different with values between 0 (different) and 1 (the same).

Tables 2 and 3 provide at each cell average SSIM between the ground truth and the de-blurred images of the chess and letters pattern, respectively. Cells in the same row represent the de-blurring of the same input but with different window sizes. The values in parenthesis are the amount of information "gain" computed by eq. (3). Table 1 shows the values of the average SSIM between de-blurred and without blur images. Value 0.1 was set to p in all tests. One may notice that the proposed algorithm could improve the SSIM metric by 17.08% at most.

$$\text{SSIM gain} = \frac{\text{Average of SSIM between } \textbf{deblurred} \text{ and without blur images}}{\text{Average of SSIM between } \textbf{blurred} \text{ and without blur images}} - 1 \qquad (3)$$

Table 1. Average of SSIM between blurred and without blur images

Blur kernel size	1	2	3	4	5
Average of Chess pattern SSIM	0.999	0.965	0.926	0.888	0.852
Avgerage of Letters SSIM	0.999	0.976	0.954	0.932	0.910

Table 2. Average of SSIM between de-blurred and without blur chess pattern images

5	0.923 (+8.41%)	0.970 (+13.94%)	0.989 (+16.16%)	0.996 (+16.96%)	0.997 (+17.08%)
4	0.961 (+8.25%)	0.991 (+11.68%)	0.997 (+12.36%)	0.998 (+12.47%)	0.999 (+12.50%)
3	0.988 (+6.75%)	0.998 (+7.86%)	0.999 (+7.96%)	0.999 (+7.96%)	0.999 (+7.96%)
2	0.999 (+3.55%)	1.000 (+3.64%)	1.000 (+3.64%)	1.000 (+3.64%)	1.000 (+3.64%)
1	1.000 (+0.08%)	1.000 (+0.08%)	1.000 (+0.08%)	1.000 (+0.08%)	1.000 (+0.08%)
Blur / Win	1	2	3	4	5

Table 3. Average of SSIM between de-blurred and without blur letters pattern images

5	0.942 (+3.56%)	0.947 (+4.06%)	0.940 (+3.30%)	0.941 (+3.38%)	0.942 (+3.53%)
4	0.968 (+3.85%)	0.973 (+4.37%)	0.970 (+4.09%)	0.971 (+4.17%)	0.972 (+4.27%)
3	0.987 (+3.44%)	0.991 (+3.85%)	0.991 (+3.82%)	0.990 (+3.78%)	0.991 (+3.80%)
2	0.999 (+2.30%)	0.998 (+2.25%)	0.998 (+2.23%)	0.998 (+2.23%)	0.998 (+2.22%)

Table 3. *(Continued)*

1	1.000 (+0.07%)	1.000 (+0.07%)	1.000 (+0.07%)	1.000 (+0.07%)	1.000 (+0.07%)
Blur ╱ Win	1	2	3	4	5

Table 4. Letters with various blur sizes applied with different window sizes

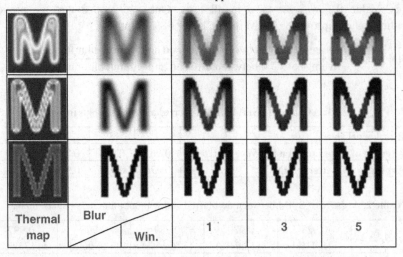

Thermal map	Blur ╱ Win.	1	3	5

Table 4 shows some results of processing the examples used for Table 3. The first column shows the blurred images thermal map for each blur level, with red representing the stroke color (black) and blue the background (white). The second column show the blurred images used as inputs.

Images with the Gaussian radius set to 1, is possible to recover most of the stroke. The thermal map of blurred "M" with 3.0 radius shows that only the upper part of the stroke is red, thus only it can be totally recoverable. Although, the corrected images appear to be restored properly as the blurred pixels are too close to black.

The same is not observed to the correct images of radius set to 5. The thermal map shows that most part of the stroke are green, showing that the blur affected the character structure. The quality improvement is observable in all images on Table 4.

3.2   Blurred Images Generated from Scanned Images

The dataset presented on previous section has noise-free images. In order to evaluate the proposed algorithm with more realistic scenarios, 3 documents were digitized by a scanner flatbed yielding into images with low noise level, which is considered as the ground truth. Analogically to previous section, the blurred images and the effectiveness of the correction were obtained. Table 5 shows the SSIM performance results.

Table 5. Average of SSIM between de-blurred and scanned images

Blur \ Win	1	2	3	4	5
5	0.898 (+3.02%)	0.899 (+3.05%)	0.895 (+2.62%)	0.893 (+2.36%)	0.890 (+2.12%)
4	0.924 (+2.52%)	0.920 (+2.05%)	0.916 (+1.61%)	0.914 (+1.37%)	0.912 (+1.16%)
3	0.944 (+1.32%)	0.938 (+0.58%)	0.934 (+0.18%)	0.931 (-0.10%)	0.929 (-0.37%)
2	0.960 (-0.25%)	0.952 (-1.11%)	0.946 (-1.67%)	0.942 (-2.15%)	0.938 (-2.58%)
1	0.969 (-2.94%)	0.946 (-5.27%)	0.928 (-7.04%)	0.915 (-8.40%)	0.905 (-9.42%)

The scanned images present a low degree of blur; thus the similarities between the scanned and weakly blurred images are too high. Therefore, the gains of the SSIM quality are negative for the images with 1-3 radiuses on Table 5.

The de-blurred image provides image with sharper edges than the ground truth and input images, thus it has better visual quality than both of these images. Figure 8.a shows the scanned image; a zoomed part can be seen on (b); (c) shows the blur level 1 applied to (b) with the de-blurred version on (d). It is noticeable that Figure 8.d is more pleasant to see than Figures 8.b and 8.c.

For the strong blur (4 and 5 radius), the SSIM gain is positive; this shows the proposed algorithm improves the quality of the image. One can be seen on the de-blurred version of Figure 8.e (8.b blur level 5) on Figure 8.f.

Fig. 8. Example of processing the scanned images

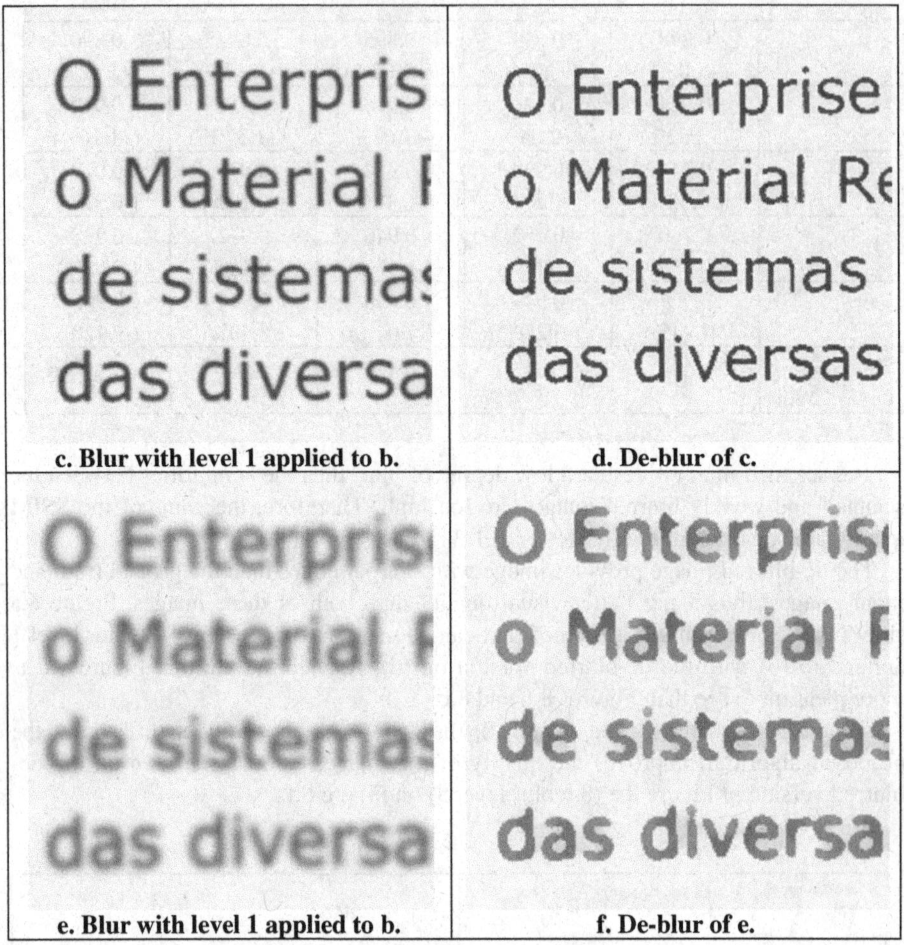

O Enterpris o Material I de sistema: das diversa	O Enterprise o Material Re de sistemas das diversas
c. Blur with level 1 applied to b.	**d. De-blur of c.**
O Enterpris o Material F de sistema: das diversa	O Enterpris o Material F de sistema: das diversa
e. Blur with level 1 applied to b.	**f. De-blur of e.**

Fig. 8. *(Continued)*

3.3   Elevated Plane Image Analysis

The images obtained with the elevated plane model [1] shows the blurred stroke combined with other noises. Figure 9 shows the results of applying the proposed algorithm to Figure 3 using a 7x7 window for p equal to 1.00 (a) and 0.25 (b). One may observe that vertical line grid was recovered until blur kernel got larger than a 7x7 window (dashed rectangle of 8.b); although the blurred horizontal line on the bottom part could be partially recovered. Increasing the window size is possible to recover the area were the blur is larger, which is shown in Figure 9 with windows of sizes 11x11 (c) and 19x19 (d) for $p = 0.25$.

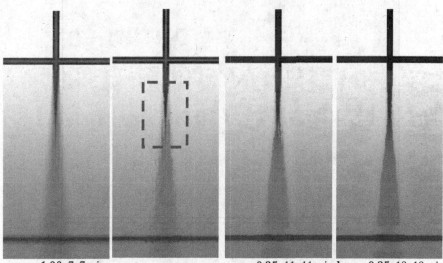

a. $p = 1.00$; 7x7 win   **b.** $p = 0.25$; 7x7 win   **c.** $p = 0.25$; 11x11 win **d.** $p = 0.25$; 19x19 win

Fig. 9. Output with 7x7 window

3.4   Document Images

Finally, some examples of de-blurring applied to real document images are presented. Figures 10 and 11 show the output at different window sizes and values of p. The resulting image was improved by the proposed algorithm.

4   Conclusions

The study performed here shows that focusing the scope of the application of a de-blurring algorithm stands a better chance of more adequately and efficiently removing such complex noise that may appear due to several different sources: physical, digitization, filtering and storage. This paper presents an algorithm to compensate the digitization non-constant blur that appear in scanning bound grayscale documents, for instance. The algorithm performance was confirmed by high values of SSIM metric in computer generated images.

The automatic inference of the parameters of the algorithm through the use of blur intensity classifier such as the one described in reference [8] is under implementation and shows some promising results already.

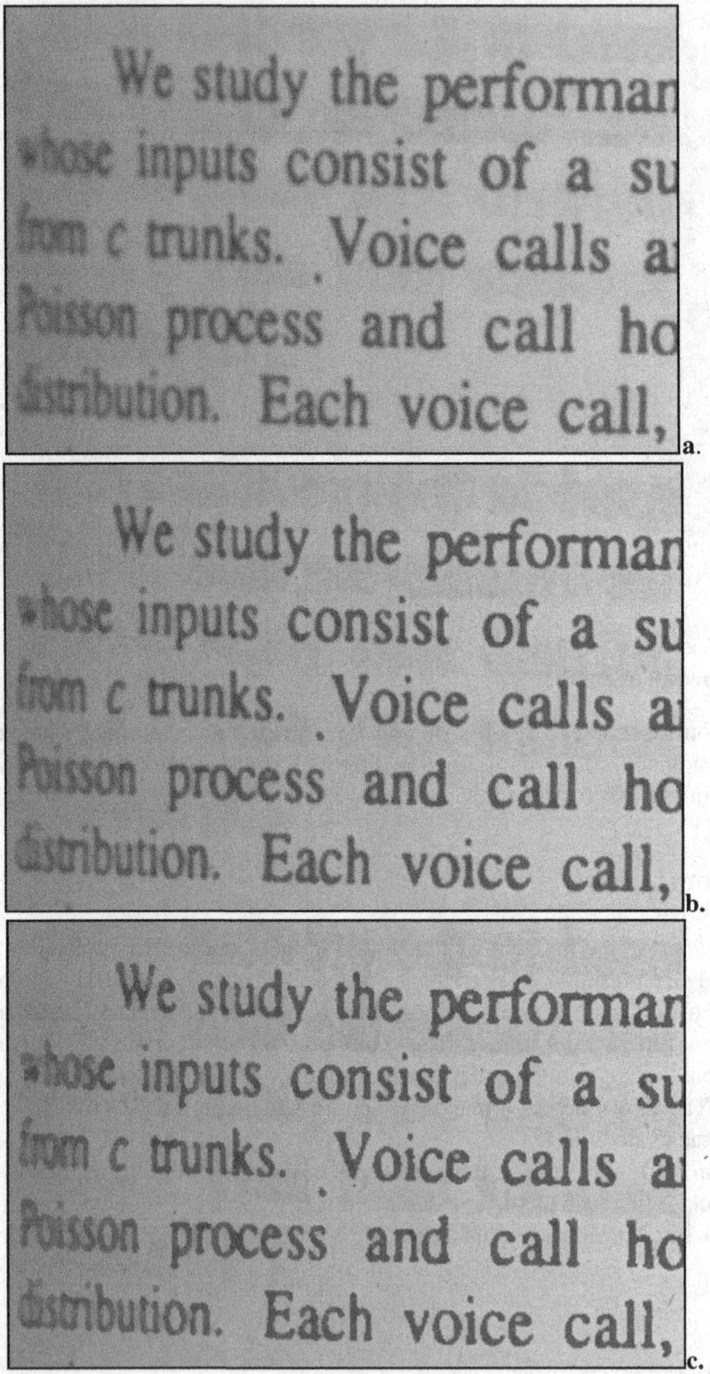

Fig. 10. Result with 5x5 window: original image (a); $p = 0.50$ (b); $p = 0.06$ (c)

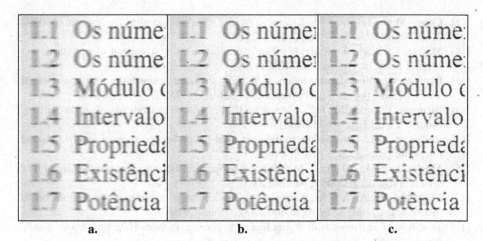

Fig. 11. Result with p=0.5: original image (a); 3x3 window (b); 7x7 window (c)

Acknowledgements. The research reported herein was partly sponsored by CNPq and MCT-Lei de Informática grants both from the Brazilian Government.

References

[1] Ukida, H., Konishi, K.: 3D Shape Reconstruction Using Three Light Sources in Image Scanner. IEICE Trans. on Inf. & Syst. E84-D(12), 1713–1721 (2001)

[2] Demoment, G.: Image reconstruction and restoration: Overview of common estimation structures and problems. IEEE Transactions on Acoustics, Speech, & Signal Processing 37(12), 2024–2036 (1989)

[3] Neelamani, R., Choi, H., Baraniuk, R.G.: Wavelet-based deconvolution for ill-conditioned systems. In: Proc. of IEEE ICASSP, vol. 6, pp. 3241–3244 (1999)

[4] Chambolle, A., Lions, P.L.: Image recovery via total variation minimization and related problems. Numerische Mathematik 76(2), 167–188 (1997)

[5] Rudin, L.I., Osher, S., Fatemi, E.: Nonlinear total variation based noise removal algorithms. Physica D 60, 259–268 (1992)

[6] Roth, S., Black, M.J.: Fields of experts: a framework for learning image priors. CVPR 2, 860–867 (2005)

[7] Joshi, N.S.: Enhancing photographs using content-specific image priors. Phd thesis, University of California, San Diego (2008)

[8] Lins, R.D., Silva, G.F.P., Banergee, S., Kuchibhotla, A., Thielo, M.: Automatically Detecting and Classifying Noises in Document Images. In: ACM-SAC 2010, vol. 1, pp. 33–39. ACM Press (March 2010)

[9] Lins, R.D.: A Taxonomy for Noise in Images of Paper Documents - The Physical Noises. In: Kamel, M., Campilho, A. (eds.) ICIAR 2009. LNCS, vol. 5627, pp. 844–854. Springer, Heidelberg (2009)

[10] Lins, R.D., Oliveira, D.M., Torreão, G., Fan, J., Thielo, M.: Correcting Book Binding Distortion in Scanned Documents. In: Campilho, A., Kamel, M. (eds.) ICIAR 2010, Part II. LNCS, vol. 6112, pp. 355–365. Springer, Heidelberg (2010)

[11] Chang, M.M., Tekalp, A.M., Erdem, A.T.: Blur identification using the bispectrum. IEEE Trans. Signal Process. 39(10), 2323–2325 (1991)

[12] Mayntz, C., Aach, T., Kunz, D.: Blur identification using a spectral inertia tensor and spectral zeros. In: Proc. of IEEE ICIP (1999)

[13] Cannon, M.: Blind deconvolution of spatially invariant image blurs with phase. IEEE Trans. Acoust. Speech Signal Process. 24(1), 56–63 (1976)

[14] Biemond, J., Lagendijk, R.L., Mersereau, R.M.: Iterative methods for image de-blurring. Proc. of the IEEE, 856–883 (1990)

[15] Rekleities, I.M.: Optical flow recognition from the power spectrum of a single blurred image. In: Proc. of IEEE ICIP (1996)

[16] Moghaddam, M.E., Jamzad, M.: Motion blur identification in noisy images using fuzzy sets. In: Proc. IEEE ISSPIT, Athens (2005)

[17] Lokhande, R., Arya, K.V., Gupta, P.: Identification of parameters and restoration of motion blurred images. In: ACM-SAC 2006, Dijon (2006)

[18] Jain, A.K.: Fundamentals of digital image processing. Prentice-Hall, Inc., Upper Saddle River (1989)

[19] Wang, Z., Bovik, A.C., Sheikh, H.R.: Image quality assessment: From error visibility to structural similarity. IEEE Transactions on Image Processing 13(4), 600–612 (2004)

[20] ImageJ. GaussianBlur (ImageJ API), http://rsbweb.nih.gov/ij/developer/api/ij/plugin/filter/GaussianBlur.html

[21] Thouin, P.D., Chang, C.I.: A method for restoration of low-resolution document images. In: IJDAR (2000)

Statistically Analyzing RGB Histograms to Remove Highlighting in Aged Paper Monochromatic Documents

Ricardo da Silva Barboza[1], Rafael Dueire Lins[1],
Diego de A. Barros[2], and Edson da F. de Lira[3]

[1] Universidade Federal de Pernambuco, Recife-PE, Brazil
rsbarboza@gmail.com, rdl@ufpe.br
[2] Universidade do Estado do Amazonas, Manaus-AM, Brazil
dbarros_eng@gmail.com
[3] Centro Universitário do Norte, Manaus-AM, Brazil
edinhoestat@yahoo.com.br

Abstract. Text highlighting is often used to emphasize parts of a document for some reason. As highlighting is a personal choice of the reader, it can be seen as physically "damaging" the original document. A recent paper shows how to remove felt-pen highlighting in monochromatic documents with a white paper background. This paper generalizes that result to filter out highlighting in monochromatic documents with non-white background due to paper natural aging.

Keywords: highlighting, paper documents, filtering, aging.

1   Introduction

Interested readers always used some kind of marking to emphasize some part of texts in books or documents. Making symbols or writing on the margins or text underlining. The modern felt-tip marker was invented by Yukio Horie in Japan in 1962. A highlighter, marker pen, marking pen, felt-tip pen, or simply a marker, is a pen which has its own ink-source, and usually a tip made of a porous material, such as felt or nylon. This sentence is an example of highlighted text, which draws the readers' attention to it at once. Highlighters are permanent markers that come in bright, transparent, often fluorescent colors, which glow under a black light. The most common color for highlighters is yellow, but they are also found in blue, green, orange, and magenta varieties. Red highlighters can be purchased along with a green translucent sheet used to hide the highlighted material. Some yellow highlighters may look greenish in color to the naked eye. Table 1 presents the most usual colors of highlighters and the components they affect most of the original image [1].

There is a personal outlook in document highlighting. What one reader may stress and emphasize may be considered irrelevant to another. Thus, in general, highlighting may be perceived as "noise" physically damaging the document [2].

Y.-B. Kwon and J.-M. Ogier (Eds.): GREC, LNCS 7423, pp. 251–259, 2013.

Table 1. Component alteration due to highlighting

Highlight	Color	Components
	Yellow	Blue
	Blue	Red/Green
	Green	Red/Blue
	Orange	Green/Blue
	Cyan	Red/Green
	Magenta	Red/Green/Blue

On the other hand, the highlighted text offers a summary of the most important parts of a document. The recent paper [5] presents a general algorithm for extracting the highlighted text and making summaries. It even allows generating different summaries for each color of marker used. One of the referees in ICDAR 2011 to the paper [5] drew the authors' attention to the existence of two patents that address the same problem [3] [4]. The solution proposed in reference [5] seems to be more general (as different colors of markers are allowed) than the one in the patents [3][4], that seems to focus only in yellow highlighting. Besides that, for the yellow marker the solution in [5] seems to be more time efficient than the scheme in [3] and [4], whose effectiveness in is still to be examined as those documents do not present any real example.

Highlighting removal is far from being a simple task as the ink often fades non-uniformly and interacts with the paper background. To the best of this paper authors' knowledge, the first reference in the literature for highlighting removal of monochromatic documents printed on white paper is [1]. If the paper darkens with age highlighting removal becomes even more difficult.

This paper generalizes the results presented in reference [1] by addressing the problem of any (Yellow, Blue, Green, Orange, Pink and Cyan) color highlighting removal in aged documents, in which the paper has darkened. A comparative statistical analysis between highlighted and non-marked areas after performing the contrast enhancement of the original image is performed as the key for finding and removing the effect of any color of markers in documents with white or aged background.

2   Contrast Enhancement

Contrast enhancement is a technique widely used in areas that range from medical [6] to satellite [7] imaging. Linear, quadratic and logarithmic functions may be used in contrast enhancement. Such functions map the hue variations of a RGB component, onto a suitable interval, widening the original range of hues in the original image.

The choice of the suitable mapping is driven by the analysis of the RGB-color histogram of the image. Normalized histograms are used to compare highlighted and non-marked regions of the image, as the number of pixels in such regions may be different. The normalized RGB-color histogram is seen as a probability density function. For a given image X, the probability density function $p(X_k)$ is defined as:

$$p(X_k) = \frac{n^k}{n} \tag{1}$$

For $k = 0, 1, ..., L - 1$, where n^k represents the number of times that the level X_k appears in the input image X and n is the total number of samples in the input image [8].

The work developed in [1] allowed observing that there is a linear relation between the highlighted and non-marked areas of an image. Thus, the choice of a suitable linear function $y = ax + b$, is the key to cancel the effect of highlighting. The approach followed in reference [1] for the yellow marker is similar to the inverse linear transformation proposed here, but in that scheme [1] satisfactory results were only obtained through several iterations.

3   Finding the Inverse Linear Function Though the Average and Deviation of the Highlighted Histogram

A typical example of highlighting may be observed in Figure 1, where a cyan marked area is presented. The normalized histogram is presented by the red curve in Figure 1b and the yellow one stands for the non-highlighted are (paper background). Both of then exclude textual areas of the document, as markers do not significantly alter their appearance (and histogram) [5].

As one may observe in the distributions in Figure 1, the marker widened the distribution of the hue of the Red components and deviated its center towards the left part of the plot, altering the average and deviation of the non-highlighted distribution. A similar phenomenon was observed for the Green and Blue components of the highlighted and non-marked images. One may also observe that the "shape" of both distributions are similar and that may be taken as Gaussians. Thus, it is reasonable to assume that the marker performs a linear transformation on the histogram.

The idea here is then to find the inverse linear transformation for each RGB-component that would cancel the effect of the highlighting. Several factors affect this choice: the color of the marker, the kind of its ink and solvent [9], the kind of paper, its porosity, opacity, etc. Even if all these factors were known at a given time, they change with time due to paper aging, ink fading, etc. Figure 2 presents an example of highlighting fading within one year.

Due to these complicating factors, the solution proposed here is to analyze two different areas of the same image with and without highlighting to determine the parameters of the filter. Having as starting point the normalized histograms as shown on Figure 1, calculated following equation (1) and using the following properties of the expected value $E(X)$ and of the deviation $\sigma(X)$ [10]:

$$\sigma(aX + b) = a\sigma(X) \tag{2}$$

$$E(aX + b) = aE(X) + b \tag{3}$$

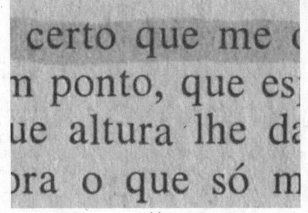

(a)

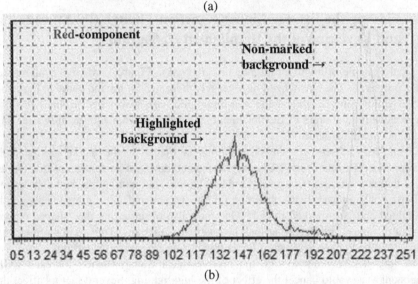

(b)

Fig. 1. (a) Image highlighted with cyan marker. (b) In Red: normalized histogram of the Red-component of cyan-marked background of the image shown in (a). (b) In Yellow: the Red-component of histogram distribution of the paper texture of the image in (a). Axes: x- hue of red; y-percentage of pixels.

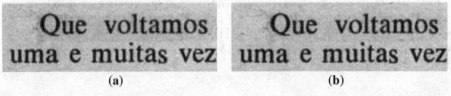

(a)   (b)

Fig. 2. Example of highlighting fading within one year. (a) Image scanned immediately after highlighting. (b) The same image scanned one year later than (a).

As $\sigma_1(X)$ is the original deviation of any RGB component of the original texture, the marker affects in a similar way the original deviation of some RGB component of the original texture, such that the deviation becomes $\sigma_2(aX)$. Notice that b is a shift in the intensity of a component and does not alter the deviation of the distribution. Thus, one may apply equation (2) to find an approximate value to the coefficient a (4) of the linear equation $y = ax + b$ and find the original deviation multiplying a by the intensity of the component under analysis.

$$a = \sigma_1(X)/ \sigma_2(X) \tag{4}$$

Applying the coefficient a to the normalized histogram presented as the red plot of Figure 1 one obtains the histogram shown by the green curve in Figure 3.

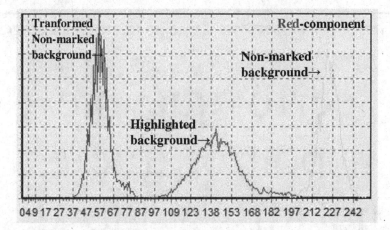

Fig. 3. Norm. hist. of the R-component of Figure 1a. (a) In Red: normalized histogram of the Red-component of cyan-marked background of the image shown in (1.a). (b) In Yellow: the Red-component of histogram distribution of the paper texture of the image in (1.a). (c) In Green: histogram transformation after application of coefficient a without in background area. Axes: x- hue of red; y-percentage of pixels.

One may also observe that besides the change in the deviation of the distribution, the expected value was also altered, as described by equation (3). Now, one needs to shift the histogram of coefficient b, which may be found by the difference between the expected values of the distributions in the yellow and green plots of Figure 3.

Applying the value of coefficient a to equation (3) one wants the mathematical expectancy to be the same for both distributions, and then one has to shift the distribution of b units, thus:

$$b = E_1(X) - E_2(X) \tag{5}$$

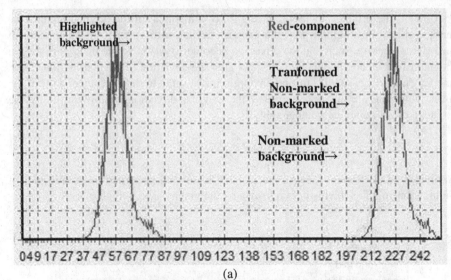

(a)

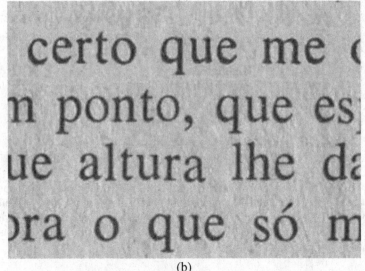

(b)

Fig. 4. (a) Normalized histogram of the Red-component of the image shown in Figure 1. In Yellow: the Red-component of histogram distribution of the paper texture of the image in (1.a). In Red: normalized histogram of the Red-component of cyan-marked background of the image shown in (1.a) after applying coefficient a. In Green: histogram transformation after application of coefficient b in non-marked background area. Axes: x- hue of red; y-percentage of pixels. (b) Zoom into the image of Figure 1(a) with the cyan marker removed.

$E_1(X)$ is the expected value of the original texture of the RGB-component under analysis and $E_2(X)$ the mathematical expectancy of the intermediate histogram, obtained through the application of coefficient a already found. Figure 4 (a) presents the final result for the histogram of the Red-component of Figure 1a. Figure 4 (b)

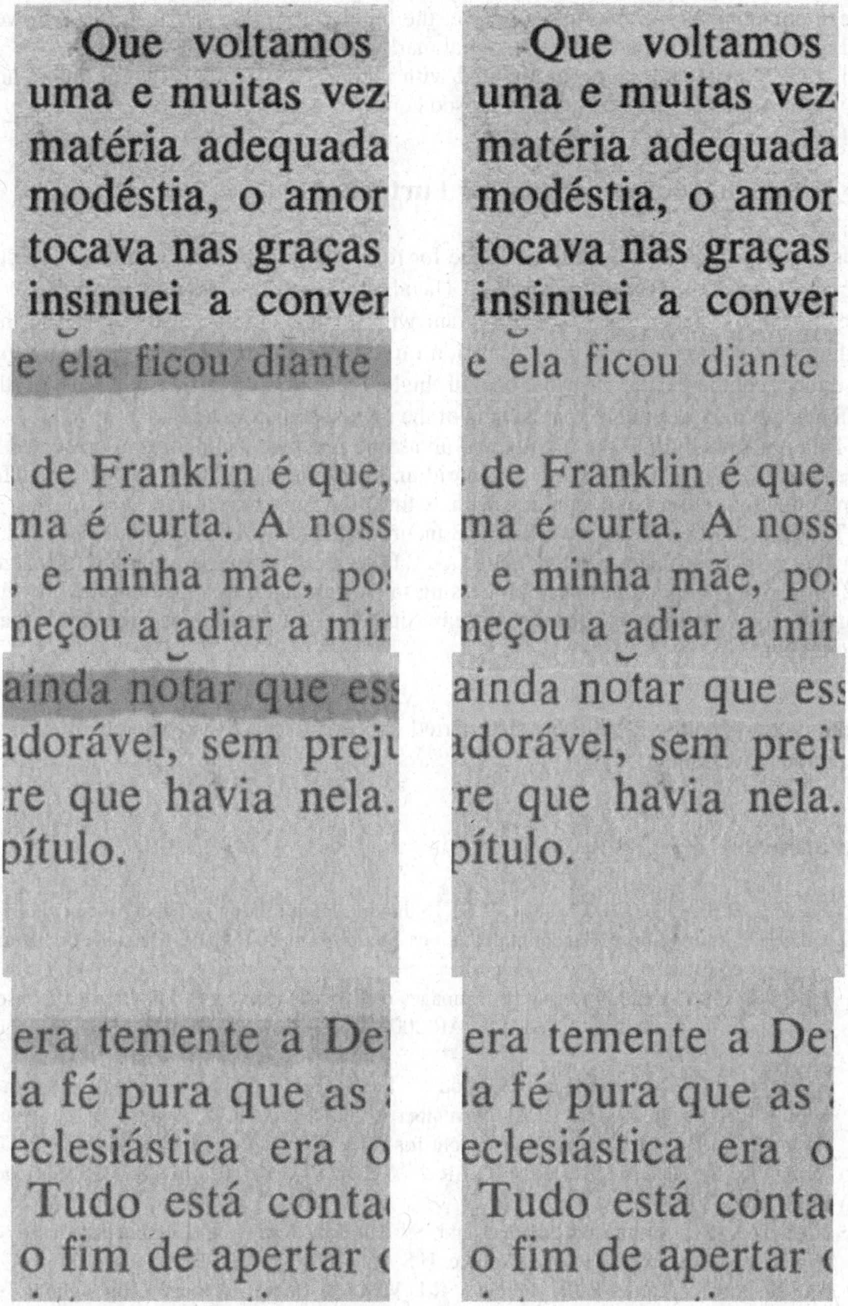

Que voltamos
uma e muitas vez
matéria adequada
modéstia, o amor
tocava nas graças
insinuei a conver
e ela ficou diante

de Franklin é que,
ma é curta. A noss
, e minha mãe, po:
neçou a adiar a mir
ainda notar que ess
adorável, sem preji
re que havia nela.
pítulo.

era temente a De
la fé pura que as :
eclesiástica era o
Tudo está conta
o fim de apertar (

Que voltamos
uma e muitas vez
matéria adequada
modéstia, o amor
tocava nas graças
insinuei a conver
e ela ficou diante

de Franklin é que,
ma é curta. A noss
, e minha mãe, po:
neçou a adiar a mir
ainda notar que ess
adorável, sem preji
re que havia nela.
pítulo.

era temente a De
la fé pura que as :
eclesiástica era o
Tudo está conta
o fim de apertar (

Fig. 5. Example of highlighted images of aged paper background on the left hand side with different colors of markers and their removal using the algorithm described herein presented to the right hand side.

shows the final filtered image obtained by applying the same technique to the Blue and Green components. As one may observe, the highlighting was satisfactorily removed and only an almost imperceptible vestigial mark is left.

Figure 5 presents images highlighted with markers of several different colors and their removal using the algorithm proposed here.

4   Conclusions and Lines for Further Work

This paper presents an efficient technique for removing highlighting in monochromatic documents with aged paper background. The algorithm assumes that aging gives rise to a texture in the paper that has a histogram with a Gaussian-like distribution and that highlighting acts as a linear transformation on the original distribution. The algorithm described compares the distributions of highlighted and non-marked areas of the document to find the suitable parameters of the inverse transformation.

To automatically find the highlighted areas one may use the algorithm presented in reference [1], which is still the best algorithm, known to the authors of this paper, for removing highlighting of documents with "white" background.

The algorithm presented here has been incorporated to the HistDoc Platform version 2.0 [11], which is freely available. HistDoc 2.0 besides working as a plugin to ImageJ [12] it also allows parallel image processing in clusters and grids meeting the growing demand for a document processing environment that can reach industrial scale throughput.

Acknowledgements. The research reported herein was partly sponsored by CNPq-Brazilian Government.

References

1. Barboza, R.S., Lins, R.D., Mattos, V.S.: Removing Highlighting in Paper Documents. In: VII IEEE International Telecommunications Symposium, ITS 2010, Manaus-AM, Brazil (September 2010)
2. Lins, R.D.: A Taxonomy for Noise in Images of Paper Documents - The Physical Noises. In: Kamel, M., Campilho, A. (eds.) ICIAR 2009. LNCS, vol. 5627, pp. 844–854. Springer, Heidelberg (2009)
3. Nagarajan, R., et al.: Automated Method for Extracting Highlighted Regions in Scanned Source. U.S. Patent 2007/0253620 (November 1, 2007); Lins, R.D., Ávila, B.T., de Araújo Formiga, A.: BigBatch – An Environment for Processing Monochromatic Documents. In: Campilho, A., Kamel, M.S. (eds.) ICIAR 2006. LNCS, vol. 4142, pp. 886–896. Springer, Heidelberg (2006)
4. Nagarajan, R.: Automated Method and System for Retrieving Documents Based on Highlighted Text from a Scanned Source. U.S. Patent 2007/0253643, No. 1 (2007)
5. Barboza, R.S., Lins, R.D., Pereira, R.D.V.M.S.: Using Readers' Highlighting on Monochromatic Documents for Automatic Text Transcription and Summarization. In: Eleventh International Conference on Document Analysis and Recognition (ICDAR 2011), Beijing, China. IEEE Press (September 2011)

6. Stetson, P.F., Sommer, F.G., Macovski, A.: Lesion contrast enhancement in medical ultrasound imaging. IEEE Trans. Medical Imaging 16(4), 416–425 (1997)
7. Starck, J., Murtagh, F., Candès, E.J., Donoho, D.L.: Gray and color image contrast enhancement by the curvelet transform. Presented at IEEE Transactions on Image Processing, 706–717 (2003)
8. Chen, D., Ramli, R.: Contrast Enhancement Using Recursive Mean-Separate Histogram Equalization for Scalable Brightness Preservation. Computer Journal of IEEE Transactions Consumer Electronics 49(4), 1301–1309 (2003)
9. Schmid, C., et al.: Ink Compositions for use in highlighter markers and associated methods. U.S. Patent 2005/0093949 (May 5, 2005)
10. Baclawski, K.: Introduction to probability with R. Ed. Taylor & Francys Group, USA (2008)
11. Lins, R.D., de França Silva, G., de Araújo Formiga, A.: HistDoc v. 2.0 - Enhancing a Platform to Process Historical Documents. In: International Workshop on Historical Document Imaging and Processing, HIP 2011, Pequim, pp. 230–239. ACM Press, New York (2011)
12. ImageJ, http://rsb.info.nih.gov/ij/

A Parts-Based Multi-scale Method for Symbol Recognition

Feng Su, Li Yang, and Tong Lu

State Key Laboratory for Novel Software Technology
Nanjing University, Nanjing 210093, China
suf@nju.edu.cn

Abstract. We present a new parts-based multi-scale recognition method for graphic symbols, especially those connecting or intersecting with other elements in the context. The main idea is to decompose the symbol into the set of multi-scale local parts, some of which are not or less affected by the contextual interferences, and then recognize the symbol based on detecting and integrating individual symbol parts. An ensemble learning and classification scheme is employed, which combines three ingredients: 1) the multi-scale spatial pyramid representation of the symbol that consists of local parts for matching. 2) the random forest based classifying of symbol parts and discriminative learning of the mappings between parts and the symbol. 3) the probabilistic aggregation of individual part detections to form the symbol recognition output. The experimental results on simulation datasets show the effectiveness of the proposed method and its promising properties in handling non-segmented symbols.

1 Introduction

During the last two decades, many recognition methods have been proposed for graphic symbols, i.e. symbols made of lines, arcs and simple geometric primitives [24,16,25,27,10,9], which can be roughly categorized into three schemes: statistical approaches, structural approaches and hybrids of both, according the way the method representing the symbol, extracting the feature and constructing the recognition algorithm. Among them, considering the shape is the one of the most intrinsic characteristics of graphic symbols, many methods focus on developing sophisticated descriptions of symbol shape features, for which recent works are mainly devoted to combing the statistical descriptions, which capture the pixel distribution of symbol instances and are generally robust to local noises or degradations, and the structural descriptions, which describe relationships between elements of the symbol and are more robust to compositive changes.

Besides the methods for extracting descriptive features, another category of methods focus on constructing sophisticated discriminative algorithms for symbol classification using various machine learning techniques [9,19,18] and usually on the basis of relatively simpler and primitive features. Methods adopting this

Y.-B. Kwon and J.-M. Ogier (Eds.): GREC, LNCS 7423, pp. 260–274, 2013.

strategy are typically effective after sufficient training on the target sample set, but may be less generative to different datasets or different degradation models.

In real and practical usage of graphic symbols, however, various contextual interferences to the symbol are common, such as intersecting or touching, resulted from either the insufficiency of the segmentation method or the inherent composition of the graphical document. Such interferences will cause large intra-class variance of symbol shape features and consequently the reduced performance of some statistical descriptors, especially when they are used on the holistic symbol. On the other hand, as long as the interferences are local, which means there are parts of the symbol left untouched (i.e. preserving the shape integrity) relative to its prototype, there could be possibilities for a bottom-up, part-based methodology, where the detections of individual symbol parts are further integrated to reason about the whole symbol.

For such part-based recognition scheme to work, two key technical ingredients should be addressed: the definition and representation of the parts, and the integration mechanism for combining the processing of local parts to the final recognition of the whole symbol. For the former, the definition of the parts of the object can vary with the problem being addressed, as long as they reflect various local features of the object and altogether constitute the collective representation of the object. For example, the parts can be simply the uniform decompositions of the object region, or, they can be characteristic components of the object like the Scale-Invariant Feature Transform (SIFT) [17] feature points. Various bag-of-feature or bag-of-words methods [22,23] can also be considered a form of the parts model, in which the object is described by a set of visual features or words extracted from it, which are further transformed into a single flat histogram that counts the frequency of occurrence of some pre-defined (quantized) feature prototypes. In our problem, however, because the contextual interferences to the symbol can occur in various scales, a multiscale representation of the symbol and its parts is necessary, for which many parts-based schemes usually lack of. For the latter aspect of the part-based recognition scheme, several strategies can be exploited to combine the processing of local parts into the inference of the whole object, either at the feature level or the label level. As the first strategy, the matching of two objects can be formulated as looking for the optimal correspondence between their parts, which can then be solved using a dynamic programming method, or more efficiently, using the pyramid matching method [13], which finds an approximate correspondence between two sets of vectors by multiresolutionally histogramming the high-dimensional feature space with a sequence of increasingly coarser uniform or non-uniform grids. Another strategy, as adopted by this paper, is to aggregate the local intermediate recognitions (i.e. the labels) of individual parts by certain voting-based schemes [21]. Because it does not pursue a (holistic and optimal) matching between parts of two objects, this strategy is flexible and efficient in computation and capable of dealing with the unequal cardinality of the parts models.

In this paper, we present our work on a novel parts-based multi-scale symbol recognition method. The focus is put on developing robust discriminative

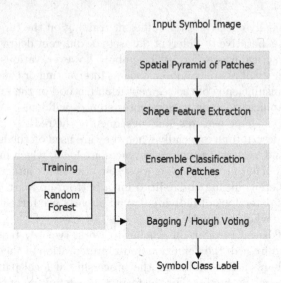

Fig. 1. Block diagram of the proposed symbol recognition algorithm

algorithm to recognize non-segmented symbols, i.e., those connected or inter-
sected by other primitives in their context. For the symbol representation, since
no priori knowledge about the position and scale of the interference is available,
we recursively decompose the symbol into finer patches, resulting in a multi-scale
spatial pyramid representation of the symbol, in which the unaffected symbol
parts reside on respective levels. To classify various symbols, we extract multiple
simple shape descriptors to form a composite feature vector for each local symbol
patch, and learn the mapping between shape features of constituent patches and
the symbol within a random forest based ensemble classifier framework, in which
the probabilistic votes by each patch on the potential category of the symbol are
aggregated to give the holistic recognition result. The framework of the proposed
algorithm is outlined in Fig. 1.

The paper is organized as follows. In Section 2, we describe the process of
constructing the multi-scale pyramid representation of the symbol and extracting
the shape features. In Section 3, we describe the part-based recognition algorithm
for the symbols. In Section 4, we present the experimental results of the proposed
method and some discussions.

2   Pyramid Representation and Feature Extraction

Multi-scale analysis has been an effective and widely exploited processing method
to many vision problems. It's applicable whenever one wishes to implement an
algorithm that involves iterative coarse-to-fine processing or the object of interest exhibits variant properties when analyzed at different scales. The basic
procedure is to construct a tree or pyramid representation of the object and to
start processing at the coarsest level, popagating to the increasingly finer levels

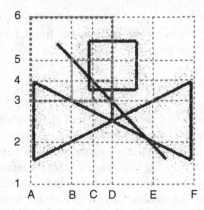

Fig. 2. Illustration of multi-scale spatial pyramid decomposition of the symbol into patches. Rectangles colored in red, green and blue denote the examples of symbol patches in different scales. Notice that, though patches such as D-1-F-3, D-2-E-3, B-4-C-5 and those colored are interfered by the intersecting line, most other patches remain untouched.

until reach the finest level, or vice versa. The pyramid representation of images [20] widely exploited in computer vision and image processing is one such type of multi-scale methods. In shape-based object modeling, for another example, Del Bimbo and Pala [6] present a multiscale hierarchical shape representation in which shape details are progressively filtered out while shape characterizing elements are preserved. Similarly, [11] describes a shape-tree-based hierarchical representation of contour curves of two dimensional objects that captures geometric properties at multiple levels of resolution.

In this section, we construct a multiscale spatial pyramid representation similar to [7] for a symbol, which describes the pixel distribution in each symbol patch instead of approximating the contour shape as [11], and extract shape descriptors for each subregion in the pyramid. The symbol is then described by this set of multi-scale local shape features, which will be further ranked and encoded later by the ensemble classifier as an implicit codebook of features specific to the symbol category.

2.1 The Spatial Pyramid

We construct the multi-scale spatial pyramid for a symbol by successively partitioning its image region along the $x-$ and $y-$ axis into increasingly finer subregions, as shown in Fig. 2, resulting a hierarchic structure of spatially nested subregions of symbol, called *symbol patches*.

Specifically, supposing we construct a L-level quadtree pyramid, each upper level patch is splitted into 4 sub-patches of half the width and height, and the whole set of patches P_i at the i-th level is:

$$P_i = \{p_1^i, p_2^i, \ldots, p_{N_{P,i}}^i\}, \qquad N_{P,i} = 4^{L-i}$$

where, the number of patches $N_{P,i}$ decreases with the level. p_1^L corresponds to the whole symbol image region while p_j^1 is at the finest level. The size $[D_h^i, D_w^i]$ of each patch at level i increase with the level:

$$D_h^i = \frac{D_H}{2^{L-i}} \qquad D_w^i = \frac{D_W}{2^{L-i}}$$

where, D_H and D_W are the height and width of the symbol image, respectively. We can see that the pyramid representation also encodes the multi-scale structural information of symbols by spatial organization of patches at each level.

The basic idea of decomposing the symbol into a spatial pyramid of patches is to isolate patches that are small enough so that not affected by other intersecting graphical objects, supposing such interferences are local to the symbol. By comparison, the distribution of shape features usually exhibits high variance for the whole symbol that involves much of the interferences, making it difficult to perform holistic shape matching. On the other hand, small patches are less discriminative for different symbol classes, for which we need sophisticated classification models to map patches to the potential symbol. We will address this later in the paper.

2.2   Shape Features

Various sophisticated shape descriptors have been proposed in past research [26,4,25,27,10,9]. Considering our purpose is to evaluate the effectiveness of the parts-based processing framework, however, we intentionally exploit some 'weak' shape descriptions to focus on the performance gains by the method rather than those by the specific features, while the latter is also explored in the experiments. Specifically, for each symbol patch, we extract three categories of shape features from its contour points: *HoA*, *HoL* and *GS*, each describing one specific aspect of the distributions of geometric constraints of pixels in the patch.

- The HoA feature is the contour point orientation histogram, which is built by going over all points that lie on object contours, and histogramming the angle associated with a point, either the orientation of the vector connecting the point to the centroid or the local contour tangent orientation. Denoting the index of contour point by i ($i = 1..N_S$, N_S is the number of points), the corresponding orientations of all points by $\{a_i\}$, and dividing the value range $[0,2\pi]$ of a_i into Q_A equal bins $[y_0, y_1] \cup [y_1, y_2] \cup \ldots \cup [y_{Q_A-1}, y_{Q_A}]$ ($y_0 = 0$ and $y_{Q_A} = 2\pi$), the HoA is a Q_A-dim vector $[HoA_1, HoA_2, \ldots, HoA_{Q_A}]$, where

$$HoA_k = \frac{1}{N_S} \sum_{i=1}^{N_S} h(a_i; y_{k-1}, y_k)$$

and

$$h(a_i; y_{k-1}, y_k) = \begin{cases} 1, & a_i \in [y_{k-1}, y_k) \\ 0, & else \end{cases}$$

- The HoL feature is the contour-to-centroid distance histogram represented as a Q_L-dim vector $[HoL_1, HoL_2, \ldots, HoL_{Q_L}]$, which can be computed similar to HoA by substituting the angle a_i at a contour point with its distance d_i to the centroid of the shape, normalizing d_i by $\max(d_i)$ and binning in the value range $[0, 1.0]$.
- The GS (Grid Statistics) feature encodes the internal spatial distribution of contour points or statistics derived from these contour points in the patch, which is a Q_S-dim vector $[GS_1, GS_2, \ldots, GS_{Q_S}]$ with Q_S being the number of spatial bins dividing the patch region (Q_S can be set equal to the number of subpatches that the current patch is splitted). Each GS_k can be the proportion of contour points of the k-th subpatch relative to the total points of the patch, or, as an example of statistics, the variances of HoA/HoL features in the subpatch.

The choice of above shape features is mainly owing to their computational efficiency, mostly with the $O(N)$ complexity. Moreover, the computation of the GS feature can be accelerated utilizing the inter-level patch correspondences of the pyramid. Note that the HoA feature is not invariant to rotations and the contour tangent is usually sensitive to noises and degradations. For better performance and robustness, we can easily replace above simple features with more sophisticated ones, for example those discussed in [26] or the SIHA descriptor [25] explored in our experiments, which are possibly also more costly in computation.

3   Ensemble Recognition of Symbols

In this section, we develop a random forest based ensemble method for symbol recognition, which learns the mapping between the shape feature of a symbol patch and its probabilistic votes on the potential categories of the symbol instance. Combined with the multi-scale spatial pyramid representation of the symbol, it allows local symbol parts at the finer scale (smaller ROI), which are not affected by intersecting entities, to be recognized with high accuracy and help reason about the whole symbol.

3.1   Random Forest Classification Model

Random forest [8] is a collection of binary decision tree predictors/classifiers, each taking the input feature vector, classifying it and outputting its own vote on the possible class label. The final classification output of the whole forest is then the majority or other measurements of integration of individual votes. The binary test at each non-leaf node of random forest performs thresholding on one feature in the feature vector to determine the branch it goes down, and the choice for the feature and the threshold are learned in the training stage by, for example, minimizing the impurity of sample classes at the node.

Compared to a single decision tree or other type of simple classifier, random forest assembles together several trees, which are trained in a randomized way (random subset of the training data for each tree or random subset of binary tests at each tree node), and usually achieves superior generalization and stability. For this reason, random forests have recently attracted many attention in computer vision [12,14], and in graphics recognition, despite relatively less investigated, random forest has been used in pragmatic handwritten digit recognition [5] and character detection from natural scenes [15] as a robust classifier.

In our work, after having determined the relevant parameters (number and maximum depth of decision trees, minimum sample count per node, etc.), the learning of the random forest from a set of symbol samples is as follows:

1. Initialize a set of N_T decision trees $\{T_1, T_2, \ldots, T_{N_T}\}$.
2. Convert all symbol images in the training set into pyramids of multi-scale patches. Denoting the number of patches by N_P and the number of symbol classes by K, each patch p_i $(i = 1..N_P)$ is attached with the class label r_i $(r_i \in [1..K])$ of its parent symbol.
3. Extract the composite shape feature vector v_i for each patch as described in previous section, and use $\{[v_i, r_i]\}_{i=1..N_P}$ to train the random forest.

Once trained, the leaf nodes of forest trees encode the characteristic local shape features for every specific symbol class.

Given an unknown symbol image, the classification using the random forest is as follows:

1. Decompose the image into the pyramid of multi-scale patches and extract the shape feature vectors $\{v_i\}$, as in the training process.
2. Send each patch v_i down every tree in the forest and collect the outputs, either the class label or the training sample set, at the predicted leaf node of every tree.
3. Aggregate the outputs to obtain the estimated class label for the input symbol, as described in next section.

The outputs of all forest trees provide the posterior probabilities of the symbol class given the whole set of patches, which can be used as the probabilistic votes for the symbol.

3.2   Probabilistic Aggregation of Patches

Given the set of classification outputs by the random forest for all patches of an unknown symbol image, we aggregate the probabilistic votes casted by every tree to infer the potential symbol class. Two methods for such aggregation are employed in this work.

Given the test image x and one of its patches x_j, the first method, *bagging* [21], computes the probability $p(c_k|x_j)$ of the symbol class k, where $p(c_k|x_j) = N(k)/N_T$, $N(k)$ is the number of trees that predict x_j to be of symbol class k and N_T is the total number of trees. Then, the probabilities from all patches $\{x_j | j \in [1..N_P]\}$ are summed up to form the total class likelihood:

$$p(c_k|x) = p(c_k|x_1, x_2, \ldots, x_{N_P}) \propto \sum_{j=1}^{N_P} p(c_k|x_j) \qquad (1)$$

The class $k = \arg\max_k p(c_k|x)$ is considered the final class for x. A simpler variation of the method is to have $p(c_k|x_j) = 1$ if the majority of trees predict class k, otherwise $p(c_k|x_j) = 0$.

The second method, *Hough voting* [12], uses a generalized Hough transform to aggregate class votes casted by the training samples associated with the tree nodes during the training stage. Let $R_t = \{p_i | i \in [1..N_{P,t}]\}$ is the set of training samples p_i stored in the leaf node of the t-th tree reached by a test patch x_j. We initialize a 1D Hough vector $H_C(k)$ $(k = 1..K)$, each element containing the accumulated votes for the corresponding symbol class. Then, for each sample p_i in R_t whose class is k, we add a contribution to the bin $H_C(k)$. After all the patches $\{x_j\}$ are processed, the peak in $H_C(k)$ indicates the MAP estimate for the potential symbol class.

4   Experiments

We tested the proposed part-based symbol recognition method in simulations on technical line symbols from the symbol recognition contest datasets of GREC2005 [1]. Since the main goal of our experiments is to evaluate the method's performance on non-segmented symbols that connect to or intersect with other graphic primitives, we generate synthetic symbol samples [3] by randomly adding lines or arcs (in the same degradation patterns) to the GREC2005 test images. To ensure the intersecting, the added lines or arcs are positioned crossing the image center, with random orientations.

For the experimental purpose, the original symbol samples we use in syntheses are from the first category of tests in [1] with 150 symbol models, whose shapes are degraded by 6 different models or levels of binary noises but without rotation/scaling transformations. To simulate different intersecting complexity, we generate 5 test datasets [3], with 1 line (L1), 1 arc (A1), 2 lines (L2), 2 arcs (A2), 1 line and 1 arc (LA) added to the original symbol images, respectively. Some examples of these synthetic samples are illustrated in Table 1.

Our random forest framework is based on the implementation in the standard OpenCV library [2], with our customization of the Hough voting mechanism for symbol patches. In all experiments, we set 16 for the maximum depth of the decision trees and use totally 100 trees in the random forest classifier (hereafter abbreviated as RF). For one symbol image, we extract its contour points and generate the 3-level pyramid of patches. For each patch, we extract shape features with following empirical settings: 8 orientation bins for the HoA feature, 8 distance bins for the HoL feature and 12-dim GS feature (4-dim proportions of contour point numbers, 4-dim variances of HoA and 4-dim variances of HoL features), which hereafter are denoted as the ALGS feature for convenience. To investigate the effectiveness of the proposed random forest based method on different feature compositions, we also extract the 128-dim SIHA shape descriptor proposed in [25] from the symbol image, with histogramming bin number $M = Q = 8$ for both the length-ratio and angle constraints, and use it alone or together with the ALGS feature. For comparison, the same holistic matching

Table 1. Synthetic intersecting symbol samples [3] with randomly added lines and arcs in different degradation models. The first row is the original symbol samples from [1].

based classification criterion for SIHA descriptors with the $L1$-norm similarity measurement as in [25] is also adopted, to reveal the influence that the intersecting interferences bring to general holistic (in contrast to parts-based) recognition schemes.

We set up two groups of testing experiments, each covering all 6 degradation models in [1]. The first group of experiments treat each degradation model separately, that is, a separate random forest classifier specifically designated for one degradation model is trained with the non-synthertic symbol samples in this degradation model, and the intersecting symbol samples synthesized from these training prototypes are used as the test sets. This setting for classifier training

Table 2. Average accuracy of individual classifiers trained for each different degradation model

(a) ALGS w. RF

degrad. models	interference levels				
	L1	A1	L2	A2	LA
mod1	1.00	1.00	0.96	0.84	0.88
mod2	0.07	0.06	0.07	0.06	0.06
mod3	0.97	0.99	0.91	0.76	0.85
mod4	0.93	0.96	0.86	0.82	0.86
mod5	0.98	1.00	0.82	0.80	0.83
mod6	0.18	0.15	0.09	0.07	0.08

(b) SIHA w. RF

degrad. models	interference levels				
	L1	A1	L2	A2	LA
mod1	0.63	0.59	0.39	0.29	0.30
mod2	0.58	0.66	0.36	0.29	0.31
mod3	0.67	0.74	0.49	0.37	0.37
mod4	0.72	0.72	0.58	0.57	0.59
mod5	0.48	0.52	0.22	0.20	0.14
mod6	0.24	0.24	0.17	0.19	0.17

(c) ALGS+SIHA w. RF

degrad. models	interference levels				
	L1	A1	L2	A2	LA
mod1	0.94	0.97	0.65	0.56	0.47
mod2	0.42	0.42	0.25	0.25	0.20
mod3	0.97	0.99	0.87	0.65	0.77
mod4	0.97	0.96	0.82	0.79	0.81
mod5	0.91	0.96	0.65	0.61	0.66
mod6	0.25	0.25	0.16	0.19	0.16

(d) SIHA matching

degrad. models	interference levels				
	L1	A1	L2	A2	LA
mod1	0.35	0.35	0.09	0.17	0.11
mod2	0.26	0.24	0.10	0.15	0.07
mod3	0.35	0.28	0.14	0.10	0.14
mod4	0.22	0.50	0.05	0.18	0.10
mod5	0.31	0.28	0.12	0.11	0.08
mod6	0.13	0.17	0.04	0.05	0.05

corresponds to the cases that we know the degradation forms in advance. Table 2 shows the average recognition accuracies on the synthetic symbol samples with the 5 levels of synthetic interference complexities (by columns) and in each of 6 degradation models (by rows). The 'ALGS+SIHA w. RF' in Table 2 refers to concatenating the ALGS and SIHA feature vectors for a patch and using it with the random forest classification scheme, while the 'SIHA matching' refers to the holistic matching between two SIHA descriptors extracted globally from the whole symbol (i.e. the top level of the spatial pyramid), as described in [25].

Comparing Table 2d, which is given by the holistic matching scheme, with other results in Table 2 that employ the parts-based model, the proposed parts-based recognition framework achieves good accuracies on the visually heavily cluttered samples even for human eyes, and obtains significantly better performance than the holistic SIHA matching scheme, showing the feasibility and potential of the parts-based ensemble recognition scheme. We note that SIHA is not originally designed to handle such intersectings and our focus here is not on evaluating various features, the comparison still reveals the robustness of the proposed scheme.

Table 3. Average accuracy of the unitary classifier trained for all degradation models

(a) ALGS w. RF

degrad. models	interference levels				
	L1	A1	L2	A2	LA
mod1	0.53	0.44	0.19	0.13	0.15
mod2	0.03	0.05	0.04	0.05	0.04
mod3	0.72	0.72	0.42	0.27	0.32
mod4	0.92	0.94	0.64	0.60	0.66
mod5	0.57	0.64	0.22	0.18	0.20
mod6	0.05	0.05	0.05	0.05	0.05

(b) SIHA w. RF

degrad. models	interference levels				
	L1	A1	L2	A2	LA
mod1	0.29	0.26	0.18	0.10	0.20
mod2	0.17	0.19	0.14	0.15	0.14
mod3	0.17	0.18	0.13	0.09	0.11
mod4	0.31	0.28	0.16	0.16	0.19
mod5	0.35	0.37	0.17	0.16	0.10
mod6	0.16	0.19	0.13	0.14	0.12

(c) ALGS+SIHA w. RF

degrad. models	interference levels				
	L1	A1	L2	A2	LA
mod1	0.57	0.57	0.26	0.24	0.21
mod2	0.19	0.19	0.14	0.15	0.14
mod3	0.63	0.63	0.39	0.25	0.33
mod4	0.86	0.83	0.47	0.21	0.36
mod5	0.74	0.80	0.48	0.46	0.43
mod6	0.11	0.12	0.07	0.10	0.06

(d) SIHA matching

degrad. models	interference levels				
	L1	A1	L2	A2	LA
mod1	0.30	0.29	0.09	0.16	0.09
mod2	0.20	0.18	0.09	0.07	0.03
mod3	0.30	0.20	0.10	0.07	0.09
mod4	0.16	0.42	0.05	0.17	0.06
mod5	0.28	0.25	0.15	0.12	0.09
mod6	0.14	0.16	0.07	0.02	0.04

When the classifier trained for one symbol degradation model is applied to samples of another different degradation model, however, the performance of the above RF setting descends significantly in the experiments (down to below 10% for certain degradation models), implying that the learned classification model not only captures the disparity of different symbol classes that we want to distinguish, but also encodes the characteristics of specific degradation forms. Moreover, the above training setting limits its application in situations that no priori knowledge about the degradation form is available. To reduce such 'over-fitting', which is incured mainly by the small sample set for different symbol classes (actually only one sample per class - the non-synthertic symbol proto-type), the second group of experiments merge the symbol samples from all 6 degradation models altogether, and group the non-synthertic symbol samples that belong to the same ground truth class into an expanded training set. Now, for each symbol class, the training set contains original samples from [1] with different degradation forms and the undegraded model symbol, a single unitary random forest classifier is then learned from these merged training sets to predict the class label for an input sample, regardless of its potential degradation model. The performance of this category of training setting for the RF classifier is shown in Table 3.

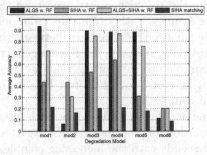

(a) degradation specific training

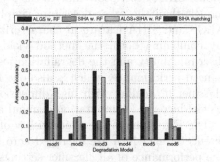

(b) training on all degradations

Fig. 3. Comparison of average accuracy in each degradation model by variant feature and classifier settings, with (a) individual classifiers trained for each degradation model; (b) the unitary classifier trained for all degradation models

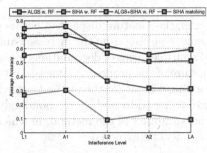

(a) degradation specific training

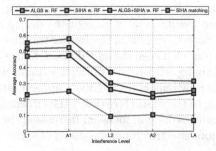

(b) training on all degradations

Fig. 4. Comparison of average accuracy at each interference level by variant feature and classifier settings, with (a) individual classifiers trained for each degradation model (b) the unitary classifier trained for all degradation models

As revealed by the results in Table 3, due to the larger intra-class variance of sample appearances (thereby the feature representations) between various degradation models in the same training set for one symbol class, the second category of RF training settings yields remarkably decreased performance, but still outperforms the holistic matching method, and on the other side, having the benefit of flexibility in organizing the training sets.

The Fig. 3 shows graphically the comparisons of the achieved accuracies by above different settings and methods, which are averaged across all synthetic interference levels. We notice that, though our focus is not on comparing the discriminability of different shape descriptors, within the same random forest based classification framework, either the simple ALGS descriptor or the more robust SIHA descriptor exhibits the lower performance for specific degradation models than the other descriptor, implying the complementary aspects of the ALGS and SIHA feature in characterizing symbols with variant degradations. By combining both, the method yields a balanced performance between the discriminability and the degradation insensitivity, resulting in an averagely enhanced performance, which is also one favorable property of the random forest classifier in dealing with high-dimensional heterogeneous features, but at the cost of increased computation demand and complexity.

The Fig. 4 shows the comparisons of the accuracies achieved for each interference level, which are averaged across all degradation models. As expected, the performance of all classifier settings descends with the increasing complexity of interferences, in which the exploitation of robust descriptors like SIHA, as we mentioned before, increases the overall performance and stableness of the proposed parts-based recognition scheme, showing its flexibility in tuning the complexity and efficiency according to variant requirements. At the same time, we also notice that, the increasing complexity of the interference causes a more significant drop of the accuracy to the unitary classifier trained on all degradations, when compared with the classifiers individually trained on each degradation model. This may because of the decreased feature prominence of one specific symbol class or the decreased inter-class feature disparities between different symbols in the former training scheme, resulting from the increased ambiguity between the added interferences and multiple forms of degradations in the training set. Because of the discriminative nature of the proposed framework, it's thereby important to choose appropriate training scheme for the method according to the characteristics of the circumstances being addressed. Correspondingly, future work will focus on increasing the generalizability of the method, in which more effective representations of symbols will also be explored.

5   Conclusion

The experiment results show that the proposed parts-based multi-scale symbol recognition method can effectively deal with partial intersection and connection of objects. It achieves a rather high accuracy even on samples with significant interferences. Its performance could be further improved by exploiting and combining various discriminative and robust features, on the basis that representative and sufficient training sets are used for better generality.

Acknowledgment. Research supported by the National Science Foundation of China under Grant Nos. 61003113, 61021062 and the Natural Science Foundation of Jiangsu Province of China under Grant Nos. BK2009082 and the 973 Program of China under Grant No. 2010CB327903.

References

1. International symbol recognition contest GREC 2005 (2005), http://symbcontestgrec05.loria.fr/
2. OpenCV (Open Source Computer Vision) library, http://opencv.willowgarage.com/
3. Synthetic intersecting graphic symbols based on international symbol recognition contest GREC 2005 dataset (2005), http://cs.nju.edu.cn/sufeng/grec05/
4. Belongie, S., Malik, J., Puzicha, J.: Shape matching and object recognition using shape contexts. IEEE Trans. PAMI 24(24), 509–522 (2002)
5. Bernard, S., Heutte, L., Adam, S.: Using random forests for handwritten digit recognition. In: ICDAR 2007, pp. 1043–1047 (2007)
6. Bimbo, A.D., Pala, P.: Shape indexing by multi-scale representation. Image and Vision Computing 17, 245–261 (1999)
7. Bosch, A., Zisserman, A., Munoz, X.: Representing shape with a spatial pyramid kernel. In: CIVR 2007, pp. 401–408 (2007)
8. Breiman, L.: Random forests. Machine Learning 45(1), 5–32 (2001)
9. Coustaty, M., Bertet, K., Visani, M., Ogier, J.M.: A new adaptive structural signature for symbol recognition by using a galois lattice as a classifier. IEEE Transactions on Systems, Man, and Cybernetics, Part B: Cybernetics 41(4), 1136–1148 (2011)
10. Escalera, S., Fornes, A., Pujol, O., Llados, J., Radeva, P.: Circular blurred shape model for multiclass symbol recognition. IEEE Transactions on Systems, Man, and Cybernetics, Part B: Cybernetics 41(2), 497–506 (2011)
11. Felzenszwalb, P.F., Schwartz, J.D.: Hierarchical matching of deformable shapes. In: CVPR (2007)
12. Gall, J., Lempitsky, V.: Class-specific hough forests for object detection. In: CVPR 2009, pp. 1022–1029 (2009)
13. Grauman, K., Darrell, T.: The pyramid match kernel: Discriminative classification with sets of image features. In: ICCV 2005, pp. 1458–1465 (2005)
14. Kontschieder, P., Bulo, S.R., Bischof, H., Pelillo, M.: Structured class-labels in random forests for semantic image labelling. In: ICCV 2011, pp. 2190–2197 (2011)
15. Kunishige, Y., Yaokai, F., Uchida, S.: Scenery character detection with environmental context. In: ICDAR 2011, pp. 1049–1053 (2011)
16. Lladós, J., Valveny, E., Sánchez, G., Martí, E.: Symbol Recognition: Current Advances and Perspectives. In: Blostein, D., Kwon, Y.-B. (eds.) GREC 2002. LNCS, vol. 2390, pp. 104–128. Springer, Heidelberg (2002)
17. Lowe, D.G.: Distinctive image features from scale-invariant keypoints. International Journal of Computer Vision 60(2), 91–110 (2004)
18. Luo, Z., Shi, Y., Soong, F.K.: Symbol graph based discriminative training and rescoring for improved math symbol recognition. In: ICASSP 2008, pp. 1953–1956 (2008)
19. Luqman, M.M., Brouard, T., Ramel, J.Y.: Graphic symbol recognition using graph based signature and bayesian network classifier. In: ICDAR 2009, pp. 1325–1329 (2009)
20. Meer, P., Baugher, E.S., Rosenfeld, A.: Frequency domain analysis and synthesis of image pyramid generating kernels. IEEE Transactions on Pattern Analysis and Machine Intelligence 9(4), 512–522 (1987)
21. Rokach, L.: Pattern Classification Using Ensemble Methods. World Scientific Publishing Co. (2010)

22. Rusinol, M., Llados, J.: Logo spotting by a bag-of-words approach for document categorization. In: ICDAR 2009, pp. 111–115 (2009)

23. Sun, W., Kise, K.: Similar manga retrieval using visual vocabulary based on regions of interest. In: ICDAR 2011, pp. 1075–1079 (2011)

24. Tombre, K., Tabbone, S., Dosch, P.: Musings on Symbol Recognition. In: Liu, W., Lladós, J. (eds.) GREC 2005. LNCS, vol. 3926, pp. 23–34. Springer, Heidelberg (2006)

25. Yang, S.: Symbol recognition via statistical integration of pixel-level constraint histograms: A new descriptor. IEEE Trans. PAMI 27(2), 278–281 (2005)

26. Zhang, D., Lu, G.: Review of shape representation and description techniques. Pattern Recognition 37, 1–19 (2004)

27. Zhang, W., Wenyin, L., Zhang, K.: Symbol recognition with kernel density matching. IEEE Trans. PAMI 28(12), 2020–2024 (2006)

Author Index